Dominique Coulon
Crossings

Actar Publishers

Buildings

Conversations

The buildings Dominique Coulon creates follow on from each other but are not alike. Since its creation in the early 1990s, the practice he set up in the Krutenau district of Strasbourg has always retained its human scale: between twenty and thirty employees work there, spread over six floors of offices, cleverly intercalated with the architect's private quarters. The particular architecture of the new building, completed in 2015, reflects the mindset of the practice: projects exist side by side, and sometimes become intertwined. There are no fixed roles or assigned posts. Each project is the result of intense and demanding collective work in which individual contributions come together and enrich each other. This reflects the way Dominique Coulon thinks, facing head-on what he calls the 'complexity' of the project, meaning all the parameters involved in the design of a building—project, site, context, users, cost, technical challenges, sensory dimension, and aesthetic. A way of thinking that is determined not to deal with the elements separately, but rather to set them in motion simultaneously: 'There is always something about a building that remains in suspense. I'm comfortable in situations where everything is not yet finalised—the long timeframe of architecture doesn't bother me at all. Precision comes when things fall into place, when the focus sharpens. Each building has to be shaped in the same way as a sculpture is shaped.'

Most of the projects completed by the practice, and all the projects presented here, are public or collective buildings: the needs and desires of different groups of individuals come together in the projects and feed the architectural thought process. Dominique Coulon's constructions are mainly located in France, and he is acutely sensitive to local particularities in the many different programmes he has designed, ranging from primary and secondary schools, conservatoires, theatres and performance venues to retirement homes and health centres, gymnasia, swimming pools, media libraries, cultural centres, courthouses, and administrative offices. Taking time out from the effervescence of his everyday work, the architect analyses his approach here. In eighteen buildings selected to reflect the diversity of the projects and four conversations on the outer edges of architecture, Dominique Coulon provides us with the keys to understanding his universe.

1996
Secondary school

Strasbourg

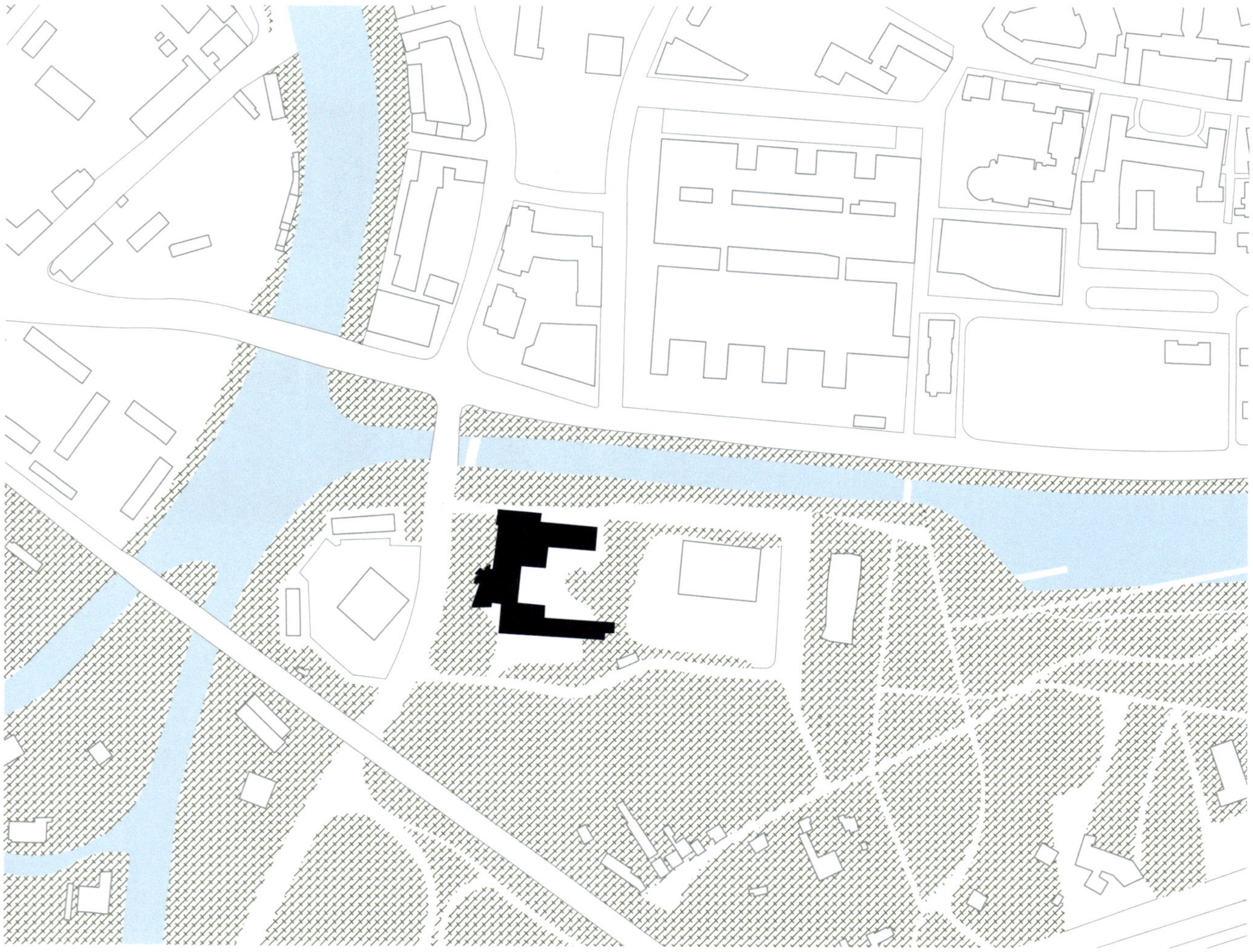

Building-free zone —— As a result of decisions made by both the French and German regimes in the late nineteenth and early twentieth centuries, a ring of unbuilt land encircles the city of Strasbourg. This greenbelt, known as the *Grene Gertel* in Alsatian, follows the path of the fortifications constructed by the German empire in the 1880s, which were dismantled in 1922–27 to provide three hundred and seventy hectares of parks, gardens and open spaces. In 1990, the decision was taken to allow a certain amount of construction in the greenbelt, subject, however, to certain limits, which include restricting it to twenty percent of the ring's surface area. Commissioned to design a secondary school for a site in the greenbelt, we imagined a building that would blend into the landscape, with a U-shaped plan opening onto the surrounding trees. Representing the official nature of the institution, the exterior on the main approach presents a united front. Inside, the complex internal layout constitutes a laboratory of new practices in an atmosphere that is at once stimulating and serene, light and transparency being used to create a *promenade architecturale* through the school whose separate sequences, each with its particular point of view, encourage different pedagogical experiences. The Virginia creeper, which over time has invaded the façades, softens the external envelope of raw light-grey concrete and redwood window frames. The building's colour varies over the course of the day and with changes in the weather. Entry to the school is gained at two points: one for pedestrians accessed via a large staircase, the other for cars and bicycles at ground level. The ground-floor entrance hall acts as the linchpin of a layout whose different, easily identified parts are linked by stairways and galleries. Visitors have no problem orienting themselves thanks to the multiplicity of viewpoints which allow the library, the canteen, the grand staircase and the courtyard to be seen from the entrance hall. Natural light is everywhere, carefully controlled to reveal the contrasting volumes and taking on their colours as it reverberates in space. In contrast to the organisational *promenade architecturale*, the classrooms—the basic units of the teaching process—are simple and straightforward. Each has its own identity, determined both by its function and by its unique relationship with the landscape outside. With nine main types of classroom, monotony is avoided, and, through their different atmospheres, a strong identity is forged for each field of learning.

N

1

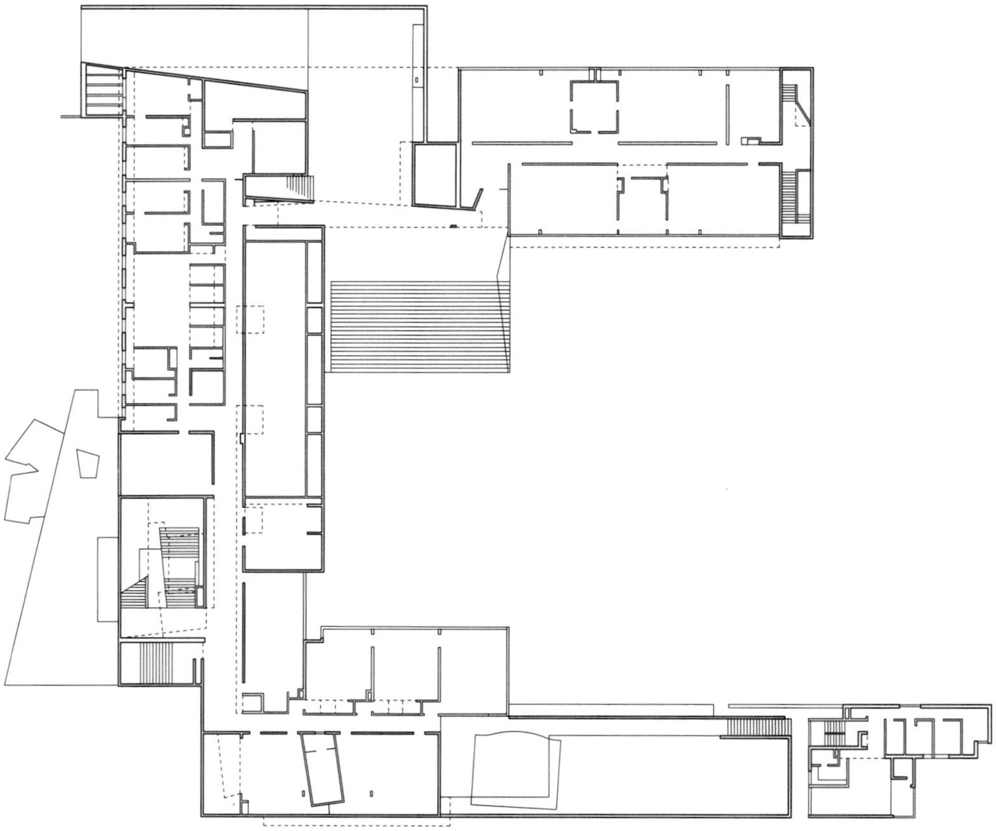

0

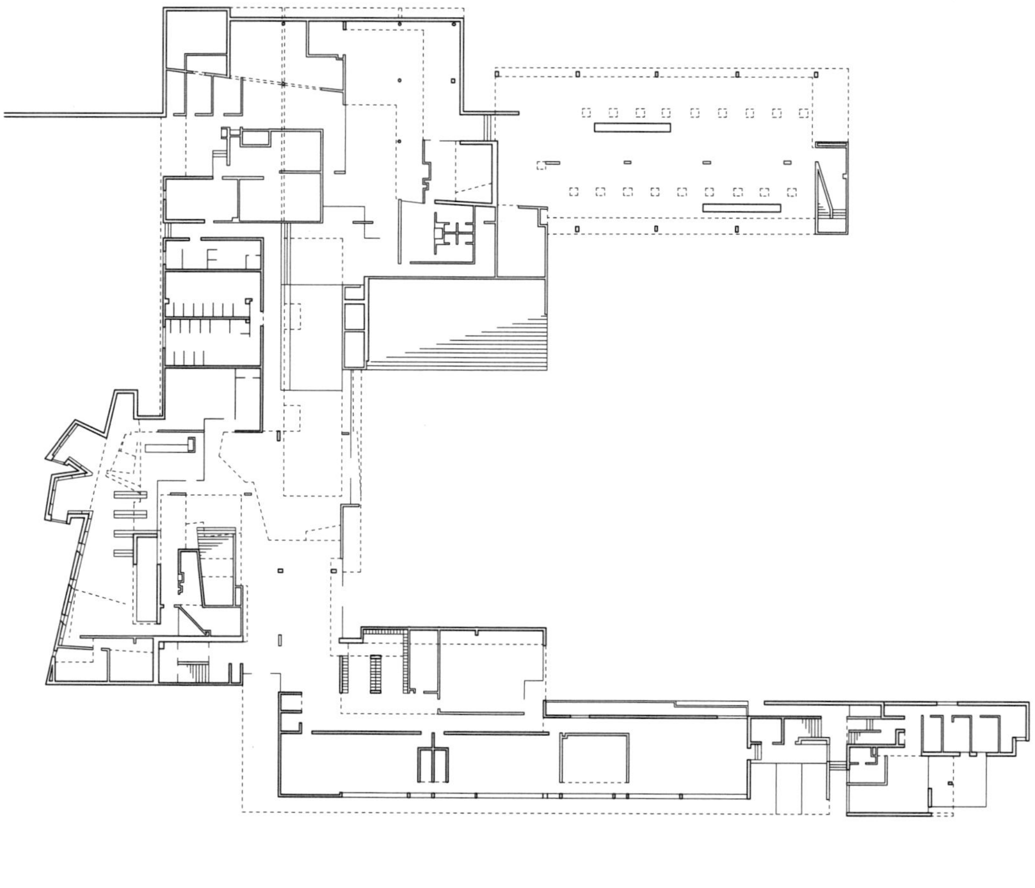

20 m

2

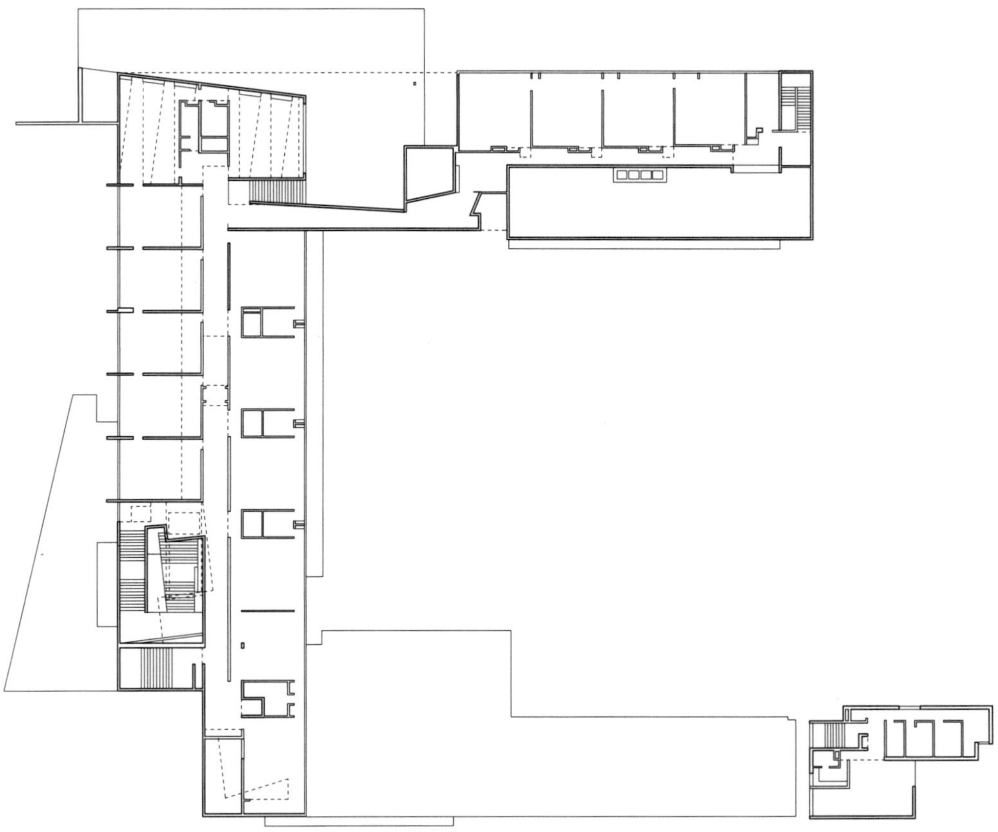

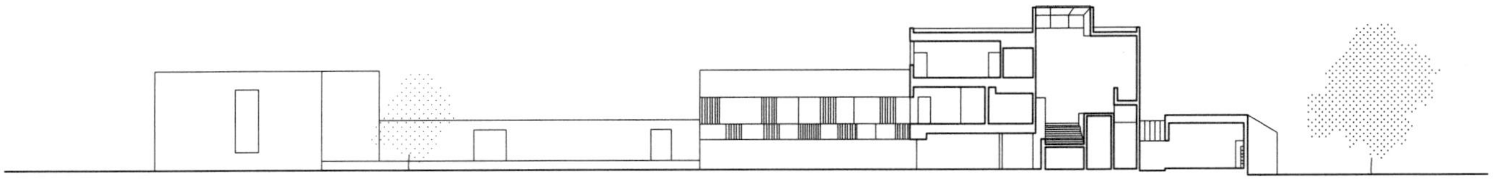

2003
Sixth-form college

Saverne

N

2

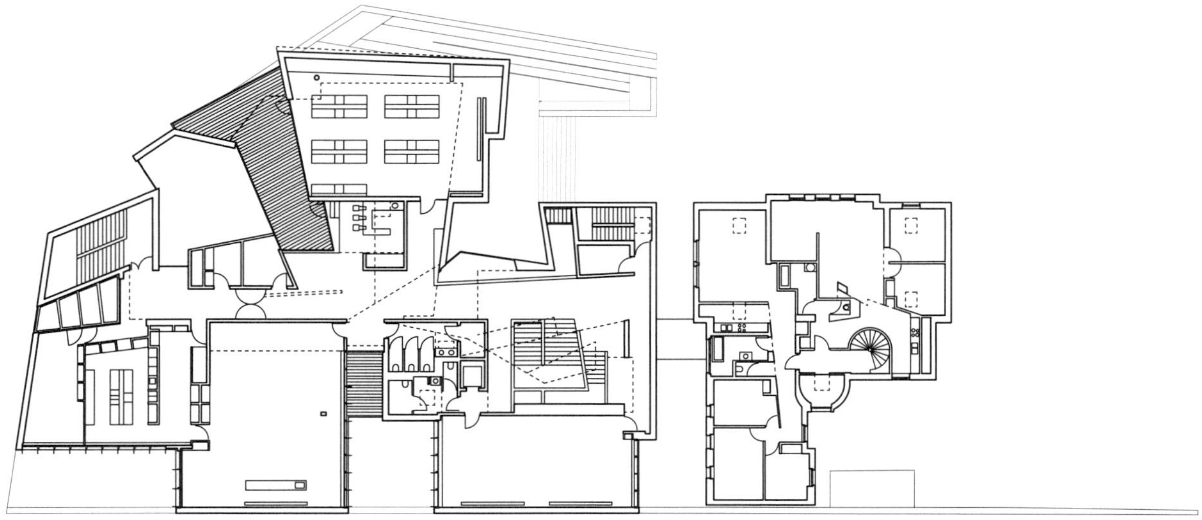

1

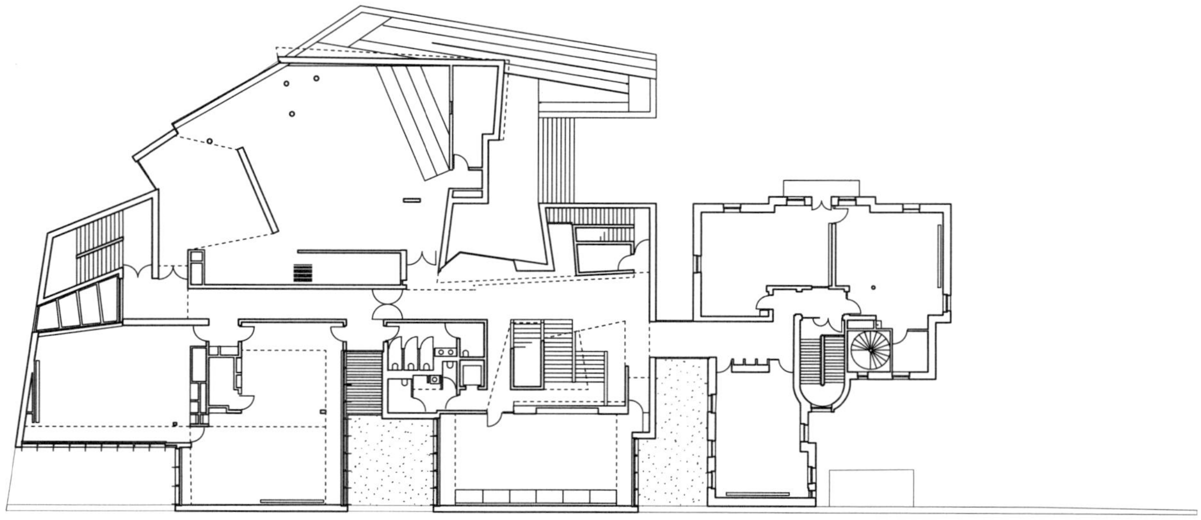

0

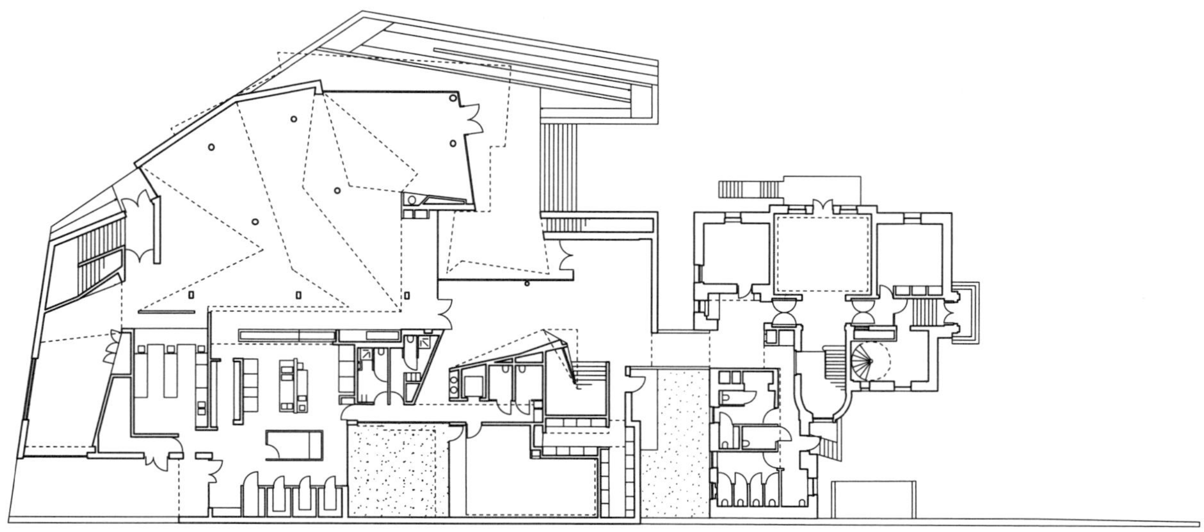

10 m

Continuity —— The sixth-form college in Saverne occupies a site that is both very small and rather beautiful: the tree-filled grounds of a nineteenth-century brick villa. The new building, an extension to the villa, follows the plot perimeter, allowing both minimal occupation of this listed natural and historic site and the creation of a clear and monumental public face on the street. Where the villa meets the new structure—at the same cornice height—there is a void, with just a discreet sliver of glass joining the two. Manufactured in the region—at the Lanter brick factory in Hochfelden—, brick is the common material, linking the old and the new and confirming the sense of place. The relationship between past and present is strongly expressed both in the siting of and the construction technology used for the extension. Its profile, the result of a manipulation of mass and thickness, plays on the complex geometry of the existing conditions, the villa becoming an anchor point that determines the correspondence between building heights and volumes—the new structure pays a certain homage to the old. On the main elevation, the principal volume—a three-dimensional trapezium with projecting bricks that catch the light—hovers above a horizontal glazed opening that allows a glimpse of the interior. The projecting bricks also constitute a humorous nod to the history of the building trade, since workmen would 'pull out' a brick when the client bought them a drink. Thick and thin volumes alternate, framing views out onto the surroundings and giving the feeling of sometimes being enclosed and at others of gazing out from a balcony. Hollows carved out of the building's mass allow glimpses, in a play of shadow, into the different elements of the programme. Inside, these cuts create breathing spaces in the circulation areas and allow views out towards the surrounding landscape. The plan was designed to bring controlled natural lighting to the teaching spaces; the building's monumental scale produces quiet interiors that are washed by daylight coming in from wall and ceiling openings, as well as from the hollows, which act like a series of light wells. The distinct treatments of ceilings, floor colours, lighting, and projecting and receding elements both conflict and harmonise in a never-ending dialogue.

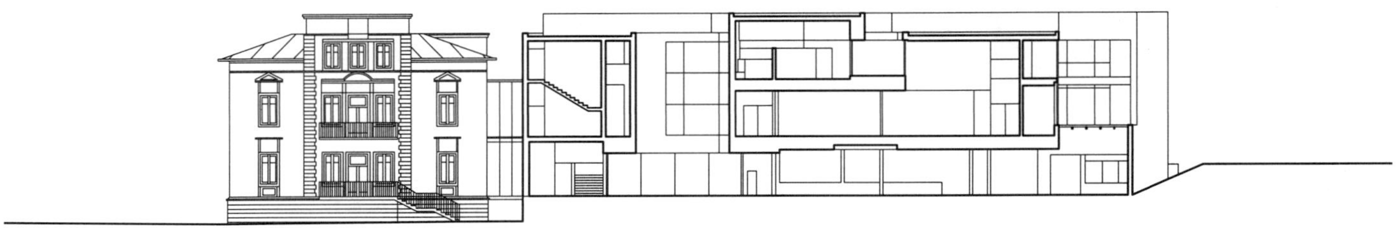

5 m

2006
Infant school

Marmoutier

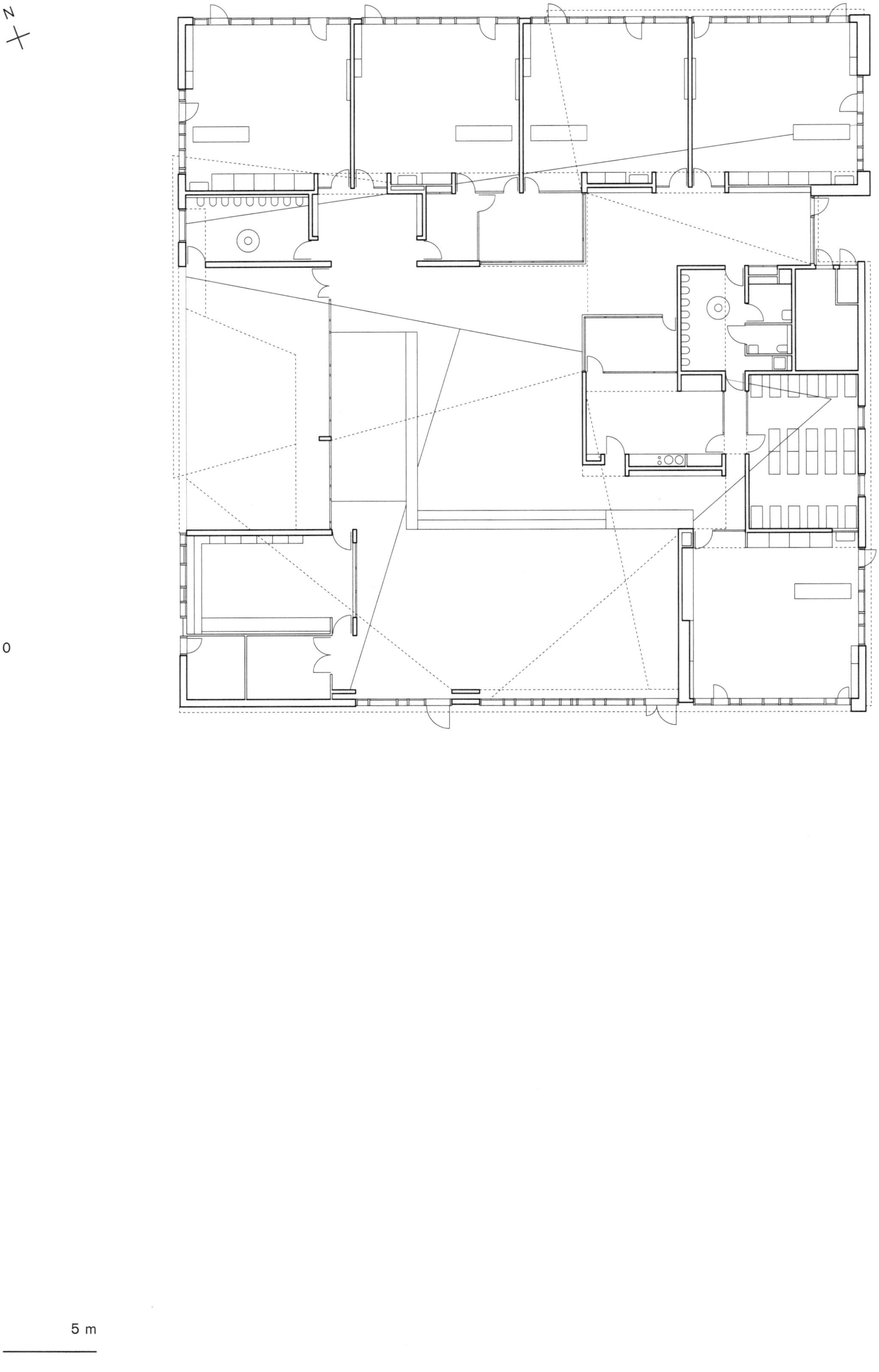

N
0
5 m

Frameworks —— Located in a former abbey garden, the school takes its cues from its surroundings: the old stone wall that encloses part of the site has been preserved, the rest of the plot is bordered with heather fencing, while the school building proper sits at the lower end of the sloping terrain. It forms a perfect square in plan, the encounter between the square and the asymmetrical folds of the roof producing spaces with their own unique sense of place—a simple layout beneath a strange shell which fractures here and there to let in daylight. Because of its compactness, the school enjoys high thermal inertia, resulting in comfortable indoor temperatures all year round. At the building's heart there is a small courtyard, which contains a rain-water pool. The thick, glazed southern bays redistribute heat in the entrance hall, while a Canadian well allows the temperature to be naturally controlled. Two internal voids, staggered diagonally in plan, cut through the building, while all the classrooms are double-aspect. Open onto the entrance hall, the sports hall is particularly generous. Lighting, colour and space division follow three distinct systems whose intersection produces playful, surprising situations. Outside, the building's copper shell, which slowly changes colour as it patinates, blends little by little into the landscape.

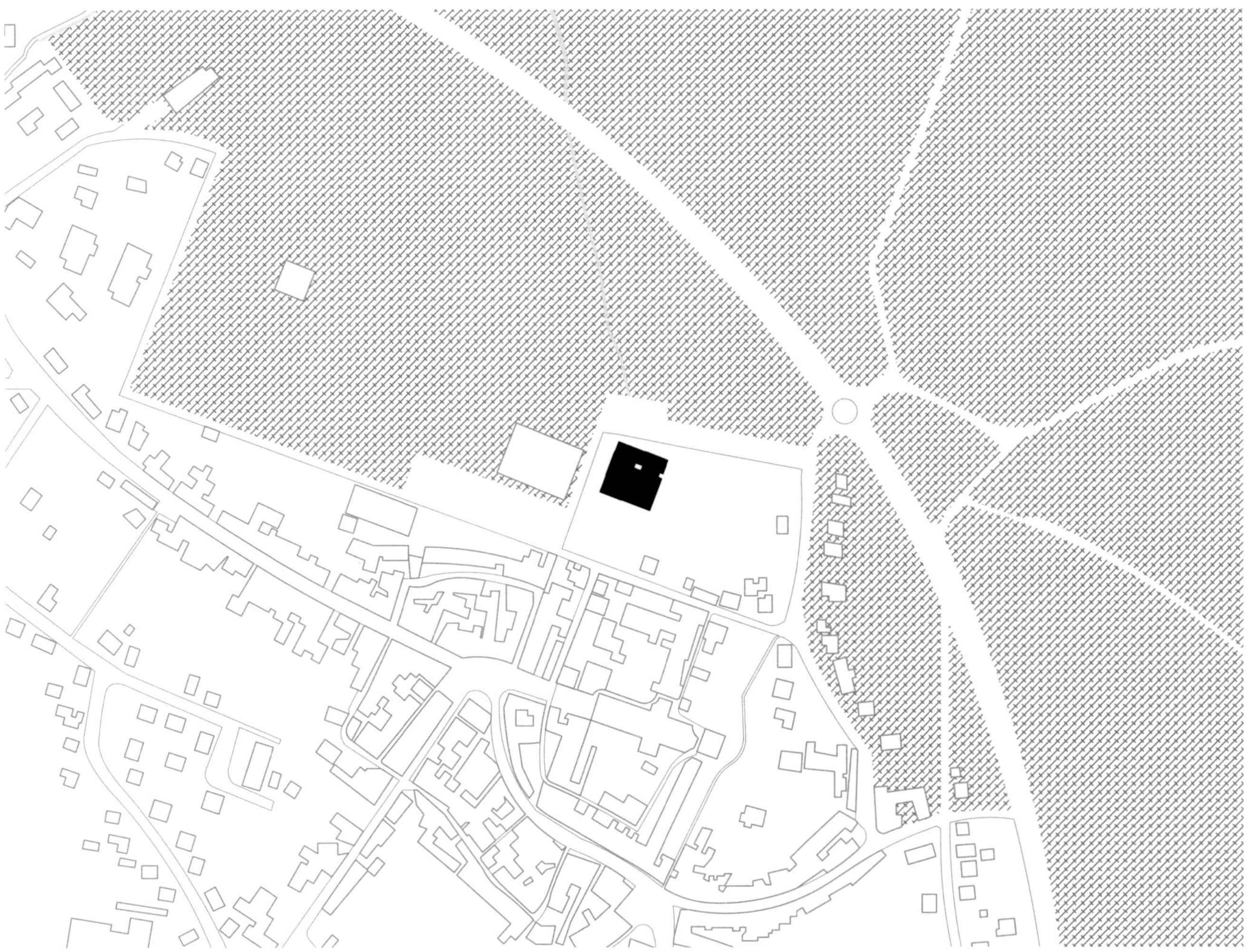

POWER AND MASS

The infant school at Marmoutier in France's Bas-Rhin *département* is a paradoxal building, at once simple and complex. It's a structure with a certain mass, comprising just five classrooms that are cautiously contained within a 36 × 36 m square plan, which also manages to establish a presence in the landscape as though it were somehow alive with a secret respiration.

Horizontal and furtive, the school puts up no fight against the sober Romanesque red-sandstone façade of the nearby abbey church, whose silhouette dominates the village. Half hidden in a hollow, it prefers to enter into dialogue with the Alsatian landscape—artfully sculpted, and subtlely criss-crossed by lines of tall trees—whose discreet charm it underlines. Large triangles of roofing are piled up willy nilly on the solid mullions of floor-to-ceiling windows that communicate directly with the outside; within the very movement that pushes it to hide itself, to disappear, the building reconciles several contradictions (stability and disequilibrium, mass and transparency, among others), and in doing so gains in density and in attractiveness so as to create its own universe, one that follows no outside references.

The design seems to have been initially conceived independently of function as the topological relationship between two distinct surfaces: the stratified surface of the ground and the triangulated surface of the roof. A polished-concrete slab with handrail and steps adheres to the slight slope of the land before brutally rising up to meld with the large plaster triangles of the ceiling, following the vertical of the central courtyard which captures and accumulates the sun's heat. The roof, with its multiple gullies, executes a complementary movement by hollowing out in the ground a rainwater-harvesting pool. The composition is thus deployed around two spatial nodes, the first of which is highlighted by an irregular bright-red ribbon that slashes the floor, the walls and the ceiling and brings to a paroxysm the torsion that folds, as though it had been twisted by an earthquake, the abstract, static figure that is the initial square plan.

Next, the programme with its system of orthogonal walls is inserted into the first spatial envelope, all the while preserving the illusion of continuity. Walls thicken into closets, while above them, ascending and descending white ceilings slip by, dilating and contracting space as they see fit. Whilst the classrooms are sensibly lined up to the north, the covered play area burrows through the eastern façade, joins up with the entrance hall and slaloms around the library, the rest room, the administrative offices, etc. until it merges down below with the sports hall, which opens generously to the south onto the exterior playground. This giant spiral of space is reminiscent of the sequence formed by the entrance and living room in Alvar Aalto's Maison Louis-Carré, another building that enters into close osmosis with the landscape while being solidly held down by the hollowing of the ceiling and the stratification of the floor.

A series of dynamic lines crosses the composition from side to side, the interlocking of yet another system with the two already described: neon lights set into the ceiling or metal wires that cut through space like washing lines and are intended for the children to hang their drawings up to dry.

The torsion motion that haunts the entire composition seems inexorably to flex some of the triangular ceilings, while outside one can clearly see where the roof attempts a slight rotation around the courtyard tower.

This *exercice de style* is totally transfigured by the careful use of materials, those chosen literally tipping the project into a world of symbols and connections, bringing the imagination into play and calling up fictions that bestow an almost animal magnetism on the bare matrix of the basic design.

Firstly, the fencing in woven heather—unexpected in this context, far from its native heathlands—seems to offer protection from the dominant winds to a whole landscape of children in movement. Secondly, the darkened copper on the roof and façades brings to the composition something of the sculptural weight of bronze. The heft of the wooden window frames transforms them into columns, whose projection beyond the glazing, both inside and out, means they also act as *brise soleil*. Finally, the sand which covers the ground in a dense, protective layer that both slows down movement and reduces the risk of injury, refers back to a prenatal, almost liquid environment. All these telluric materials pass through the registers of the primitive, the heavy and the soft, as though the building, without ever condescending to the use of organic forms, constituted a place of transition between the maternal body and a public domain of experimentation and socialisation.

Richard Scoffier, Paris, on 2 August 2007

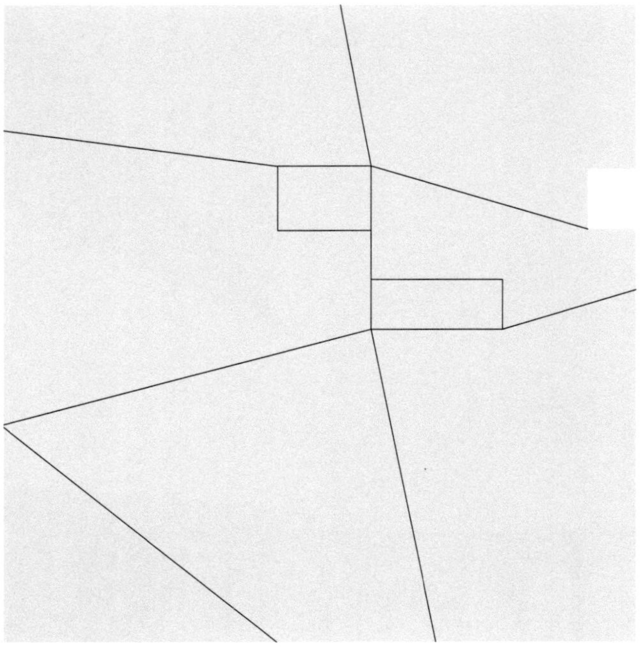

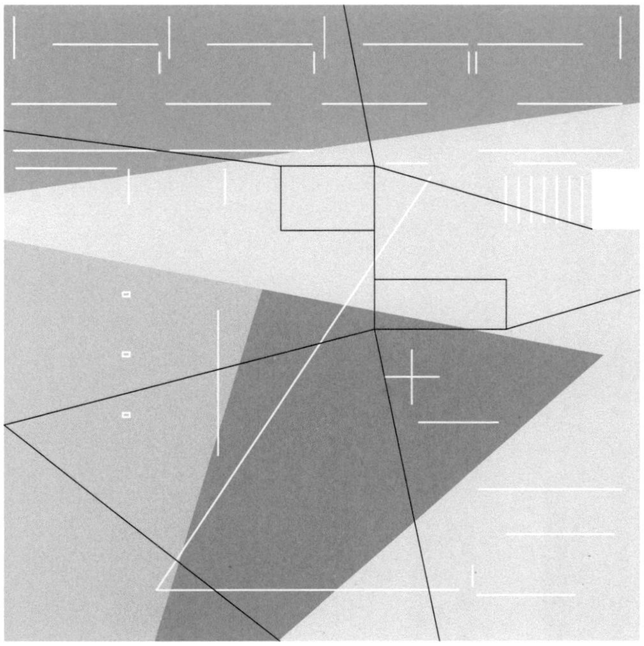

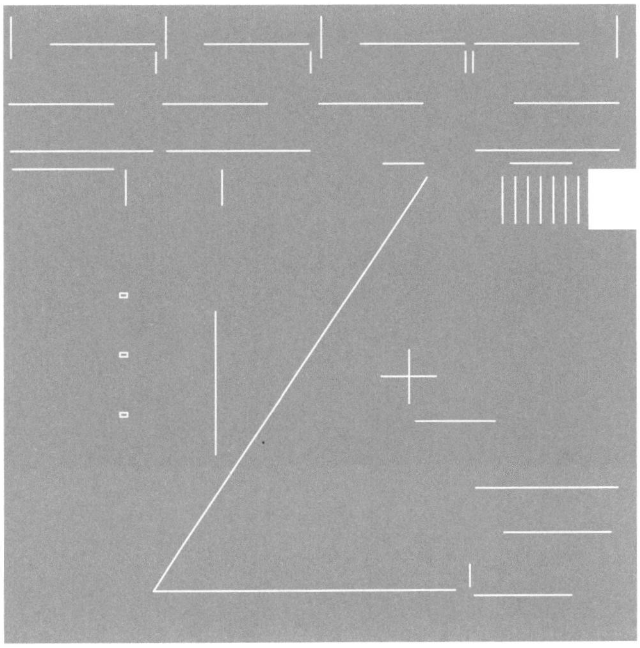

Roof, neon lights and ground layers superimposed on the square plan.

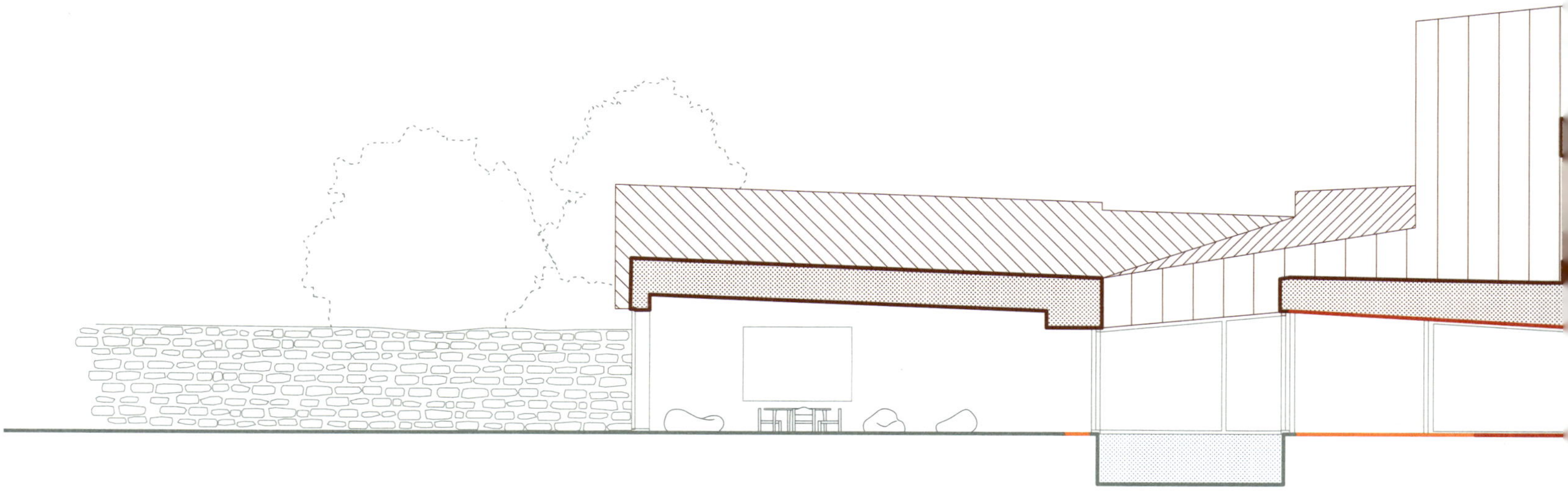

5 m

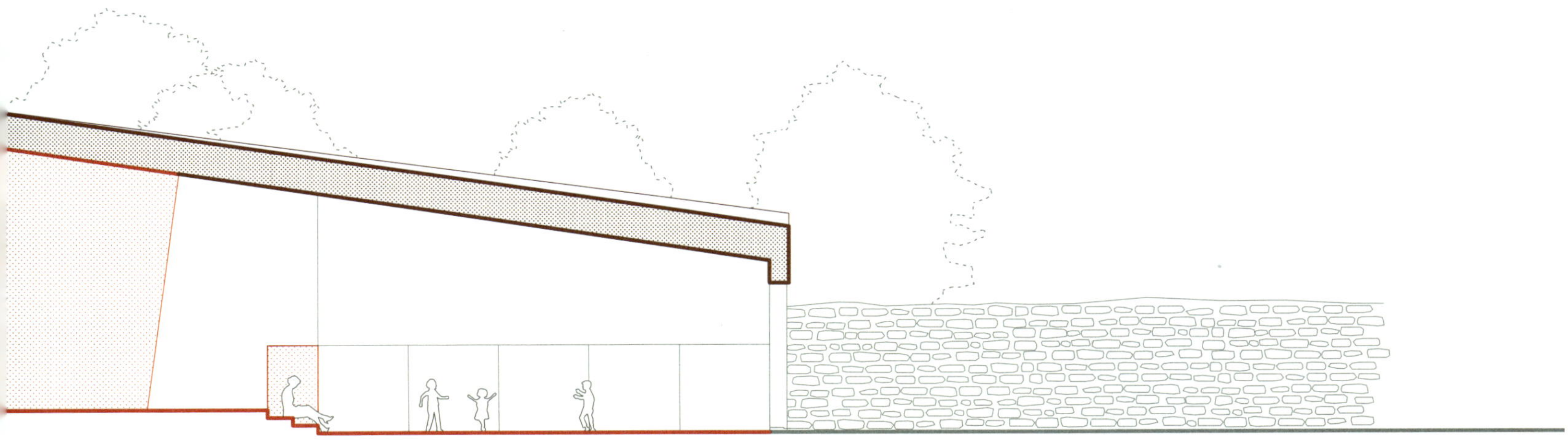

Montreuil

PHARMACIE

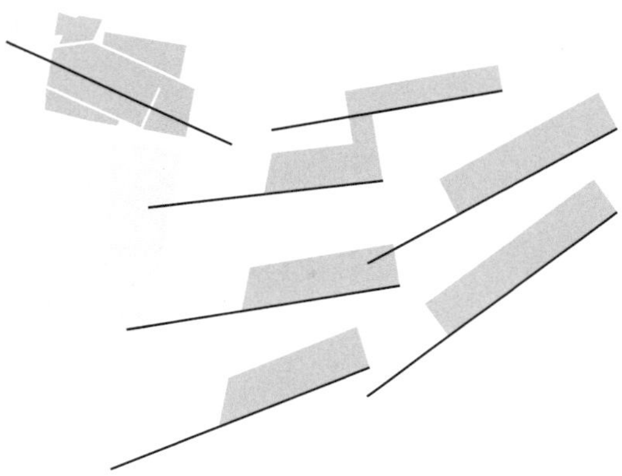

Depths —— The theatre is part of the Montreuil urban plan drawn up by Álvaro Siza in the 1990s, at the municipality's request, with a view to curbing deterioration of the historic centre and in a spirit of dialogue between old and new. The site enjoys a privileged position in Siza's plan, opening to the west and the south onto two major public spaces, the Place Jean Jaurès, in front of the town hall, and the Place Guernica, respectively. It seemed essential to us that the theatre address both these spaces and have neither a front nor a rear. The auditorium's slight rotation with respect to the plot is picked up by the entrance hall, which opens onto both plazas. In this way an incline is set up which prolongs Siza's radiating plan on the hillside of Montreuil—buildings that spread out like the fingers of a hand and which, in doing so, reveal the slope, deforming and accentuating the visual perspectives. The theatre's volumes follow this movement, changing scale from the intimate to the monumental, their white concrete reflecting back a sculptural light. Inside, the pivoting of the plan allows for a theatrical journey of contractions and expansions around the auditorium; as one climbs higher, the red surfaces become darker, accentuating the depth and density of the spaces which alternately narrow and dilate. Once inside the sober, pared-down auditorium, spectators are struck by the imposing presence of the footbridges and the lateral concrete walls: these, following a slight corkscrew movement, are gently folded to ensure good acoustics. A transition from purple to vermilion in the upholstery and carpeting spills out from the rear down to the stage. On show nights, the theatre's play of transparency is revealed, the entrance hall lighting up like a red lantern at the heart of the town.

N

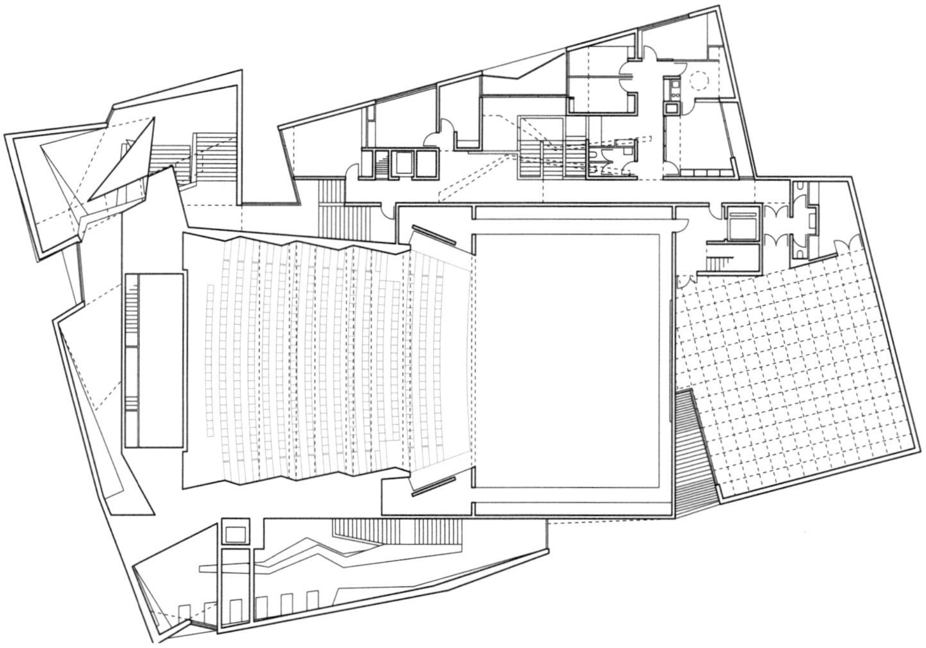

2

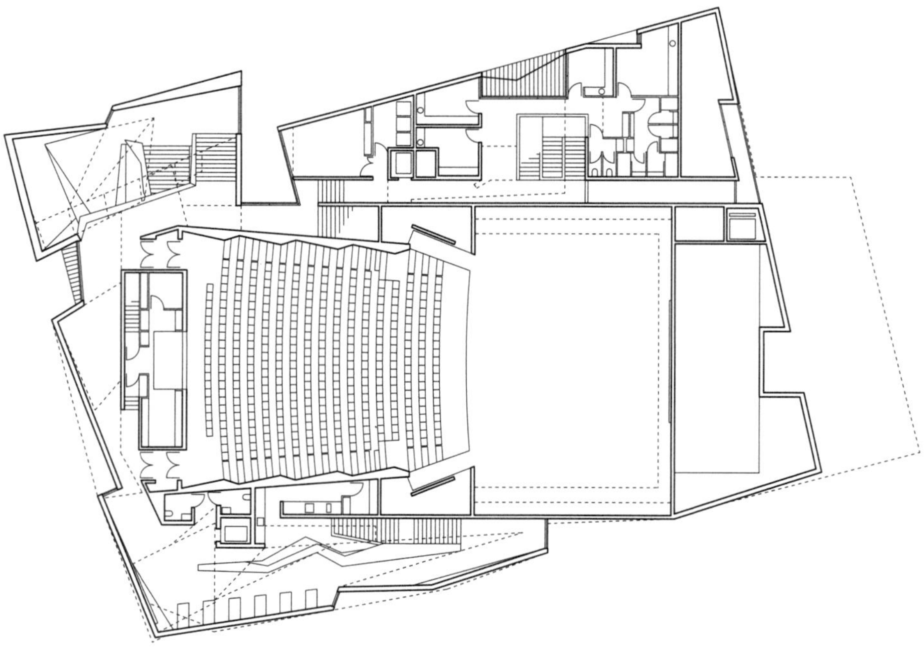

1

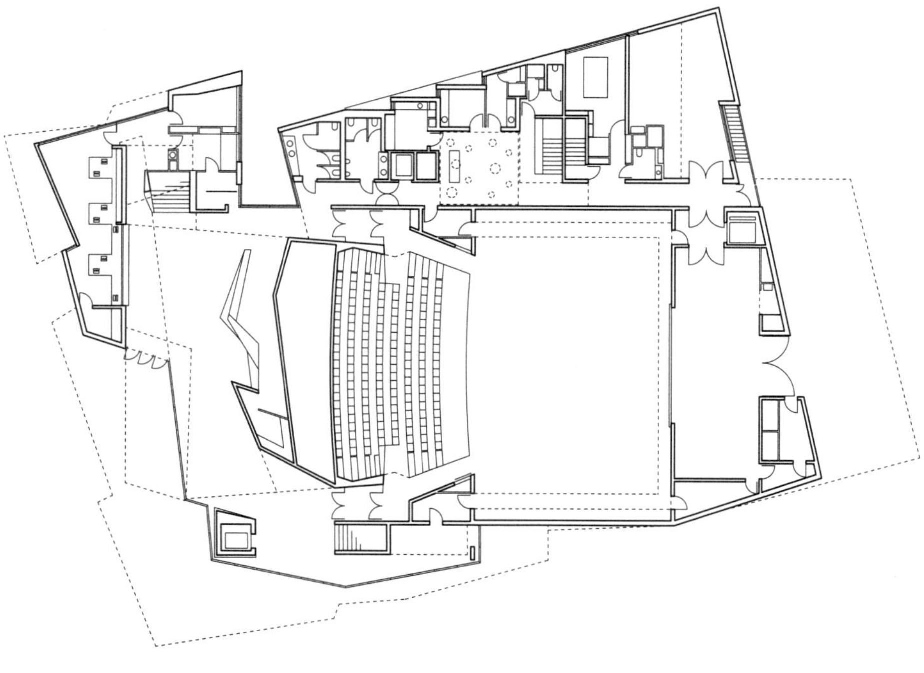

0

10 m

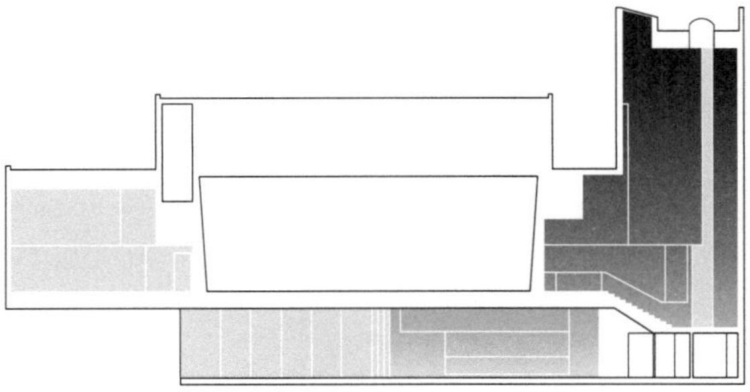
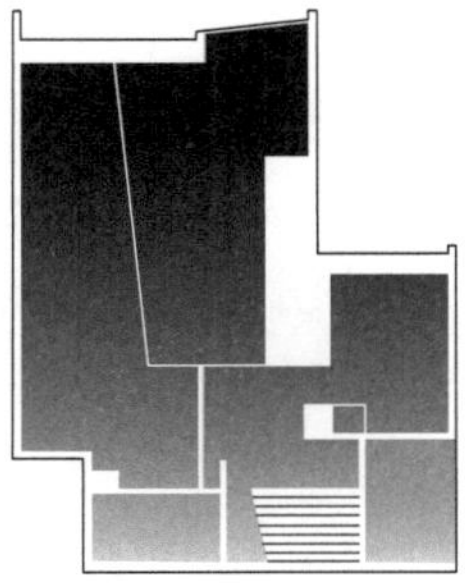
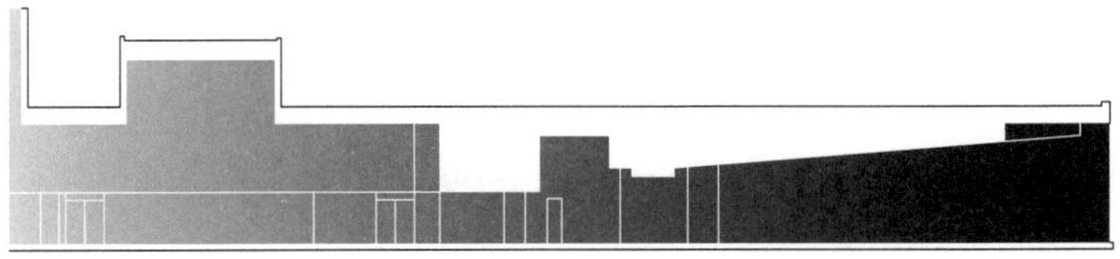
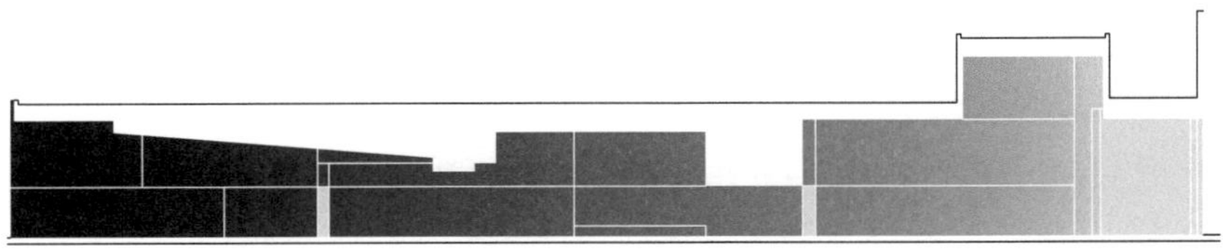
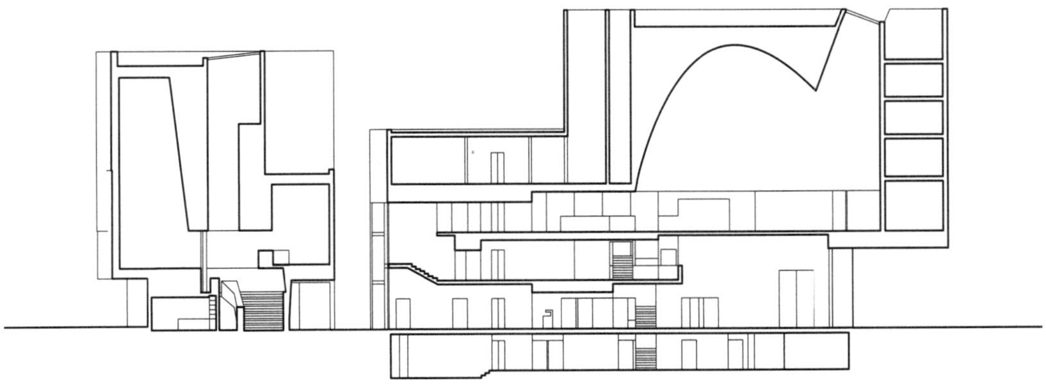
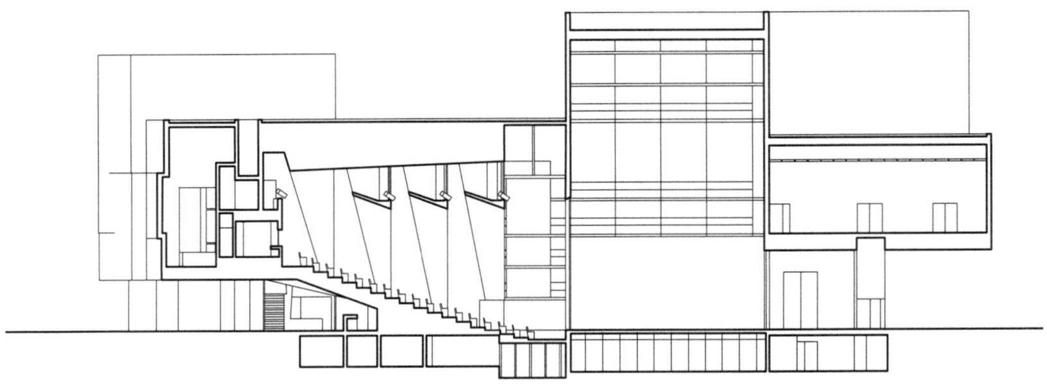

THEATRE, TOWN AND TERRITORY

The National Centre for Drama in Montreuil, completed in 2007, allows us to consider all at once the case of this Parisian suburb, the plan drawn up by Álvaro Siza, which seeks to reorganise the town-hall neighbourhood following the brutal and detrimental redevelopments of the 1970s, and the place of theatre in the urban context, a theme that is often neglected.

At the time of its inauguration, the building stood in what appeared like a battlefield whose outcome was not yet certain, where the traditional layout of a late-nineteenth-century town was confronted with the compact masses of a shopping centre undergoing renovation and autistic residential towers. The new facility, allied with recent buildings that stride up the hill, slips in between the network of closed nineteenth-century streets and the large twentieth-century volumes, and constitutes the centrepiece of a plan that aims to associate the municipality with its wider territory so as to promote the idea of a non-hierarchical environment made up of fluid spaces and nodes.

At the time of the competition, for which Patrick Berger and Antoine Stinco proposed symmetrical schemes that radiated with their own internal logic, Dominique Coulon imagined a block more in tune with the urban and geographical context. His design seems to emanate from an intimate knowledge of the site's orogenesis (a term for describing the formation of relief in the landscape), marking the point of inflexion between lower and upper Montreuil—the former dominated by an axis linking it directly to the Bastille, and thus designating it as a suburb of Paris, the latter by a more rural landscape where old peach-growing walls can still be found. The theatre, which appears like an object in disequilibrium whose parts are tightly bound together, is not formed from a laborious accumulation of levels, nor an articulation of independent components, but rather stands as an inseparable ensemble. The multiple cantilevers, cavities and corbels create an effect of tensegrity: as a result, the scaffolding was not taken down as work advanced but rather in one go, once the carcass had been completely finished. Resting less on the ground than on itself, the building seems involuntarily to recall the church of Sainte Bernadette de Nevers by Claude Parent and Paul Virilio, a precursor that arose from their fascination with abandoned bunkers, those autonomous structures whose tilting reveals the shifting of the sands on which they were built.

In the same way, to respond to the two plazas that stand either side of the theatre in a diagonal, the auditorium pivots 15 degrees, as well as lifting itself up and opening simultaneously onto the two public spaces without prioritising either one of them. This rotation also allows the problem of the town hall to be solved: since the theatre's site is not exactly lined up with the centre of the town hall's façade, a lateral protrusion jumps out from the main volume to counteract this misalignment and address head on the entrance to the monumental municipal structure of 1935. The theatre has few openings or occlusions, but rather notches and scarifications: the structural skin of white concrete is tattooed with a coloured wash that comes and goes according to the light, further reinforcing the impression of a building that is ready to uncoil and strike at any moment. Constantly on the alert, it stands on the checkerboard sketched out by the two plazas like a horse whose movements are hard to anticipate, just as capable of blocking the towers as of dragging the town hall down with it into its spiral.

The volumes containing the stairway, the foyer and the rehearsal space, which wrap themselves around the auditorium, are larger than functionally necessary so as to avoid being crushed by the visual weight of the fly tower. This strategy allows for a perfectly proportioned exterior as well as opening up vertiginous voids on the interior that could be structured and sculpted without the slightest constraint. Corresponding to the tightly closed fist-like mass which lays down the law outside, a sequence of volumes unfolds once the threshold has been crossed which recalls the dilation and contraction of the irrational spaces Lewis Carroll dreamt up for his Alice.

Recession: the entrance hall, embedded under the tiers of seating, has flooring that is interrupted by a sinuous line of fracture at the level of the welcome desk, which rises up, just like in a zone of geological convergence where tectonic plates slip under and over each other. Extension: the stairwell is covered by a high ceiling in which bits of volume float in a chiaroscuro worthy of Caravaggio; at once light and dark, vertiginously empty and saturated, this red shaft stretches out horizontally to access the auditorium and contracts to the point of blackness in the foyer.

Elsewhere in the building, the access space leading to the rehearsal room is covered with a monumental vault fragment hollowed out from the rectangular mass of the roof, an effect that remains largely invisible because of its very dark midnight-blue colour and the total absence of light, as though it were a question of operating in a world of barely perceptible forces. Fractures, which sometimes open out onto the townscape and which bring light flooding into the interior, seem to have been brought about by the varying tensions between the different spaces.

The building is also surprising in its eschewal of the forms usually associated with its function: in contrast to Konstantin Melnikov's Rusakov Club, it doesn't appear like a machine whose various parts (fly tower, tiers of seating rising towards the sky like the fingers of a hand, stair towers, etc.) affirm their independence so as all the better to fit together like a clever puzzle; nor does it reprise the model developed in the eighteenth century by Charles de Wailly at the Théâtre de l'Odéon, or by Mathurin Crucy in Nantes, buildings which allow the transubstantiation of spectators into actors when, at the end of the performance, the audience members step out onto the stage that is the foyers, before resuming their everyday existence. But it nonetheless incorporates at its heart the essence of these two examples by affirming itself as a volume and by formulating an implicit discourse with respect to the relationship between theatre and urbanity. It seems to close around a secret that is at the very origin of our life in society: the propensity to imitation which, even more than in painting or sculpture, reaches its paroxysm in drama. This guilty and uncontrollable desire of impure, animal origin, which impels us to take on and imitate the gestures and postures of others, paradoxically allows us to establish ourselves as subjects, and can be considered the very motor of humanity.

The building thus seems to resemble a node that associates the multiple dimensions of space–geographical, urban and symbolic–in the manner of ancient-Greek theatre which, cleverly set into the relief, allowed the profane and orthogonal street layout to be anchored to the landscape, and in doing so linked public life to representation. It testifies to a different idea of the city and of architecture, one that is less a question of solids and voids and more one of extension and compression, of spaces open to exchange and communication and of closed volumes stretched tight around their secrets.

Richard Scoffier, Paris, on 28 January 2008

13.1.13
PALERMO

A

B

C

D

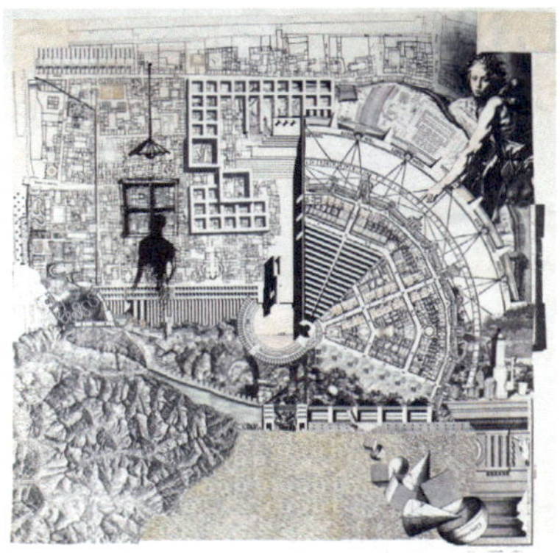

E

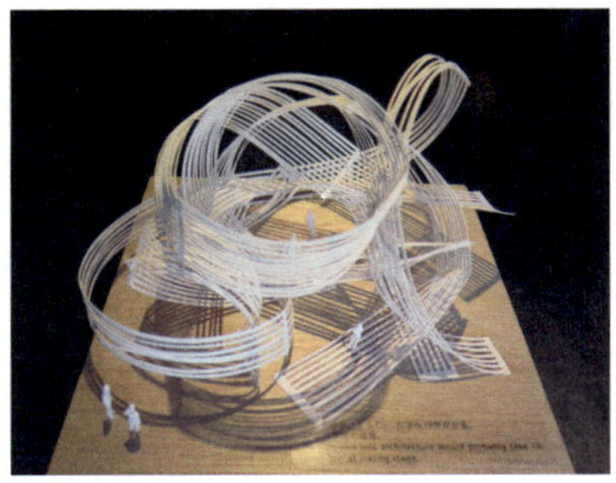

F

G

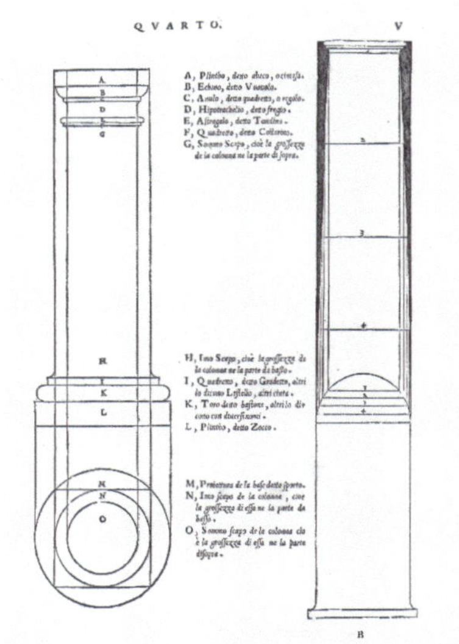
QVARTO.
V
A, Plintho, detto abaco, o cimasa.
B, Echino, detto Vuouolo.
D, Hipotrachelio, detto fregio.
E, Astregalo, detto Tondino.
F, Quadretto, detto Collarino.
G, Sommo Scapo, cioè la grossezza de la colonna ne la parte di sopra.
H, Imo Scapo, cioè la grossezza de la colonna ne la parte da basso.
L, Plintho, detto Zocco.
M, Proiettura de la base detto sporto.
N, Imo scapo de la colonna, cioe la grossezza di essa ne la parte da basso.
O, Sommo scapo de la colonna cio è la grossezza di essa ne la parte di sopra.

H

I

Architecture absorbs the things that surround it and pass through it: landscapes, society, institutions, sciences, culture. In the form of dialogues, Dominique Coulon and his guests consider the wealth of these interactions from four different interdisciplinary viewpoints: methods, spaces, city, and complexity.

Architect Luca Merlini qualified at Zurich EPF and has teached at the Paris-Malaquais school of architecture. He has published a number of works on theory and architectural stories. He worked on the Parc de la Villette with Bernard Tschumi from 1980 to 1992, and in 2014 authored *L'Archipel Tschumi. Cinq Îles*, published by Éditions B2.

Claude Bonnet is a teaching researcher in neurosciences. He regularly contributes to the 'Architecture and Complexity' master's course headed by Dominique Coulon, casting a scientist's light on the mechanisms of the perception of space that architects use intuitively in designing their projects.

As mayor of Belfort from 2007 to 2014, Étienne Butzbach accompanied a number of town planning and architectural projects and demonstrated his commitment to combating territorial inequalities in local neighbourhoods. The politician and the architect are on common ground discussing the town, its inhabitants, and the issues of the urban dynamic and shared spaces.

Daniel Payot and Alexandra Pignol are philosophers; both teach at Strasbourg University. They are well acquainted with both the philosophy of art and the school of architecture in Strasbourg, and open the way for an untrammelled consideration of complexity in architecture, ranging from theory to practise.

A Luca Merlini, *Palerme*, 2013. B Peter Märkli, *La Congiunta*, 1992. C Adolf Loos, Tristan Tzara's house, 1926. D Le Corbusier, *Chapelle Notre-Dame du Haut à Ronchamp*, 1955. E Aldo Rossi, Eraldo Consolascio, Bruno Reichlin, Fabio Reinhart, *La Città Analoga*, 1976. F Sou Fujimoto, *Futures of the Future*, exhibition in Tokyo, 2015. G Le Corbusier, *La Villa Stein*, n.d. H Sebastiano Serlio, *Regole generali di architettura*, Venice: Francesco Marcolini da Forli, 1540. I Claude Parent, housing of M. Claude Parent, Neuilly-sur-Seine: sketch of the 'dispositif séjour', 1974.

Methods
Luca Merlini
Strasbourg, on 21 February 2018

LM
Let's start with a quote from Henri Michaux that I feel describes the work we both do as architects and the research that always precedes the project: 'Before being a product, thought is a process.'[1] A process or a *procedure.* I think the way of sketching out one's thought process as a procedure for tracing out the route one's thinking will take well before a project actually takes shape, the way of sketching out the questions to be raised, forms part of the project even at that early stage—it is perhaps what the project is. In this book, drawing is ever-present, since each project is accompanied by a drawing that is specific, unique, and therefore precious. For me, this then raises the question of what role drawing plays in the research you carry out prior to a project, in relation to the words that form the framework of what you are being asked to do, in relation to the brief as it is handed down. It's a well-known fact that they are often rather brutal and administrative. For you, do the interpretations that you need to make to be able to enter into a project take place inside your head, or elsewhere? Do you go through a thorough process that includes drawing, even though your drawing may not be directly related to the shape the project is to take but rather to the type of questions that arise? There: it's the transition from words to drawings—the procedure of the project, in fact—that I'm interested in … I don't know how you approach that, and I'd like to hear you say something about it.

DC
Well, I probably work less with drawings than you do during the preliminary work. I use a range of tools, including sketches, models and diagrams … I really enjoy those hesitant moments at the start of a project. You always have ideas in your head, and you make preparations for visiting the site. The site is important for me; it can be very disappointing sometimes, yet at other times it can be quite forceful. Often there is some sort of history that you're not aware of, strange aspects that crop up, elements that are positioned in a way you don't understand … I like that preparatory time, when things are still vague, and everything is possible. Nothing is there, yet you have to imagine activities and a presence. Sometimes the site seems to be just waiting for a project and it's easy to realise that it will be of benefit to the neighbourhood or to the town. But sometimes the site is not a good choice and you can have the opposite feeling—the feeling that you are actually diminishing the place. At times that can be very frustrating.

It's not easy to understand topography and climate, for instance, before you visit a site. Yesterday I was in Saint-Jean-de-Luz—it was raining, and the sea was really grey. It didn't look particularly cheerful, but in fact it was quite pleasant. The scenery was less clear-cut. It wasn't a picture-postcard landscape, as it sometimes is. When you visit a site, it's very hard to take in everything you see and hear, what with the brief itself and the information provided at the meeting when everyone presents their intentions. The diagnosis has been made in advance, by other people. You have to appropriate it, put yourself into the scenario being proposed. It's an important moment, and you have to listen carefully. Generally, I like to see the site first and then go back with the other teams—it's not at all the same. Michel Corajoud used to say that to understand a site properly you had to place yourself on the outside. It's often on the outer edges that you find the unexpected, conflicts, or potential. I came to realise that some people only ever see a site through a camera lens.

LM
That's very true. There's too much of a tendency to create one's vision through a camera. As far as I'm concerned, I never take photographs; in fact, I don't even make any drawings at the time. I draw afterwards. Whatever the place, whatever the town where I'm going, whether it's as a tourist or in the context of a future project, I draw what my eyes think they saw, but always afterwards, because

I think the interpretation, the distortion even, that the memory carries out is absolutely essential. [A] What's left in fact is the things you want to change, ideas to build on. What's left is perhaps the concept the place can offer—although it could be something else other than the place—that could become the concept for the future architecture. I don't know if you go through a similar stage too, but I understand the notion of vagueness you referred to just now as something that is perhaps much the same; it seems to me you were saying much the same thing—slowly building up your own personal vision in the same way, perhaps.

DC

Quite so. Creating your own personal vision while things are still rather vague is well worthwhile, since it's before there's any resistance to the project. Afterwards there is some sort of struggle … for example, you have to imagine the scale of the building and everything it could become—you have to take stock more seriously. But I think that what is important is what comes before that. I like architecture that doesn't appear to be constrained by the site, architecture that appears to be on the same wavelength as its site. You rarely need a standalone object, although there are times when that does seem to be necessary. A standalone building is out of synch with its surroundings, and must stand out. In other words, it's the actual idea of an object that exudes strength. The building exerts an influence on the town and on the public space, as if it were concentrating a certain amount of energy.

I try to create a sort of interior universe in my buildings. On the one hand there is the brief that I'm aware of, and the relationships that can be imagined between the different elements of the programme, and on the other hand there are the views to be had, the views that can be achieved. To come back to Saint-Jean-de-Luz, I was rather obsessed with being able to see the sea, because it's really not far away, but you're at ground level at the time—the building doesn't exist yet, so there's the question of how to make sure the sea will be visible. I was thinking of a terrace, but at the time I had no way of checking that it would be possible.

LM

You mentioned the importance of these interior situations that you want to include in projects. That's something I really like. Georges Didi-Huberman divides his book *Being a Skull*, [2] which is mainly about Giuseppe Penone, into a series of chapters, each one about being one particular thing. He starts with 'being a box', then moves on to 'being an onion', then 'being a snail', and so on, in a series of transformations to get closer to 'being a site'. But let's stay with just the first two chapters, and the transition from box to onion. From the first attempts at drawing a human skull, when it was considered as no more than a box with holes, we have moved on to a space that has thickness, a change in vision that the author attributes to Leonardo da Vinci. This idea of depth takes us away from a group of holes towards a sequence. So Didi-Huberman talks about onions. Leaving aside the taste factor, I've always liked the concept of the onion, with its layers of skins, each one being a step towards something else.

Specialised care home
Mattaincourt, 2010

Perhaps what you're saying makes me think of this idea of 'being an onion', meaning that as one penetrates further into the thickness of one of your buildings one sometimes sees the sky, or the view, or what the weather's like … Your buildings are a series of crossings. From the outside, they often look like a suspended pebble, a closed thing, and you feel the outside sliding beneath it and expanding, building up in successive connected layers. It really is like peeling off the layers of an onion.

Sports centre
Strasbourg, 2017

What I find really interesting is when the people who enter a building are both its users and its inhabitants. They are its users because they have come to see a show, if it's a theatre. But they are also its inhabitants, because the way the building is designed makes them reach beyond its initial function. It's as if, slipped behind this initial function, there are deeply domestic dimensions—niches, relationships, or very personal places where they cease to be like all the other people, where they can watch other people live, or look at the scenery, just like when you are alone in your own home. A constant interplay of what is shared and what is intimate. What do you think? Or is that perhaps an over-personal interpretation?

DC

No, no—I think you're right. I like thickness, the fact that you can be engulfed by the building. But what I find interesting are the times when the thickness is rendered more fragile. It's perhaps the desire to give individuals a space of their own. You can have the very pleasant feeling of being in a public place and at the same time being in your own space or place. A refuge in a larger place, somehow. In cafés, for example, regulars always sit in 'their' place …

LM

What you're saying puts me in mind of a building that, expressed in purely architectural terms, is nothing like what you do—Peter Märkli's 'La Congiunta' just south of the Gothard in Ticino. [B] The building houses sculptures by the artist Josephsohn, who was a friend of the architect. From the outside it is a very closed volume, looking rather like a row of railway carriages strung together. It is located in the countryside outside the village, beneath the railway line. It's a museum, but it doesn't look anything like a museum; what I mean is that there are no staff on duty, there's no bookshop or café, or anything that would make it seem like a museum.
To visit it you have to collect the key from the village inn, you drive up by car, go over a little bridge across the river, then you reach a place where you're not too sure where to put the car because there's no car park. In the end you leave the car on a patch of grass, a bit concerned because you don't know if it's the right place. You open the door —it's rather uncomfortable, as there's a high step up to go in; once you go in, you're suddenly inside a magnificent space in terms of light, with a bare floor. And for as long as you stay there, you're the owner of the building and the works inside—they belong to you. You stay for five minutes—or for three hours—then you leave again, you go back to your car, it takes quite a bit of manoeuvring to get out, you hand in the key back at the inn, and you sign the visitors' book. And obviously if you're a bit curious you take a look to see if there's anyone you know who has already been there—when you see that someone you know was there say three years earlier, you immediately get the feeling of belonging to a very select club. You get the feeling that for the duration of your visit you have been the

owner of a very special place, even if it's perfectly obvious that other people have been there before you. In fact, I rather like this way of experiencing architecture as something precious and actually rather free. That's something I see in your projects.

I'd like to come back to my distinction between users and inhabitants for a moment. I have the impression that at the swimming pool in Bagneux, for example, people don't necessarily go there to swim—people perhaps go there for something else. Perhaps to escape somewhere to read while being surrounded by the sound of water, even though it's not really a seaside resort. At one and the same time you are with other people and alone with yourself, which I rather like. It's something that interests me in your architecture—I feel it rather like a constant presence.

It's usually said that the most difficult thing for architects to do is to build their own house or office. You had to deal with that with your combined workshop and home, which is where we are at the moment; all your 'obsessions' are here, but on a domestic scale this time. Personally, I think obsessions are a good thing; I think that to be an architect you need to be obsessive. But I have got one question—why haven't you put the project for this house in the book? How did you make the transition from 'building for other people' to 'building for yourself'? I don't know if there really is an answer to that, but it might be interesting to hear what you may have to say about it.

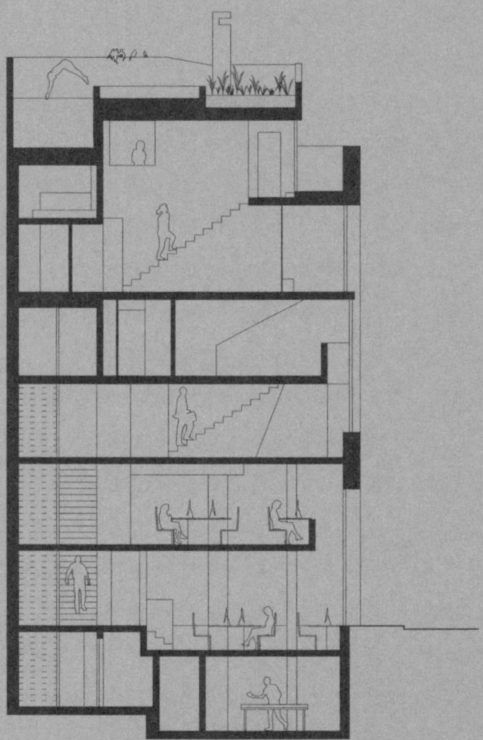

Combined workshop and home
Strasbourg, 2015

DC
You're right that my combined workshop and home isn't in the book. It's not an oversight—it's more of a choice. The agency works almost exclusively on public buildings—it's the collective dimension that interests us. So including this project in the book would have been rather out of place. Also there was nothing special about the programme to start with. But I wanted things to be not particularly ordered. That's perhaps one of my 'obsessions'. So I came up with a type of imbrication that's reminiscent of houses by Adolf Loos. (And in fact I have slept in the house he designed for Tristan Tzara in Montmartre. In the servants' quarters, more exactly, which gave me an opportunity to visit the house—I really enjoyed it.) [c]

I find that obsessions are a driving force. Where you are sitting, for example, is 'the guest's place'—the only place where you get a view of the cathedral. Everyone knows how fond Strasbourgers are of their cathedral. We incorporated a diagonal opening—the only one in the building—to be able to create this special view. There was any number of possible scenarios, partly because we weren't pushed for time in designing the project, but also because we had to think how I was going to both live and work here. It wasn't straightforward. Then, at one point, the town planning regulations changed and we were allowed to add another floor, so we redesigned the whole thing. The staircase is a central feature, allowing the imbrication of spaces between the workshop section and the private section. It's quite easy to get lost …

LM

You're right, with two parallel staircases—so you the architect can look at you the private individual. In a way, the staircase mirrors your own personality.

DC

Even here in the flat, for example, when I show people round they can't find the staircase to be able to leave. Because you turn around, and as soon as you do that you lose all your markers.

LM

I slept in the studio of your combined workshop and home two years ago while the rest of the building was still under construction. We had dinner in town and when I got back—the only person in the place at the time the double staircase was being built—I was really worried that I wouldn't be able to find the studio: I imagined myself spending all night wandering about the building. But in the end it wasn't like that—I found it quite easily: I took the right staircase straight away.

DC

Perhaps in a more domestic building it's easier to play with this kind of imbrication, particularly as I wasn't accountable to anyone else regarding the use to be made of the building. Which is never the case with a public commission, obviously.

LM

You might think that when you are building for yourself you put in everything you can't put in other projects—like an accumulation of your obsessions. But the aim is more to create a place that really matches who you are. The work is perhaps somewhere between accumulation and subtraction. So from that point of view it could be seen as a 'normal' piece of work among all your other work, except that the 'client' is easier to get on with.

DC

You're right; there's no denying that when you create your own house and workshop you have more freedom, because you don't have to be constrained by a brief imposed by a client. It was a pleasure to be rid of a lot of pointless things, and I didn't put myself under any particular pressure. In fact, it wasn't even me who monitored the work as it was being carried out, to be honest.

That reminds me of a talk I heard given by Álvaro Siza at the town hall in Montreuil, about the delivery of the town centre for which he had drawn a new master plan. When he finished, someone asked where he lived, and he replied that, because he felt it was very difficult to create one's own home, he had decided to live in a block of flats designed by Souto de Moura, one of his close friends.

Combined workshop and home
Strasbourg, 2015

He added that it suited him perfectly because it meant he didn't have to ask himself too many questions. So he eluded the problem.

LM
That's what a lot of architects do ...

DC
Yes, there was also the house Roger Diener commissioned Snozzi to design. To come back to this place, though, I didn't try to do everything. Take this empty space here, for example—it's true that it's important because there is a very large building in the vicinity that masks the sun a lot in winter. There's a gooseneck that catches all the light and redistributes it. That gooseneck was one key element of the project.

LM
Is there a hidden part to your work, some theoretical thinking or method that you don't show but which underpins all the rest? Some secret tools behind the way you work, or your teaching? For instance, when you say, 'That's the guest's place', it makes me think of the characters we sometimes invent as a scenario for developing an architectural project: I often do that myself, even as part of my teaching method. So I'd like to come back to the matter of the guest: is setting up certain key characters—who might be fictitious but have to be obsessive (because the obsessive guest would look at nothing other than the cathedral)—something that is part of your approach or something you use in your teaching?

DC
In all my projects there is at least one key area—a particular place that I manage to construct in my mind. I then imagine a certain form of space, an atmosphere into which I project uses and situations. I try to define an interior place, a place that precedes the production of the project. It's almost as if that place is the soul or core of the building. And in fact I'm not particularly bothered about knowing what the building will look like: dealing with the façades often happens at late as possible. In the same way, I don't have much faith in architecture that attempts to solve everything as if it were a maths exercise. I don't think of a building as being a well-oiled machine. I'm always surprised to hear people talking about the 'functioning' of a building. A piece of architecture isn't a machine—in fact, it's perhaps the complete opposite, a sort of living being, with its own particularities and qualities, and defects too. Something you can become attached to. I don't believe in a scientific approach to the production of a project. I think there's something empirical about architecture—something incomplete and particular. That's what makes it so interesting. Rationality is only a means for building work, not for producing a project.

For my first theatre in Montreuil, the scenographer had explained to me that there could be a sort of magic in the relationship between stage and auditorium. There are some theatres that both actors and audiences just love, and no-one knows why. Some kind of mechanism is established between the two elements, and it makes everyone like the place. The Olympia, for instance—I've never been there myself, but apparently it's very popular: there's also the historical aspect. For Montreuil, I wanted to establish a rapport of the same type. But there's no magic formula or ready-made solution. The dividing line between actors and audience is usually fairly hermetic—it was in this brief, at any rate. I made a point of ensuring that the dressing rooms—hidden places that are usually considered less important—were just as well designed as the rest of the building. And indeed when Siza came to see the theatre he wanted to see absolutely everything—he even went into the boiler-room.

LM
Were you there for his visit?

DC
Yes, I was there. Siza has always had his own particular way of observing things. When I was a student, I happened to drive him to see the chapel

in Ronchamp. D It was a very foggy day, and everyone was moaning about the weather; they would have preferred ideal conditions, but he loved the fact that it was different. And indeed the chapel in the fog had a very fluid feel, with that gentle light. And anyway it's a fact that sometimes there's fog in Ronchamp—the sky isn't always blue.

LM
Le Corbusier probably must have sometimes found himself in a fog when he visited the site there.

DC
Personally, it doesn't bother me if I haven't seen absolutely everything to do with a building, if I haven't seen everything straight away. I think it's interesting to build up my own idea of a building, or even of a town. I'm beginning to know a good number of places in France, but I haven't seen everything. I've never been to Brest, for instance. Have you ever been there?

LM
No. There are a lot of places in France I don't know; the same applies to the rest of the world, in fact. And you're right—sometimes it's worth inventing them for yourself …

DC
Yes, that's it—there's an element of fantasy in something you haven't actually seen. If we include an element of mystery in our architecture, if we introduce that element of fantasy, it's unsettling for the person living in or visiting the building. And then there are some random things—it means not everything is totally under control. For example, the particular sound of the staircase in this building, which is made of folded metal sheet, was a happy surprise. I'm sure there are some people who work here who manage to recognise my footsteps when I use the staircase—that makes it something rather playful. When you make a building, there are a number of things that are also suggested by the construction. You design everything, and yet …

LM
Architecture is rather like a story we tell ourselves, or that we tell someone else. That points us perhaps towards an interesting notion—the relationship between architecture and narrative—and to a broader question: what narrative does the architecture express? Does it come before the project, or is it a consequence of the project? Personally, I find the narrative is something that appears very early on in the project, without actually knowing if the architecture it's going to generate belongs to my narrative or if it's already someone else's narrative. In my way of teaching, and also in my way of planning a project—or for some of them, at any rate—I use the characters I invent to construct the architectural project. I make up a story before I make up the project, in the hope that the project will in fact set off other stories. Stories that no longer belong to me, and that I will probably never know. The project takes on a life of its own, it moves on … I like that. In your combined workshop and home, the question: 'Is that Dominique going up the stairs, or is it someone else?' could be the starting point for any number of narratives, or for an endless narrative … Rather like Calvino in *If on a winter's night a traveler*.[3]

Since I've mentioned Calvino—or more generally the use of a number of references, literary or otherwise, from a narrative point of view—, I could maybe mention here one of my educational experiments that's close to my heart—it's called 'sublime drawings'. What I call sublime drawings are a number of great drawings in the history of architecture: Rossi's *Analogue City*, for instance, some Superstudio drawings, or drawings by Boullée—there are some in every period, in fact. They are representations with which I feel the architect signs a kind of contract with himself and shows his deepest desire or conviction in terms of architecture. *The Analogue City*, for example, is the vision of the late-twentieth-century town as interpreted by Aldo Rossi (and those who worked on the idea with him) that comes across as a slightly mysterious combination of history, autobiography and references that are sometimes inserted almost secretly. E

At the start of the semester, as a preliminary to their project, I ask my students to do their own 'sublime drawing' and to put into it everything they believe to be fundamental in architecture. Then afterwards we start out on the semester's project. Will their sublime drawing stay the course? Will there be anything left of it at the end of the process, or not? I like the students to adopt a position quickly, even if they realise subsequently that the project has undermined their positions. If by the end the project has totally veered away from the sublime drawing it doesn't mean that the drawing was bad, but it may have clarified their processes. I also like to confront them with rather paradoxical situations, as in another exercise—'electric couples'. I discovered the notion of electric couples in a short story by the Barcelonese writer Enrique Vila-Matas. He felt Laurel and Hardy form an electric couple, for instance—he meant a couple formed by two ordinary people who, when they are put together, create a sudden energy, like a flash of lightning. I wondered whether the notion of the electric couple existed in architecture. After all, if you put a musician and a clockmaker together, the result is the little house on the lake that Le Corbusier built for his parents. I have never forced myself to dictate the characters involved—it could be Cassius Clay and Catherine de' Medici, or Madonna and the Pope. The important thing is that firstly the encounter must have some explosive aspect to it, and secondly, for something conceptual to become an actual space at some point, it's necessary to work out what tools are needed to translate the concept into a space. The exercise consists of an initial stage of producing a collage that relates the electricity of the encounter, then moving on from this collage to an architecture. I would like students to be able to position themselves as a result of these passages in the narration, and find the means of sketching out their route.

When I was a student in Zurich at the time Aldo Rossi was teaching there, all the students' projects looked like Aldo Rossi's work, even though that's not what he expected of them. I don't think being influenced by one's teacher is necessarily negative, as long as the teacher also offers resources that allow the students their freedom: and that includes being able to set the influences aside. When I came to see the final work of your students, I didn't necessarily see Coulon-type work. So I was wondering how your own theories pass into your projects and into your teaching. Have you got a secret method?

DC

Well, I have got a method, but it isn't anything truly specific; it's more of an accumulation of references and reading matter, and I won't tell you any more than that … it's a secret. To come back to teaching, I insist on setting up situations in which the students can make their own decisions. They have to find the elements of freedom. There is a learning stage, obviously, involving certain essential notions, but I think of the production of a project as a game of some kind. In my teaching I try to set up this idea of a game, and—for instance—I find that working with scale models is very important. A mock-up is something that is not particularly well made, so it's easy to turn it around, or take it apart … The material can give you hints. In other words, it's also possible to discover things by surprise. During a recent visit to Strasbourg, philosopher and sociologist Edgar Morin explained his vision of teaching in all the fields of scientific research where things are well ordered in relation to each other. He thinks it's a mistake that there's no teaching on the unforeseeable, since inventiveness is often the result of the unforeseeable. I get the feeling that there is also a random aspect to the production of a project. For my part, I have no desire to make people believe I have everything under control in a project, or in the production of a project.

LM

A lot of time in school is spent trying to make people believe there are clear-cut methods for doing a project, when in fact there aren't. In the approach to the project there is a controlled, constructed, rationalised, conceptual and formulated aspect, but there is also an intuitive aspect, and I don't think you can ever totally separate that from the rest. Everyone manufactures their own world. I agree with you about the importance of vagueness and chance. The art of teaching essentially lies in enabling the students to become the people they are, not shoehorning them into doctrine. The fact that we ourselves are constantly seeking out teaching methods is part of the difficulty of offering both tools and freedom. But precisely because of that, difficulty is perhaps a good thing. When someone comes up to me and asks how a project is produced, I don't really have an answer.

DC
You're right: there isn't really any ready-made method, but it's the teacher's role to push the students outside their comfort zone. For diploma projects, students often choose wacky destinations. On the other hand, I once had two students who found a site in Colmar. They had been attracted by the relationship with water—an area of Colmar is called Little Venice. It was all rather well-behaved. After some discussion and a bit of provocation on my part, they finally ended up in Bangkok. They didn't know the city: they had a quick run-through of the culture first, and then went out there. The final project was a great success: it included a floating market, residential accommodation, a media library—there were some wild ideas.

LM
Much better!

DC
That's right! It's good to remember that, because it wasn't obvious at the start. And that's perhaps what teaching is all about. In fact in the diploma works you supervise there is also this aspect of narrative and playfulness.

LM
The use of narrative is a way of questioning reality without wanting to do things that resemble reality. I think that's essential, because schools aren't real life, but they are places for questioning reality. I remember one diploma project I supervised recently that brought together two dangers with regard to two vital elements of common property: the disappearance of our memory contained in books, and the destructive power of water. The student had come up with a combination of a library and a dam with this scenario: the water could flood the library—in which case our memory would disappear—and the water that is absolutely vital to us would then be our enemy. What architectural form could a building take if it were to take advantage of these two contradictory forces? It raised some very up-to-date questions about the balance of the elements, the balance between memory and water, through a fictional project. From the point of view of feasibility, the project was totally realistic, rather like a Superstudio or Archigram project. The interplay of this technical hyperrealism and the enjoyment of using the imagination raises some really important questions about the state of our society: I think that's the true role of the architect. That's the kind of project I like to see come up in a school.

To come back to your work, I suppose each time you start by questioning the programme. In Anzin, for instance, you told me that originally the mayor wanted a neutral box, which he felt was more suitable for probable future developments. You managed to persuade him that the evolution of a media library was not necessarily linked to the neutrality of the space but that on the contrary the force of the space could help it to evolve. And all of a sudden, in Thionville, the media library became a public space in all its dimensions, upside down and inside out, everything coming together—it's a crossroads, a meeting place for everything that's going on in the town at any given moment. This kind of thinking is part of the role of an architect; they have a responsibility towards what a programme might offer.

DC
The brief for a programme is not something neutral; it reflects what a group of people want. To draw it up, people have got together and discussed it,

often over a number of years. It has been put together well in advance. Having said that, I always encourage students to question it, to turn it in every direction until it makes sense. The positioning of the elements in relation to each other, for instance —that's not neutral.

In competitions, the person who analyses the project and draws up its brief is the programmer; he likes his programme, so he's not too happy if it gets questioned. Rem Koolhaas happily questions programmes. It's not always easy; we do it perhaps during a second stage, once the competition has been won: it's quite strategic. It has happened that we've designed a project but in the end what we deliver isn't the same, because it doesn't comply totally with the brief for the programme. Once the contract has been signed we come back with the original project and explain why we think it's more relevant in terms of uses and potential.

There comes a point when you have to take possession of the arrangement, and when the pieces fall into place you have to push things that bit further. Coming back to the idea of using a scale model, I'm not convinced that students always see their potential. It's sometimes a bit random. In Tokyo in 2015, I had the opportunity to visit Sou Fujimoto's *Futures of the Future* exhibition. It was entirely composed of somewhat unusual scale models made from everyday objects, with a figure alongside to indicate the scale.[F] There's always an effort to produce a space in Fujimoto's work. I often show this exhibition to students because it's based on the principle of not doing the same as usual. They may sometimes think that things ought to be done in a certain way, so you have to make them ask more questions, to demonstrate that there are other ways of doing things, or at least that there are possibilities that are as yet unknown. In producing projects, it's a matter of always finding the energy to renew yourself. I like it when projects don't happen easily, when there's a bit of resistance.

LM

Like you, I get the feeling that those projects that are put together in a straight line, so to speak, without going backwards and forwards and round about, are generally lacking in something somewhere, precisely because there haven't been any major upheavals while they were being produced.

DC

To invent a project, you shouldn't project yourself into an image. If you have an image of the project, it's already completed and the image is known, so you haven't really invented anything new. So I try to put off the moment when students can hang onto something as reassuring as an image.

LM

You mentioned how students don't always see the potential of their scale models. Often the models are there, but to make the most of them you just need to change the way you look at them—then you can see what you've made from a slightly different angle. In other words, you make up a kind of dance as you look around what you've made—not just with your eyes, but with your hands as well. That's true for scale models, and it also true for drawings. I think that the breaking point, the point when you start to see the 'moment after' of a project, is when you change your viewpoint, change the type of drawing, and break with your own normality. It's at that moment that the project advances. It's habit that causes a project to cease to evolve. In *L'Archipel Tschumi: Cinq Îles* I wrote that the drawing is never the representation of the project in its final state but that it is always a representation of a moment in the life of the project. Hence the great difficulty I have with super-smooth computer graphics where illustrating the project has become more important than the project itself, with all its instability and its future …

DC

When I was a student, I chose to work on the drawings of Le Corbusier. He drew, for example, a sort of caricature of the idea of the 'architectural promenade': a drawing with lots of little passageways and stairs … Then you get the feeling he tried to domesticate his drawing in order to arrive at the final project.[G]

I use scale models a lot these days. I use them to reinforce things: you pick up a model, you look at it; you check it, you turn it around in the light. The proportions stand out immediately. Models also make it possible to check the quality of interior spaces. I often use models for my projects, but not as much as when I'm teaching, because in most cases I'm working on competitions, with tight deadlines. I think the scale model is very educational for students. It forces them to deal with the question of scale, and the way a space bends and folds. You have to learn to look at a space from different viewpoints, different angles, because everything can change depending on your viewpoint. In constructing a project there is of course always an 'image' stage, but it needs to be supplemented by the materiality a model provides—an image doesn't have that.

LM
Students also follow their teachers' obsessions: scale models seem to be yours and mine would be the 'sublime drawings'. After what we've just been saying, there might seem to be a paradox here. Using scale models is very important to you, yet there are very few models, either study models or completed ones, in this book. Is that maybe your 'hidden' side?

DC
It's true that we wondered about that. The scale models we have produced have always been made to enable us to achieve precision in the production of space. This book includes a few photographs of study models, but I didn't want there to be any more than that. I feel that photographs of scale models aren't particularly interesting: what is interesting is being able to manipulate them, and move around them.

LM
I know what you mean. In the end, it brings us back to the wonderful but hazardous question of what and how to pass something on: what is it we want to say with an exhibition, a book—and particularly a building?

DC
It's a huge question! I think each individual will want to say something different about their work. Personally, this retrospective has given me an opportunity to look back at everything I have been able to do so far, starting with the work I did for my diploma. What I wanted to do with that project was to condense all the wildest briefs I could think of into one project. So there was a theatre for performances, a swimming pool, housing for artists, a library, a fitness room, a radio station, a piano bar, a museum, archives … I thought up a number of scenarios: for instance you could walk out of a housing unit and dive into the swimming pool, which provided light to the interior of the museum. The idea was to concentrate multiple functions within a six-sided box shape in order to create new types of connections. And in fact you were on the assessment panel for my diploma, headed by Henri Ciriani—that's how we met.

LM
Yes—it was the first time I'd been on a diploma panel in France. That's when I discovered the extremely solemn side of defending a thesis in France and realised just how much the diploma represents an important moment of passage —in its content, of course, but also in its form.

DC
It's true that the diploma marks an important moment—I often tell my students that. And in fact I remember a question you asked me at the time: 'Is your project a single system or a number of systems?' I answered that it was a single system, whereas in fact it was an association of several systems but I didn't realise it at the time. I've never forgotten that question.

LM

So you were already used to the idea of complexity. Personally, I think I also remember speaking about the question of the programme itself. That's something I'm still interested in today, but at the time I was deeply involved in the project for the Parc de la Villette, where the programme was the main generator of the architectural space. Your diploma project was at a time in French teaching that was marked by Ciriani's Uno group in Belleville, with an approach that was quite different from my own; I felt it already took liberties with its academic context. I have to say it was a fantastic project. But what interested me was the route you took. When I ran into you again a few years later and you invited me to take part in assessment panels, I could see that the imposed references that had been current when you were a student had shifted towards selected references. I appreciated the freedom you had adopted in transforming the skill and knowledge you had acquired into a personal scheme with more freedom and depth—more thickness, to come back to the image of the onion.

DC

I didn't study all the time with Henri Ciriani. What I took away from his teaching was the pleasure in setting up a certain degree of interior fluidity in spaces. That was part of the quality of his teaching—projecting yourself into the interior and in the end not worrying that much about what the building looks like. I studied with him by choice from my fourth year onwards, but I've always been afraid of being fascinated by someone. That's perhaps why my influences are very diverse, although I've never tried to forget him. And in fact I realise that it's quite unusual to see the projects presented for the architect's diploma. The first project in one of James Stirling's monographs is his diploma work, and it's the only example I know of.

LM

It was a clever way for Stirling to recognise the connection between two states: the architect's diploma isn't an end—it's a starting point. There are two disturbing thresholds for students. Firstly there's the 'going in for' architecture, meaning the transition from school to university. Then there's the transition from studying to something that comes afterwards—a tipping point towards the unknown.

DC

What I've always appreciated about your contributions to assessment panels is that the comments you make are actually always open questions. There are a whole host of things behind the question, a whole host of possibilities students can latch onto to take it further—a kind of gift to take away with them. They go away with their question—it's up to them to transform the question. You have to be very strong psychologically for what comes afterwards, because architects always have moments of doubt, but the diploma serves as a marker—it's a bit like a backbone.

LM

You have to be happy with what you've done, because it stays with you forever after. I'm happy with the studies I did; I had the opportunity of meeting some top-class people who passed something on to me that's still there. On the other hand, I'm not happy with the work I did for my diploma. So ever since I regularly re-do my diploma work in my head. Honestly, I could produce a book using the twenty-five repeat diploma projects I've done! I would like the students I've supervised to be happy with their diploma work. For it to become a marker for what they do afterwards.

DC

Yes, but it's also important to learn how to work together as a group in the workshop. Indeed the fact that it's actually called a workshop says a lot, I think. Producing a project is manual work too. Being an architect involves using your hands, making a scale model, cutting things out, doing a drawing, and so on. A bit less so now that we have computers, but this material aspect—when matter and material are important—is one of the good things about the diploma: it means you're preparing things, there's a special smell, it smells of glue …

LM
These past two years I've had the pleasure of noticing the resurgence of drawing, stacking, superposition, and duels—often quite unintentional—between sketches in notebooks. The sketch, in fact, takes on substance, a material aspect …

DC
I think that has something to do with this idea of matter, perhaps also the notion of chance or accident that may arise when you do a drawing. There can always be accidental things with drawings, because the hand moves. I've been told that the Catalan architect Miralles had his own way of working on projects—he would have the plans printed almost every half-hour and then re-drew them by hand because he wanted to recapture the physical movement.

LM
I remember the time about twenty years ago when agencies were moving away from paper and using computers more; it was a difficult time for everyone, because we were all learning to work differently: there was nothing on the drawing board because everything was on the computer. I've always enjoyed walking about on my own among the drawing boards late in the evening or first thing in the morning. I always liked the idea of work left in suspense on the boards, because it starts floating around in my head. And all the coloured pencils and bits of paper lying about. That's all part and parcel of the project. So I used to find it really frustrating—the computers were switched off, and I didn't know how to turn them on. For quite a while I had the impression that I was a stranger to my own projects.

DC
In a documentary about Oscar Niemeyer,[4] you see the architect at the age of 101, sitting at his desk. At one point he draws a cross-section and a view of the actual building appears. The way the film is put together gives the impression that it's as easy as that. I've also heard that he wrote excellent copy, that he used to write very well, and that there were even some competitions he won just on the strength of his text. I don't know if it's true, though.

LM
That's quite reassuring, in fact—it means that somebody actually read what he wrote! I believe the relationship between copy and drawing is a deeply architectural question, which brings us to talk about incompleteness. I'm convinced that it's the architect's role to find the links that make things that bit more complete—not necessarily totally complete, but a bit more complete. For architects, in the relationship between words and drawing, each says something, and each is incomplete in the way in which it says it. Together, they have a kind of wholeness. Writing and drawing are forms of architecture: we work on landscapes that are incomplete and that we perhaps need to complete, we work on bits of towns that are incomplete. Rather than wholeness, I think it's more like solidarity. Asking how words and a drawing come together to form a single unit is much the same as asking how a project forms part of its context. Niemeyer's copy only becomes complete when the work has been completed, but on its own and incomplete, it makes you want to see the finished work. There is of course also the question of whether things should be completed. That's a different question, but it's a good one. The world aspires to a form of completeness, but its perpetual and inevitable incompleteness is a wonderful thing.

DC
I like it when the words evoke something larger, and refer to something vague. Words make it possible to initiate the imagined aspect of a project. They are important for producing a project.

LM
The notion of vagueness came up several times while we've been talking—it's as if vagueness

is something rather precious. But when I look at your work I see that it's absolutely precise. Is there a need to pass through a stage of vagueness in order to reach that absolute precision? Does it not refer back in some way to that concealed part of our work that we can't explain?

DC

I think you're right. Producing a project sometimes involves seizing an opportunity when you find some random thing, working out how to organise the vagueness or the conditions so that it can happen. It's not about demonstrating something, demonstrating has something very scientific to it—it's about suggesting something that will be faultless. I'm not really interested in absolute precision—I find it a bit pretentious. When you try to demonstrate something, you can get it really wrong, too! Don't demonstrate—take risks instead. In Thionville, for example, the brief for the media library had real potential. It had been drawn up by a philosopher who proposed producing what's called a third place,[5] an intermediate place between work and home. There was a desire to move things around, to ask questions. We appropriated the programme and took the suggestions right through to their conclusion. The building has become a focal point in the town and is extremely popular with teenagers, even though they don't usually frequent media libraries. You know that you don't know who the users will be: that's what I find interesting about public buildings. You know they will probably be there for several generations to come, so you're almost obliged to stand back from the person you're working for, because nothing is permanent. So it's quite pleasant that there's something left floating. All that to say that you can actually reverse uses and functions, and create subversive situations. An architect has the power to create places, and I rather enjoy working on public buildings when I don't know who the public is. You need to know how to plan for the future, because the buildings will last much longer than we will.

1 Henri Michaux in *Tent Posts* (original title *Poteaux d'Angle*), English translation by Lynn Hoggard, Copenhagen: Green Integer, 1997.

2 Georges Didi-Huberman, *Being a Skull. Site, Contact, Thought, Sculpture* (original title *Être crâne. Lieu, contact, pensée, sculpture*), English translation by Drew S. Burk, Univocal Publishing, 2016.

3 Italo Calvino, *Se una notte d'inverno un viaggiatore*, 1979.

4 Santiago Stelley, *Oscar Niemeyer 101*, 2009.

5 A 'third place'—a notion that emerged in the United States in the early 1980s in the work of the sociologist Ray Oldenburg—is a space separate from but complementary to the 'first place' (the home) and the 'second place' (the workplace)—an informal area for socialising and interacting. The model of the library as a third place began to develop in the United States in the 2000s. Cf. Ray Oldenburg, *The Great Good Place*, New York: Marlowe & Company, 1991.

Spaces
Claude Bonnet
Strasbourg, on 29 and 30 January 2018

DC
Claude, you're a neuroscientist; you've been a researcher and a teacher, specialising more particularly in the perception of space. For several years your research has guided the works of students in my workshop at the school of architecture in Strasbourg. Could you perhaps start by telling us a bit more about your career?

CB
I started out as a researcher in the experimental psychology laboratory at the University 'René Descartes'–Paris V (in partnership with the French national body for scientific research: the Centre National de la Recherche Scientifique—CNRS), then I became professor of cognitive psychology and head of the laboratory. At the end of my term as director I wanted a change of air, and that's what brought me to Strasbourg, where I continued with research and teaching until I retired in 2007. I taught cognitive psychology and neuroscience[1] at the University of Strasbourg, and introduced a course in these disciplines in the second year of the course leading up to a master's degree in architecture and complexity that you supervise at the ENSAS school of architecture in Strasbourg.

I was initially trained in experimental psychology from an essentially behaviourist[2] point of view—behaviour and nothing else. The approach evolved in the 1960s and gave birth to cognitive psychology, which focuses the interpretation of experimental results on the play of mental representations. Recent developments in neuroscience have led to some rapprochements and occasionally even a merger of the disciplines of psychology and neuroscience. I am in that current of research.

DC
How we apprehend a space is extremely dependent on our visual perception. Could you briefly explain the mechanisms of this?

CB
What interested me firstly in the study of perception was exactly that—highlighting the mechanisms[3] that underpin perception. There are several ways of approaching the study of perception. If we define perception as the *awareness* of objects in our environment and its spatial characteristics, it is impossible to highlight the mechanisms an individual's organism uses to achieve this. What is essential in these mechanisms cannot be accessed consciously. To shorten the explanation—we only have access to the finished products of the mechanisms of perception.

The definition of perception from the neuroscientific point of view concerns all the mechanisms for processing sensorial information originating on the outside (*exteroceptive mechanisms*) or on the inside (*proprioceptive mechanisms*). This processing enables the organism to act appropriately within its environment, by checking on its actions, ensuring its survival and the acquisition of knowledge of that environment and its activity. We can see that this definition concerns all animal species, to varying degrees. If we think of just visual perception, we can see that from the stage of retinal image through to conscious perception, the nervous system carries out a succession of activities to process the information contained in the retinal image. Each neurone in the visual system is activated by just one small area of the retinal image: its receptive field. What's more, it is only sensitive to certain characteristics of the stimulation, such as the orientation of a spatial contrast,[4] colour, or the direction of the movement of such a contrast.[5] So these sensors are specialised, receiving information that is primarily local, since the receptor fields are small in size. The processing is organised in a hierarchical fashion according to their functional specialisation.

The visual system carries out an analysis so that different areas of the brain are more particularly activated by different characteristics of the visual stimuli such as colour, faces, movement, etc. There are two main neural visual pathways. One, called the ventral pathway, processes visual information about shape. It is involved in the recognition of objects, faces, letters, etc. The other, called the dorsal pathway, processes spatial information (volume, depth) and movement. It's this last type that is more specifically involved in processing architectural information.

These functional specialisations can be observed in animals and in humans by using electrophysiological or brain imaging techniques. Although they aren't used in situations in our everyday lives, they can be observed in a neuropsychological context in patients suffering from a limited cerebral lesion that produces some dysfunction. Thus, depending on the location of the lesion, patients have difficulty with the visual recognition of faces (prosopagnosia), or deficient colour vision (achromatopsia), or are unable to perceive visual movement (akinetopsia).

All this research shows that perception, from the point of view of the mechanisms involved, is never a *direct reflection* of the subject's environment, but a *reconstruction* that involves not only a processing of the different dimensions of the physical stimuli but also a number of mental representations. All perceptive and physical (motor) activity leaves a trace in the brain. These traces are what constitute memory and learning, and enable us to form habits and representations. Thus representations are made up of knowledge, conscious or otherwise, that results from our past experiences. It is not made up of pure ideas: it is biologically inscribed—literally *embodied*. Knowledge comprises mnesic traces that can be noticed in various structures of the brain. On this point, the neurobiologist Francisco Varela refers to 'the embodied mind'.[6]

DC

So, as the product of a reconstruction that calls on each individual's specificities, perception is always dependent on the individual: personal mental representations are the result of our experience. This means that processing in relation to visual perception makes it possible for a person to apprehend his environment and the space that surrounds him in a very personal fashion, even though a certain number of elements are common from one individual to another. How would you define the notion of space?

CB

From the point of view of the psycho-biological mechanisms involved, there are at least three types of space:[7] perceived space,[8] lived space,[9] and conceived space.[10] For the sake of convenience we talk of the perception of space, but as far as perception is concerned, there are spaces, plural. *Perceived* space refers to the neurosensorial mechanisms of the specialised neuronal systems that process proprioceptive, motor, vestibular[11] and auditive information in addition to visual information. In normal functioning, there are very many interconnections between the different mechanisms described here. Thus the mechanisms of visual perception are in constant interaction with the mechanisms that are more directly connected with the movements of the body. Perceived space is involved in coordinating movements and actions. Making a movement yourself (picking up an object in front of you, for example), watching someone doing the same thing, and even just looking at a fixed image of a person making the same movement all activate the same areas of the brain. Rather diagrammatically, you could say that we understand another person's movements and actions because our brain recognises them, and mimics them. *Lived* space is the result of the combination of this neurosensorial processing with not only the subject's concomitant intentions but also his emotions. In turn, it carries out actions on the perceived space. The individual's affectivity and cultural components produce differentiated lived spaces. *Conceived* space refers to the different more or less formalised shared cultural representations of the geometric and dynamic properties of the space. So from the point of view of the perceptive mechanisms, we can speak of the architectural space on a number of levels.

DC

So we are wrong if we refer to space in the singular! Seen in this light, the architectural space is only initially produced by the architecture; it constantly changes thereafter as a result of these different mechanisms of perception. For example, taking as a starting point or an initial environment pretty much any building—we would need to imagine a building that is neutral in terms of conceived space, removed from all human conception of its architecture. That's impossible, of course; for the sake of argument, let's say four walls, an entrance, and a roof; or even a sort of primitive cave dwelling. This elementary architecture would act firstly as a set of items of objective information that are characteristic of it: dimensions, shapes, colours, sounds and so on, making up an initial perceived space. It is only then, when this neurosensorial processing comes up against the emotions of the people moving in that space, and these emotions influence their perception, that the architecture becomes a lived space. And the conjunction of this perceived space and this lived space could at this stage give rise to an initial conceptualisation of the architectural space by the 'prime architect', whose modelling would then create a first non-neutral structure. Any new reading of this architectural space by visitors would be a new lived space, which might then in turn alter the schemes of the conceived space, i.e. the collective representations. It is in this way that architects consider their buildings. Each new building adds its share of physical inventions that are perceived and experienced differently, constantly adding to the loop, gradually building up a cultural and social conception of architecture as we know it today, with codes that have been established over several millennia of history. But perhaps you could explain in more detail the specific features of these different spaces—starting perhaps with perceived space?

I Perceived space

CB

Visual space, like the space in which our actions take place, is three-dimensional. But the retinal image is flat: depth, volume and relief seem to have been lost. Yet our everyday experience is of a three-dimensional space! So the visual system has to reconstruct the three-dimensional space using various items of information—clues, so to speak.

When we look at something, in the near distance (less than five metres away), ocular accommodation and convergence[12] are the only clues to the absolute distance between the observer and the object. These are motor activities that function in the same way as reflex actions. Convergence is a valid clue to depth if neurones in the occipital cortex are able to extract the information of depth from the retinal disparity, i.e. the fact that the images of two objects at different distances are not geometrically identical on the two retinas. This is the mechanism of stereoscopic binocular vision. If you cover up one eye, you eliminate that clue and the evaluation of distances is disturbed. These clues—often called physiological clues—cease to be particularly effective for distances of more than five metres. It's just as well that the visual system is able to use other clues to reconstruct depth, volume and relief.

Other clues are referred to as kinetic because they are the result of movements of retinal images: monocular parallax,[13] dynamic changes in the retinal size of the images (expansion or contraction of the image of an object), optic flows, and differences in speed. In interior spaces more particularly, hearing plays a role that is often underestimated in the perception of volume, in localisation, and in how ambiences are felt. Lastly, there are clues referred to as pictorial, such as relative size, linear perspective, aerial perspective (decrease in contrast as distance increases, a bluish colouring in the distance), gradients in texture, and interpositions.

In a given environment, these clues usually provide concordant spatial information. It is possible to show that they are processed separately by placing them in competition, in contradiction, and that pictorial clues, pictorial representations, are not the most efficient clues to depth and relief. Basically, pictorial clues comply with the laws of physical optics. Everyday use has taught our brains to know these laws and to use them in practice. These mnesic traces are representations. Their effectiveness doesn't depend on our ability to conceptualise them.

The separation of the processing of these various clues can be illustrated by putting them in conflict. The English artist Patrick Hughes, for example, produces three-dimensional paintings in which perspective clues supply information that contradicts the convergence clues and binocular vision. He calls these paintings *reverspectives.* At relatively short distances, the perspective clues take priority: we see the outlines clearly in the foreground whereas they are in fact in the background.

Happily, our everyday experience of space doesn't usually have to deal with such conflicts. The brain generates coherent representations of space. Sometimes, however, the observer may experience an illusion similar to that of a train in a station (also called *vection)*: this is when you are sitting in a train that isn't moving but you're waiting for it to set off, and the visual movement of a train setting off from the platform alongside your train makes you feel as if your own train is moving. Yet the vestibular system has given the body no signal of the body's movement. The illusion disappears as soon as you look elsewhere, at a fixed object in your surroundings.

What I have set out so far supposes an immobile observer facing what's going on. In normal life, the observer is not usually quite so passive. Firstly, his eyes are constantly moving, either as a result of small spontaneous movements, or in exploratory ocular movements that guide movements of the body. The observer moves about in an environment, exploring it and taking action in it. All these movements of the body generate not only changes in the visual information being supplied, but also proprioceptive, motor and vestibular information. Let's take a straightforward example. When we look at different parts of a visual environment, the retinal images of that environment move. And yet, generally, we perceive it as a stable visual environment. Movement of the eyes generates proprioceptive and motor information that the brain will compare with the visual information available before concluding that the visual world is stable. This perceived stability is a reconstruction carried out in the parietal cortex which combines the visual information of the movement of the images, the efferent signals[14] of the motor commands of the extra-ocular muscles, and the proprioceptive signals of the contractions of these muscles. This wonderful machinery can be disturbed by medication, alcohol or drugs: that's when it looks like everything is moving!

II Lived space

But I still haven't said much about either lived space or conceived space. Above all, I haven't stressed the importance of the body's actions in the constitution of spatial representations. A fundamental concept here is the body schema,[15] a set of representations of the body, its posture and the position of the different members. Basically, these representations are non-conscious. That's the essential condition for the production of automatic skill. They are the result of the integration of sensorimotor information.[16]

Let's take an example. To go down a flight of stairs quickly, the brain, having perceived the characteristics of the steps, has to calculate the position of the members and coordinate them or adjust the speed and length of pace. The processing of this information is orchestrated unconsciously by the body schema. There are norms for the dimensions (rise, tread, head room, tread length) and regularity of steps and staircases. Which means that, for an adult, the behaviour for going down a flight of stairs can be automated. An initial glance allows the person to note the characteristics of the stairs and generate the appropriate motor programmes. This behaviour will be all the easier to automate if the individual's measurements correspond to the norms for staircases. Obviously, in order to acquire perfectly automated behaviour of this kind, the conjunction of physical development and repeated practice is a minimum requirement.

This means that the brain contains an internal model representing the biomechanical characteristics and orders of scale that would also enable us to situate our body—defined by its spatial coordinates—in space, and to have a topographical representation of all and part of our body, without which we would not in fact be able to move at all.

Situating ourselves, locating ourselves in a given space is a vital function, and the mechanisms involved are starting to be deciphered. The 2014 Nobel Prize for Medicine was awarded to John O'Keefe, May-Britt Moser and Edvard Moser for their work on rats, whose hippocampus cells —the area of the brain involved in spatial memory— form a geo-positioning system in the brain, rather like an internal GPS. A similar mechanism has been identified in humans. These cells constitute a spatial memory that may become damaged, in cases of dementia for example. On the other hand, long practice in a complex environment improves it: London taxi drivers, for example, who undergo intensive training to memorise every last nook and cranny in the city, have an enlarged hippocampus!

Lived space is therefore essentially a space where actions take place. As far as architecture is concerned, it's a space to explore, if only to find out where you are or choose an itinerary, and for constructing representations of the paths we take.

Housing for the elderly
Huningue, 2018

Infant school
Reims, 2001

Combined workshop and home
Strasbourg, 2015

Our conceived space, for its part, is basically Euclidean. It's a kind of mental model that doesn't correspond to perceived space. This is because the structure of perceived space is curved, as demonstrated by much experimental work. In 1947, in a theoretical exposé, Luneburg had shown that if a subject is required to arrange lights regularly along the length of a path, he will arrange them not in accordance with the Euclidean laws of perspective but in a hyperbolic curve.[17] The curvature of perceived space is not constant.

Architects and painters didn't wait for this experimental work to be carried out to realise empirically that perceived space has a curved structure. One classic example is the colonnades in Greek temples. To give the visual impression that the pillars are perfectly cylindrical, they bulge near the middle and converge towards the top. To give the impression that they are regularly spaced, the intervals between them expand from the centre to the outer edges of the colonnade. [H]

This Euclidean conception of space is cultural. It is perhaps this divergence between conceived space and perceived space that explains, at least in part, the negative impact of over-Euclidean constructions. They are perceived as being too uniform and as a result are felt to be tiresome, or even alarming. They don't offer any surprises. Sometimes embellishments are added to break up the monotony. This means that some architectural spaces offer no surprises while others, on the contrary, play on the surprise effect by breaking away from what is expected of a Euclidean space. More often than not, the space is made more complex (I won't go into the details of the notion of complexification here) by using, for example, rounded shapes that are supposed to imitate or be reminiscent of natural elements. The cultural aspect plays an important role in the reactions of non-professionals to an architectural environment.

Playground of the 'Saint-Jean' school complex
Strasbourg, 2013

DC

So the more an architectural space plays on these different perceptions, the more complex it becomes, and the more likely it is to diverge from the Euclidean dimension of conceived space: reintroducing curves into the architectural space is a way of getting closer to the space as it would be perceived without the rigid filter of conceived space—and in fact conception of the architectural space is more rigid in the West than in the East, where emptiness and absence are much more important in the definition of images and places. As an architect, I am always keen to offer spatial wealth and complexity—I don't see that as meaning complicated architecture, because complexity lies less in the formal geometry of the projects and more in the articulation of the separate elements within a whole, with all the parts working together yet retaining their singularities. And in these complex spaces, each route may reveal something unexpected: a kind of surprise that intensifies the experience and, if I've understood correctly, leaves its mark on the lived space.

CB

In order to construct a structured, stable mental space, certain information on the limits is necessary all the same—the horizon, for instance, is a limit. And surprise is, by definition, an effect that doesn't last! When we are faced with a new example of architecture, our affective reactions are relatively substantial—whether positively or negatively. When we familiarise ourselves with its environment, our reactions fade: we refer to this as habituation —it's the most elementary form of learning among all living organisms. For humans, of course, this habituation is not necessarily accompanied by a lack of interest. How do you think the effect of the initial surprise that the architect wanted to create evolves as a place is used?

DC

Ah—that's a trick question! Once they have been constructed, buildings are out of our hands. But we could hope that happy surprises will turn into a form of affection for the place. I think it's the recurrence of normalised and standardised elements in our built spaces that encourages the emergence of these mechanical, unthinking habits, and their accumulation eventually makes us less attentive to our environment; a lack of daily stimulation could almost go as far as causing a form of apathy. And as an architect, that's the very thing I fear.

So I try to create surprising spaces, spaces that turn routines upside down. I'm convinced, for instance, that over-regular structures standardise buildings. If the structure, the limits of a building are too marked, there's no longer any room for manoeuvre. Will we want to look more closely at a place if we are given the keys to interpreting it straight away? And conversely, if the structural frame doesn't fit into an orthonormal grid, a form of movement or dynamism is created and it becomes harder for the user to create a mental image of the building he is standing in—taken to the extreme, this logic may call for considerable effort, a commitment that's both mental and physical. In Lausanne, for example, the Learning Centre at the Polytechnic School, designed by the Japanese agency SANAA, incorporates an unusual topography inside the building itself: visitors can't escape the bulging floor, and in places you have to make a real physical effort. In Thionville, the garden ramp of the media library is in fact nothing more than a surface that rises us as it passes from the inside to the outside of the building. The principle is the same: through their geometry and their plasticity, places invite us to imagine other ways of positioning ourselves and moving about. They also create the possibility of spending time in places that would otherwise have been transit areas, like in the oblique architecture theorised[18] by Claude Parent.[I]

But I'm also convinced that the mere thought that there is something we can't see, that there are concealed elements still to discover, stimulates the imagination and keeps a place attractive. In the book he published in 1957, *La Poétique de l'Espace*, the scientific philosopher Gaston Bachelard looked at the value of the poetic image in spaces that wonderfully escape from the constricting geometry of the real world: 'With a single poetic detail, the imagination confronts us with a new world. From then on, the detail takes precedence over the panorama, and a simple image, if it is new, will open up an entire world.'[19] Thus the initial surprise can be converted into renewed attention, into an alert, playful, inquisitive state of mind.

To provoke these triggers of surprises, complex architecture as an assembly of autonomous systems develops a whole vocabulary, a whole grammar of space that opens up to interpretation and appropriation. The creation of contrasting 'syncopated' sub-spaces, for example, generates unexpected situations. Because it's possible to create syncopations in a space as in a musical rhythm: the breaks produced by displacing the rhythmic accent away from the place where it is expected, disruptive events that upset the regularity of a sequence—it could be no more than a variation in size between two spaces, or an irregularity supplied by the work on colour. In the theatre in Freyming-Merlebach, once you have walked calmly through the soft, uniform shades of the foyer, you push open the door into the theatre itself and you are plunged suddenly into an explosion of bright colours. Elsewhere it is a contrast of sounds —in fact it can be applied to any one of the elements that constitute a perceived space. At the Human Rights sports centre in Strasbourg, the hall in untreated concrete is particularly sonorous —everything echoes—, whereas the multi-purpose hall, which has a soft, cottony sprayed plaster facing on its walls, has a pleasantly muted acoustic. Lastly, natural light—even though it's an element that's external to the building—should be considered an integral part of every project: it adds a unique colour and quality to the appreciation of shapes, colours and atmospheres. And I think daylight is one of these mobile factors that directly affect our perception of space: a place that receives daylight will be different every time you visit it. These constant changes, driven by nature, also contribute to maintaining interest in a place once the initial surprise effect has worn off, because they constantly reiterate the surprise in a different way each time.

Restructuring of the Administrative Centre
Strasbourg, 2007

Generally, I think that everything that consists of adding movement to things that appear to be evident, shifting or challenging elements that seem to have been adopted in the architectural space—meaning whatever has the value of a conceived space in the architecture—provides an additional source of stimuli and calls for new learning, and I think that constitutes an enrichment which adds to visitors' experience and encourages them to use their imagination.

CB
So many possibilities! And as an architect, how do you experience these different relationships with spaces? How do your work of imagination and the way you feel the spaces that you move in influence the spaces you are going to design?

DC
When I imagine a building, I can't really say that I walk about in it. It's more a case of mentally constructing and projecting a space that doesn't yet exist—a constructive thought, so to speak. At the agency, we have a number of tools to help us with the different stages of design. The most obvious is probably sketching, which enables us to put approximate ideas down on paper as we go along while we are still structuring our thoughts, but we don't use it all that much because we choose to deal with the content of programmes quite quickly, setting all the elements in motion and looking for initial articulations on the basis of their singularities. After that we do our initial plans and cross sections; these are crucial because they enable us to assess the balance of the programmes and their flows, so that we can then adjust the relationships between the central places of the programme in order to harmonise the whole. Axonometric perspective—a Euclidean tool par excellence—also enables us to stand apart from the space and consider it from a suitable analytical distance. And at some point, of course, we move on to volume, with our first experimental scale models. But at this stage we are still distant outside observers, looking at a miniature project—rather like Gulliver among the Lilliputians. These tools don't allow a real immersive experience—and indeed there's nothing to say that such an experience would be a better design tool—but this range of representations enables us to carry out a very fine, polymorphous analysis for each project. You have to wait for the building-site stage for the scale of the project to be inversed: that's the real passage from design to reality, a stage when we can at last physically feel the space we have designed and which henceforth is out of our hands.

Building a scale model
Media library, Thionville, 2016

Architectural design is a complex process. It's not just a matter of using our technical knowledge to produce a structure that makes it possible to put programmes together. We also have to take into account very many factors of a physical, psychological, sociological, cultural, historical, economic and ecological nature, and to grasp what is at stake and the context in order to produce an architectural idea that gives meaning and coherence to the whole. Just as a space is a combination of the different ways in which we perceive it, architecture is a combination of these very varied factors. I like using this diversity to consider each building as a prototype, rendered totally unique by its position in a specific context. Every set of technical, contextual, empirical and sensitive elements can be combined in many ways, each one in turn having the potential to produce a unique project that goes far beyond mere functionality.

CB
I'm provoking you here, but shouldn't architecture be first and foremost functional?

DC
Yes—of course, a space has to be functional, but that's just the minimum! Architecture has a non-negligible impact on the shaping and evolution of societies: the architect's work can't be restricted to merely putting up utilitarian buildings.
I totally agree with Louis Kahn's concepts of served and servant spaces—they make it possible to translate the function of a place into reality.
I think architecture should combine the practical and the artistic seamlessly. Architects should add something extra to their projects. I'm absolutely convinced that architecture cannot merely respond to the uses to be made of it: it must also provoke pleasure—a physical pleasure that should increase as we move through a place.

CB
Pleasure—a form of emotion. We know that the emotions play an essential role in cognitive functioning and that they influence our perception of space, but according to the neuropsychologist Antonio Damasio they are also motor and trigger elements in human culture: he says the different forms of culture (arts, sciences, technologies, etc.) constitute firstly a form of response necessary for certain feelings such as suffering and pain.[20] From this point of view, architecture is indeed not only for us a source of emotions, but also, and intrinsically, a response to our emotions.

DC
I think that I personally agree with those who, like Bruno Queysanne in 1987,[21] still prefer to 'feel' architecture by walking: with their steps, with their actual feet, as the first and essential actors in the architectural survey drawing, which is also one of the stages in the perception of a building. I feel the need for architecture that is constantly on the move: to provoke emotions—of whatever kind—the architect must bring movement into these spaces and invent systems that mobilise all the senses. Users must be given the opportunity to be part of the action. They have to be encouraged to act, not by imposing rules on them but on the contrary by making them forget the rules and giving them a great sense of freedom as they move through the place. Through the feelings we experience, architecture has the ability to change our state of mind. I feel the variety of architectural spaces is fundamental as a reflection of the individualities that make up societies: an open, contrasting place that can be read in several different ways will attract users with widely differing profiles.

1 Cognitive psychology is a branch of psychology that seeks, by using an experimental approach, to elucidate the mechanisms of the major mental functions. Research in neuroscience is concerned with the structure and functioning of the nervous system in general and the brain in particular.

2 Behaviourism is a concept in psychology that concentrates solely on the relations that are observable between external stimuli and behaviour. In principle at least it excludes any call on psychological concepts.

3 Claude Bonnet, Francis Lestienne, *Percevoir et produire le mouvement*, Paris: Armand Colin, 2003.

4 Contrast: difference in luminosity between the light and dark areas of an image. As a result, the dividing line between the two is, at least locally, linear and therefore has a spatial orientation.

5 Direction of the movement of a spatial contrast: movement –the spatial shift from the dark area to the light area–is in a direction perpendicular to the orientation of the contour.

6 Eleanor Rosch, Evan Thompson, Francisco Varela, *L'Inscription corporelle de l'esprit. Sciences cognitives et expérience humaine*, Paris: Seuil, 1993; published in English under the title *The Embodied Mind: Cognitive science and human experience*, Cambridge: MIT Press, 1991.

7 Alain Berthoz, Roland Recht (eds), *Les Espaces de l'homme*, Paris: Odile Jacob, 2005.

8 Perceived space: The initial perception of a space, made possible by a set of mechanisms for processing information of different kinds: visual, proprioceptive, motor, vestibular, auditive, etc. Perceived space presents a particular negative curve that makes it a Riemannian non-Euclidean space.

9 Lived space combines perceived space with the subject's experience, intentions and emotions: lived spaces are more differentiated than perceived spaces.

10 Conceived space is a set of representations of the geometric and dynamic properties of a space, sometimes far from physical reality or the perceived space; it is an essentially Euclidean archetype that marks the collective unconscious and is shaped by human cultures.

11 The vestibular system, which has receptors located in the inner ear, receives and transmits information on the acceleration of head movements and on the gravitational vertical.

12 Ocular accommodation: reflex action adjusting the curvature of the eye's lens to provide a clear retinal image.
Ocular convergence: rotation of both eyes towards the nose, more marked the closer the object, ensuring the continuity of binocular vision.

13 Monocular parallax: change in the relative position of images of objects at different distances from the observer.

14 Efferent neuronal signals are those which emanate from the central nervous system.

15 The body schema is the representation of the biomechanical properties of the body. On a genetic basis, it develops with our motor experiences. It is different from *body image*, which is conscious and does not necessarily coincide with reality.

16 Sensorimotor information refers to sensorial information and the corresponding motor activity.

17 Cf. Rudolf Karl Luneburg (1903–1949), *Mathematical Analysis of Binocular Vision*, Princeton: Princeton University Press, 1947.

18 Claude Parent, *Vivre à l'oblique*, Paris: L'Aventure urbaine, 1970.

19 Gaston Bachelard, *La Poétique de l'Espace*, Paris: Quadrige et Presses Universitaires de France, 2004, p. 129:
« Avec un détail poétique, l'imagination nous place devant un monde neuf. Dès lors le détail prime le panorama. Une simple image, si elle est nouvelle, ouvre un monde. » Re-published in 2014 by Penguin Classics, London; English title: *The Poetics of Space*, translation by Maria Jolas.

20 Antonio Damasio talking about emotions during the radio programme *La Grande Table* broadcast on France Culture on 22 November 2017. Cf. Antonio Damasio, *L'ordre étrange des choses: la vie, les sentiments et la fabrique de la culture*, Paris: Odile Jacob, 2017

21 Bruno Queysanne, 'Penser l'architecture, c'est penser autrement' in *Mesure pour Mesure*, Paris: Cahiers du CCI, 1987, pp. 95–8.

City
Étienne Butzbach
Paris, on 15 January 2019

DC
I remember with pleasure our meeting when the conservatoire was being built in Belfort, particularly on the building site: you were asking questions, looking at the cross sections—you were paying a lot of attention.

EB
Our discussions about the conservatoire have left me with good memories too. You knew how to listen to our suggestions and incorporate them in the project; things resonated with a very human dimension of empathy. We have been working for more than twenty years with the architects and officials at the town planning agency in Belfort, as well as with the town's engineers, and during that time we have tried to construct a way of really thinking about the town in all its sociological, anthropological and philosophical dimensions. But the devil's in the detail, as they say: a door frame, the height of a step … that's why I was paying so much attention on-site! We were lucky to meet some very interesting architects, and we learned to draw on that and come up with some very different ideas.

DC
What I'd like to talk about here is the public —political—dimension of architecture. That means throwing light on the way we do things, on the way we think, and on what public projects mean for architects and their clients. You have worked in neighbourhoods where it's important to give everyone an opportunity to speak. In our work in the agency, we also ask this central question: how are people going to experience the spaces the programme offers? We try to construct by starting on the inside. That's perhaps our subject—the social dimension of architecture. What relationship do you have with the town, with architecture?

EB
Fifty thousand residents means fifty thousand different ways of living in the town: you can visit every part of the town, you can anticipate as much as you like, there will always be something that escapes you. It's essential to find out what people's positions are and take an interest in how they do things, in order to understand how things work. The way we talk about architecture and town planning is a central question.

I've always been fascinated by everything to do with towns: towns are liberating. In '68—I was sixteen at the time—we thought everything was possible. The only problem was knowing how to construct what was to come next. For me, urban civilisation was one of the answers: even then I thought that towns were fascinating places. One of my first ways of approaching towns was by practising Situationist *dérive*: discovering a town on foot, testing its value according to the people I met, its unexpected nooks and crannies, urban follies—shapes and places that humans have charged with a type of magic. And in fact the history of such places is often fascinating. I like walking through a place and imagining what has happened there. A town is like that too: an agglomeration of items of heritage just waiting to be brought back to life. Later, I felt the topographical spirit of places was very important, not only their ecosystem but also the strata that had been laid down over the years: all these treasures that allow us to stand on the shoulders of giants and to build on the knowledge and experience that humanity has accumulated over the centuries.

So how does architecture embody a certain idea of the town or urban living? I have always thought of urban policy as being policy for the whole town and not just a particular neighbourhood. In my mind, a town is like the city of ancient Athens: it's not the enclosure that we have seen in recent decades. That's the problem with the production of common ground, which comes up regularly in questions of urban mix. It's said that it takes an entire village to bring up a child, but you could just as easily say that it takes an entire town. Belonging to a collective group is what makes us human, but conflict cannot be dissociated from that. There's no point trying to avoid the issue. Children and adults are constructed through conflict—on condition that some way out is possible. Personally, I think it's better to fight by using political arguments: politics is a conquest of mankind to build societies by thinking about what we share—because without common ground, nothing is possible.

As for the production of public spaces, I think you have to combine a Structuralist vision of things—meaning a lucid vision of the determinisms that constitute societies—with a degree of open-mindedness—meaning a disposition to embrace everything that escapes these determinisms. We have to develop a notion of the public space that incorporates its non-physical, relational, communicational dimension. We also have to know how to combine the pessimism of Gramsci's intelligence, which recognises in economic forces and sociological determinants a number of powerful elements in the structuring of societies, and the ability, the determination of the human being to escape from that structuring. These are fundamental questions—humans are what they do. I am part of a generation that was faced with extremely structured visions of the world, visions that were desperately hopeless because they were so specific. But there is something irrepressible about human beings that we must manage to cultivate: the city—whether it is political, urban or physical—is simultaneously enclosing and emancipatory.

So we have to constantly go back and forth between what constrains shapes and what allows them, on the contrary, to be as rich and dense as possible, aggregating sociology, politics, history—and at the same time remaining open and conducive to the individual being able to inhabit and appropriate the shapes. Jean Nouvel's work on the theatre in Belfort goes in that direction: leaving the marks that are on the walls, keeping what already exists. In my previous house, I refused to paint the skirting boards and door frames, so as not to 'freeze' them in place. I see signs —the marks of time—on them.

I'm making this detour through urbanity and the city because I don't think architecture, which at a given point embodies a specific object —an amenity, a building or a public space—, has any meaning except in the understanding of the context in which it is situated. That's what public architecture is: an object that is made unique by its particular context. Like the Conservatoire project, which forms part of the Fort Hatry site and is related to the Fort's history. What I found very interesting in the work your agency does was that ability to draw inspiration from the spirit of the place. We also had a happy experience when we were building the Congress Centre in Belfort: Gilles Bouchez had won the competition as he had best understood the relationship with the town. His building opened to the south into the town, in line with Vauban's plans, whereas those of his competitors overlooked a boulevard running alongside the site. But even so it was still relatively enclosed, rather like a shell. Taking inspiration from an idea I had seen somewhere else, I suggested to Bouchez that we should lift the mass up slightly to achieve an element of transparency that would also link the building to the rest of the town. Then during the building phase there were some trees that made things a bit complicated, but sometimes it's interesting if the architecture has to deal with some constraints rather than being allowed to just wipe out everything that's there already and build something new—something that could just as easily have been designed in a vacuum. The ability to blend in with what is already there is the strength of any building: architecture isn't just the construction of an object, it's more the construction of an object in relation to something else—in relation not only to its users but also to a space, and in this case to a public space.

DC

You're right: without interactions, architecture has no reason to exist. Public architecture constitutes our main activity, and it's also a commitment, almost a political choice on our part, to following a French—or European—movement to constantly invest in and support public commissions that continues to believe that it's possible to come up with programmes for everyone. This investment is a distant echo of France as a culture-driven country, where there are historical layers, strata that form one of the country's specific features. And at some point certain local councillors, at the local level, are the bearers of a local project and become the go-betweens between the public and the architect. The ideal is obviously when the architect meets the local councillors during a competition procedure, when architects are in competition with each other: that means that the choice will be in favour of the best response, or at any rate the response that seems to be the closest match to what is wanted. It is then up to architecture to carry or transform what is set out in the programme—which is in fact a kind of device constructed by the users, by the local councillors; a mayor who has decided at some point to invest a certain budget in such and such a building. I think a clear statement is often made, and there's a real generosity. When a mayor decides to build a group of schools in a neighbourhood that needs it, that's a political decision that the architect will have to translate into the corresponding buildings. That's where I believe context comes into it. A building must demonstrate a degree of soundness in relation to the place it occupies: you're right that it's not an object that you can move about from one place to another. It's an object that has to integrate, feel or enter into resonance with a site, and with the use to be made of it, and with a human community.

EB

And once the project has been entrusted to you, how do you grasp the programme, with its political determination? How do you approach that tipping point, when it still seems that everything is possible in terms of architecture?

DC

I try, with each project, to transcribe in the spaces I create the generosity of intention that already exists in certain programmes. It's often the only link we have with any consultations there may be, with what has gone before, and that can give rise to a form of frustration. The architect picks up the story on the move. The project may for example be located in a town he has never visited before, in which case he has to make an initial effort to understand the place. Consultation also often involves an attitude or a political choice, and you have to both understand the history being proposed, and transform or reinterpret it using the force of architecture.

Sometimes the programme remains very abstract, even if we are lucky enough during the competition stage to meet the client and receive an explanation from him, as with your project, of why he has chosen to put this building in this particular place, why he has invested his money here and not elsewhere—it's not always the case. So we take hold of all these elements, all this background, and transpose it into our architectural response. The site for the Conservatoire in Belfort was rather peculiar, with a building backing onto woodland and facing the town—an entire landscape was already there, and we tried to echo that, or at the very least come up with a very individual response.

Rehearsal studio
Conservatoire, Belfort, 2015

And in fact that's an interesting point about a project for a conservatoire—we don't yet have archetypes for music schools. They are buildings that are too recent for us to be able to ask: 'Well, what does a conservatoire look like?' For a courthouse, for example, you expect something fairly specific: there's a known history of architecture for courthouses. But for a programme for a music school there's no expected form, no expected writing. Quite the contrary: it seems to me that there's something to invent in the vocabulary of these new places—something to invent in the architectural language. That's what I'm interested in.

More generally, I try to produce places that gather people in, that bring people together, and that allow uses that relate to more things than the programme is being asked to achieve. As far as I'm concerned, a building is successful when it does more than is expected of it, when it goes that extra mile—when it has an extra dimension. That's perhaps what gives us the impression, when we go into some buildings, that they have a soul: they have an unforgettable atmosphere. And places like that stay in our minds because we experienced something there.

'Saint-Jean' school complex
Strasbourg, 2013

Media library
Thionville, 2016

That's how personal stories are created, too. We all have certain memories of the schools we attended as children; they aren't always extraordinary but they leave their mark on our personal history and it is these memories that later in our lives enable us to situate ourselves, to make choices, to adopt attitudes. That's why I want to make schools as un-monotonous as possible: I try, for example, to set up routes that are scattered with specific events. I want to make the schools as non-repetitive as possible so that the buildings don't have a crushing weight that puts all the children on the same level. I like schools to be a bit rebellious.

EB
You try to make schools that respect a certain form of mystery—the unexpected; schools where things aren't always where you would expect to find them.

DC
Yes, it's exactly that.

EB

I'd like to come back to what happens in the early stages of a project. Before the architecture, there is the commission, either public or private. Urban and architectural social action isn't limited to public commissioning: there are enough tools these days—numerous and varied regulations, local urban plans and so on—for us to be able to have real conversations and carry out urban projects worthy of the name with private promoters. But when the market dominates, there is a tendency to reaffirm the prevalence of public action in town planning. And of course when the role of the State is challenged, when freedom of expression seems to be the watchword yet the market regulates everything, it's essential to support and protect public commissioning, which provides assurance of a dialogue between clients and specialists. This dialogue, which must be a constant iterative process from the planning stage right through to completion, is enriched by the multiple contacts between the programmer, the technicians, the engineers, the architect and the users, and its accumulated energy is ploughed back into the architecture that is being produced.

As for the social function of the architecture, we are agreed that a public facility has no meaning other than the uses made of it. Yet we can't reduce it to this function alone: that would mean disregarding its symbolic role, its aesthetic role, its role of magnifying the community. It is these roles that are threatened when the production of towns is delegated to the market or to the management of income from property: we have seen the problems this causes in the industrial areas of certain towns, with a multitude of high-rise buildings and standardised architecture. The guarantee of a diverse town, then, is above all public control over town planning and development—an urban project, in other words, that links, for example, roads and the ecological constraints of mobility: a background that needs to be worked on before the architecture can be brought in. When we then call on an architect to magnify this work and embody it in specific facilities, it's important that we pass on to him our vision of things, although we also need to be prepared to supplement or enrich our original thinking.

Architects also bring us the experience they have already been able to gain in other places. I expect a lot from travelling and comparing these experiences, but I expect even more from the programme when it is actually in place and the changes that are bound to come up. This leeway is valuable, and hard to maintain when things become rigidified. In this respect, anonymous jury panels are a disaster: the best moment in a project is when you talk to the teams. That allows us to draw attention to certain aspects of the programme, and to pass on what we would like to see, beyond the cold descriptions in the technical specifications. Things start to settle out even during this initial discussion. Anonymity is absurd: faced with a complex object, reading a summary or looking at scale models just isn't enough. Even if you already have a bit of experience and can adopt some critical distance, you still need words. It's in such times that I believe emulation is absolutely essential.

DC

I totally agree. The architect's response expresses his interpretation of the programme and I'm convinced that you have to be able, at some point, to narrate that interpretation. And the best way to narrate anything is to say it out loud, with a physical presence. The filter of anonymity detracts from the discussions in a way that a text given to a jury panel can never make up for.

EB

Yes, it's a very strong feeling of loss that I've also had between the before and after of certain projects. We have to have as many meetings and competitions as possible, like Europan.[1] It's fascinating to see so many outside eyes applying their creativity to our territory. In Belfort, in the 1980s, we hosted an international seminar on contemporary architecture that gave us food for thought for the next twenty years. The teams came from all over the place, some of them included students; we offered them about ten days' immersion in the town, with the local authority providing them with excellent accommodation.[2] It's the kind of experience that makes it possible to draw up an inventory of plots of land, carry out site diagnoses, and also quite simply to be in contact with architectural practices: not all local councillors know spontaneously how to read a scale model or a map.

Architecture can't solve all the problems on its own: it's a joint effort. Some types of architecture are so hemmed in that the facilities themselves are enclosed. We were talking about rebel schools a moment ago—let's take for example an open school, which is considered in relation to other times of day—time spent outside the classroom. How can it be associated with a leisure centre or a library that has its own opening hours? The absolutely central part of the school must open towards the outside, for example with a room specially for parents that can be reached from the street. Of course, you also have to have a certain number of precise rules that frame recreational time and make it possible: you don't want the kids just to run off! The children are free, but within an enclosed space and for a limited amount of time. The idea we have of schools and education produces a certain type of architecture, and the architect may challenge some of the aspects of a commission according to his own idea of education—he's a go-between who also has something to say. School today is an exciting subject: we have moved away from basic, standardised constructions; contemporary mutations call for objects that are more flexible, more open—benevolent objects.

As for the Conservatoire in Belfort, part of the reason for positioning it on the hill occupied by the Fort Hatry site was because there was land available there, of course, but it was also partly because this made the project part of the link we were trying to create between the difficult residential neighbourhoods to the west and the city centre in the east. When the Fort was developed as a park, with the Passagers des Villes agency in Lyon, we had already made a gap in the fortress: on the inside, we put a gym and some housing, to combine public and private areas. The Conservatoire came to be there too, opening onto the town and Vauban's citadel on one side and with the other side looking out towards the Vosges mountains. It was important that it should open onto its neighbourhood because at the time we were also implementing a policy of democratising music-making, encouraged by the teaching of music at school which was already well established in Belfort. Young people wanted to make music but their social environment made it difficult, so we proposed lending them an instrument for a year—including a mute—if they were living in subsidised social housing. You have to go down to the smallest detail sometimes, and that's one of the fascinating aspects of being a mayor. A friend came to see me one day: she was very anxious as her project was going to have to stop because there were kids playing the trumpet in social housing units and the director of their music school didn't have the money to buy mutes for them—they cost two hundred euros apiece. Finding three thousand euros to buy mutes for trumpets—sometimes that's what being a mayor is all about.

So the concept for the Conservatoire was much more than just its shape; it involved thinking about an attractive, open space where individual music-making that calls for suitable small soundproofed cells could be combined with collective music-making in large theatre areas. It was then enriched by your contributions: traffic through an open space, huge staircases that transform the hall and allow types of music-making we hadn't thought of—choirs, for instance. All that to reaffirm that things are included in a mechanical fashion: a piece of architecture is more or less social depending on whether or not it incorporates certain types of use that already bear the mark of social policies, meaning uses that demonstrate egalitarianism and solidarity.

DC

And it's easy to imagine that it would be difficult for some policies to result in buildings of use to the public! You were talking about schools as *benevolent* objects: it's a word I'm very fond of. In a group of schools, the elements of the programme are often gathered together: a nursery school, a primary school, premises for out-of-school activities, a library, a sports hall. I think architecture ought to put in some real work there, both to open things up, and to reassure. In some Scandinavian countries, even in Germany, playgrounds stay open after school hours. In Strasbourg—and perhaps in Belfort too?—associations are allowed to use sports halls in the evenings and at the weekend. There are small music schools in nearly every group of schools, and often the facility becomes porous, opening up to the town. Individual uses get stronger and the school becomes a place of generosity, a pleasant place to be. A form of sharing and benevolence sets in; when you pass in front of a school, looking at it conjures up all the stories that have gone on there. Architecture must carry these stories, it must conjure up that generosity. That's what we try to do—by using colour, for instance, as in the group of schools at La Courneuve. We designed the building rather like a jewel at the centre of the 'Cité des 4000' housing estate—you can see it from all the surrounding blocks of flats. The local community was really looking forward to the facility, and I felt it was important that it should radiate out into the surrounding neighbourhood. At the inauguration party in 2010, you could actually feel the local residents' pride: it made a very strong impression on me.

EB
I know La Courneuve well—I used to live there. The people must have felt well-regarded.

DC
Even though the building is almost entirely white, there has never been any graffiti or vandalism. The mayor had supported my idea of making large bay windows open onto the town; the local councillors felt the school was extremely important for the neighbourhood, and their attitude was extremely generous. That trust, that assistance, gives me, as an architect, an even stronger feeling of responsibility, a desire to surpass myself. Schools are places where you learn to become emancipated. I believe that architecture should also evoke that freedom: translating it into spaces, producing architecture that moves, architecture that communicates the pleasure to be had in moving about.

EB
That's the direction things seem to be moving in: there are more and more recommendations with regard to quality of life in the school environment. School architecture has passed out of the hands of the standardised Ministry of Education into the hands of the local authorities, and nowadays everything depends on how attached local councillors are to their schools and getting what they want done. It's sometimes cheerfully disorganised, although a number of aspects are fixed so that the important things are borne in mind when a school is being built.

DC
The paradox, when you add all these rules to the different elements dictated by the programme, is that you wonder what latitude is still allowed to the architect. Part of our freedom consists of imagining the relationships that are going to be created among the users, giving them as much freedom as possible, or provoking specific freedoms in particular places. That sometimes takes a very imaginary, very conceptual turn: we wonder who these users are whom we often only meet at inaugurations. But everyone involved, whether local councillor or architect, has to be capable of projecting themselves into the future: one of our responsibilities is to make buildings that last. The architect is faced with a two-fold demand: he must both respond to an immediate need that is specific and topical, and imagine how his building is going to stand up to the passage of time. He has to be able to win over the users and stakeholders of today, and at the same time dare to imagine the building in the future:

it may be avant-garde, or merely offer some aspects that are capable of taking it beyond its present use. That's what's difficult about our work, but that's also what makes it interesting: we have to stay the course and look further into the distance, to see what the strength of the building will be in ten or thirty years' time, and what will enable it to survive and absorb society's evolutions. The architect must be able to grasp this dualism, seize on it. His work on space enables him to produce these strong places that are capable either of reaching across time or passing through the ages with more ease. We can all remember the places that we find moving and which have stood up to centuries or merely years of history. This constant dimension of architecture is very important: the problem lies in achieving a certain degree of 'rightness' in your own age and then ensuring that it continues.

EB

There is indeed a permanent tension between the need to take account of contemporary usage and the contrary and imperative need to escape from that usage, in as much as things are bound to change, as is society and its expectations. You expect that something that is supposed to last for forty years will be able to anticipate at least some of the changes likely to occur in the future, and it's a good idea to not tie your hands by drafting technical specifications that only take present uses into account. Not all that long ago it was fashionable to get residents to come up with ideas for their neighbourhood of the future; people would meet, but it didn't take into account the amount of time personal decision-making takes—it's not the same as decision-making for public production: it takes five, ten or fifteen years to work out a priority town-planning area, and in the meantime the people present at the start of the concertation have already bought property elsewhere—if you only take the users' prescriptions into account, it's bound to be a failure. What's needed is not so much a balance as a real dynamic that needs to be found between the current needs that are noticed and the ability to project into the future. This is one of the essential features of public commissions: the ability to embrace the unexpected, the ability to call yourself into question.

Concertation only works if you come to it with some clear ideas; you can't just hold out a pencil to people and say: 'Go on, do the work of a town planner, an architect, an engineer'—it would be mayhem. As a local councillor, you have to show that you have a project, even if the project is not completely finalised. If some interesting elements or objections come up and add something to the project, you can always put things back on the table. I'll take an example: in 2016, there was a 'citizen dialogue' in Toulouse on the initiative of the local government office (*Conseil Général*) on a project aimed at resolving a certain problem of social mixing. After four months of concertation, the original hypothesis had been invalidated and the Conseil Général had changed the direction of its project. Something had been brought to the project—that's what I expect from an architect: that he will contribute things I haven't thought of, possibly obliging me to revise part of my programme. But before that stage you have to express the constraints clearly—a financial framework, for instance, remains valid until such time as there are sufficiently strong arguments for changing it. You can't say to the architect, 'That's fine—we'll add things as we go along!' Particularly with public resources becoming scarcer. It's not possible nowadays to start on a site and overshoot by thirty percent by the time it's finished. You have to follow the outlines, yet stay capable of playing a trump card if one comes up, or taking an opportunity that would take you outside the intended framework. It's not easy—the architect mustn't feel he can do whatever he feels like doing! There are often solid reasons for defending a programme.

DC

I remember the first meeting for the competition for the Conservatoire: we had already put the cat among the pigeons by telling you straight out that the budget wasn't appropriate. But you listened to me very carefully and I was able to give you my reasons: in a conservatoire, the acoustic norms are stricter than in a school. You told us you understood and that you would think about it, and that's what you actually did: as head of the authority of the agglomeration, you proposed an extra million euros—although you did say that it wouldn't be reconsidered …

EB
That's true, and I was very pleased with the choices made. We got the project passed in 2009, right in the middle of the financial crisis. Some of the local councillors said that we were pouring money down the drain building a conservatoire, but we got an absolute majority with about sixty percent in favour in a joint assembly of about forty municipalities, including a number of people who certainly didn't put culture at the top of their list of concerns.

DC
It's funny, because that's one of the things you feel, as an architect: when a project is being carried along even by just a handful of people, you feel that there's real trust being passed on.

EB
And vice-versa, since we're more likely to defend an architectural project that we've found convincing. It's a dialectic: on the one hand you need openness, and on the other the intelligence or strength of the project to be able to overcome the constraints. Architecture also involves education: I believe a good architect doesn't consider the local councillor to be someone who has no understanding, but as someone who needs to be convinced.

DC
Trust is essential. The local councillor entrusts a sometimes quite considerable budget to a team, and that trust carries with it a great deal of responsibility. We are aware of the weight of it: it is usually reflected in a desire to make the building as successful as possible.

EB
It has to be said also that, at the time of the competition for the Conservatoire, you were one of the few architects to have any experience in this type of programme: that was one of the factors that brought the balance down in your favour.

DC
Yes, we had just finished the Conservatoire in Maizières-lès-Metz. The mayor there was a structural engineer and it was a generous programme, with a conservatoire, an auditorium, a reception hall, a kitchen, and an out-of-school reception centre. On the other hand, it was very tight budget, and the site was quite terrifying, in a fairly new low-rise residential neighbourhood with no anchorage potential—a fairly catastrophic suburban set-up, close to the motorway to Luxembourg.
In that type of context, there's no way of getting round the question of insertion in the urban fabric: we proposed a very closed building, a huge monolith bringing together all the elements in the programme and featuring a giant cantilever above an entrance that takes you in … to something completely different.

Conservatoire
Maizières-lès-Metz, 2009

EB

It was the building that was going to create the anchorage in the neighbourhood: the first time I saw it, it reminded me of Le Corbusier's chapel at Ronchamp. I don't know why—perhaps it was because of the shapes in the concrete, something organic that stood out. The facade is a statement: there's something intriguing, very aesthetic, about it—it has real shape.

DC

It's true that it has this strength as a very deliberate building that fully assumes its scale. Yet the initial idea was to stress above all the areas inside the building so that you would forget about the context of the Conservatoire as you walked through it, to produce a dissociated space. We hadn't managed to find any aspect of the landscape to hang the project on—not even an interesting view; on the motorway side, it was necessary to provide protection from the noise. In the end, the Conservatoire is dotted with interior patios: what there is to see is the sky—the sky is always beautiful. And the building stands up, it's coherent, and it has its contrasts: a certain roughness on the outside, with a softer inside, which we felt was the best response. Once again, the context made a huge difference to the architectural writing.

EB

That's what I found particularly interesting about this project: it's an assembly of lots of different things, yet there's real cohesion. There's a formality that links everything and gives the outside the look of a shared object, an object that creates something that is shared. Another thing I really noticed, compared with other things I've seen where people were more concerned with uses, is that what we had in the end was a real collection that showed the complexity of the programme, the motley collection of different sized rooms, yet articulated them and gave them some form of unity. It's not something that's obvious, and that's what I liked about your plan for Belfort: the large cube shape supplies *de facto* unity.

The volume of the library, suspended above the main stairway. Conservatoire, Belfort, 2015

DC

That's right; these programmes are the sum of a number of very small elements—some of the studios measure less than six square metres. How does one manage to bring them together? Personally, I find the federating role is played by the group area. The smaller the elements are, the more I want to produce a central space and make it large, make it a place that brings people together. The organisation of the smaller elements can also be extremely important: the library at the Conservatoire, for instance, extends out into empty space. It's one of the elements in the programme that cuts through all the others, and although it's small, the fact of suspending it like that within the space available gives it a preciousness, a weight, a presence. Perhaps the very fact of providing a kind of public place or space inside a building reconstructs a social dimension of the town actually within the architecture.

EB

I don't know how people use it nowadays, but it's true that we fell in love with the suspended library. But I don't know if I would make the analogy between these federating spaces and towns. In a town, something is always left to juxtaposition, but in your projects, on the contrary, there is a lot of work on composition. Like in Belfort, with the two halls, the central space, the patios, the library and the almost monk-like cells for rehearsal rooms, and the opening systems that mean that the building breathes and you can both see and be seen. I liked all that very much—and proof of that is that I'm still capable of saying something about it!

DC
It's the memory we have of places ... Some places give us the feeling of having grown: a place we like, or a place that has a certain strength, can suddenly release something that marks our body and is reflected later in a positive emotion—the kind of emotion you can feel in certain buildings.

EB
Exactly, and that's why architecture is a strongly structuring element in the feeling of belonging and the pride you can feel in a place. It's an element in my pride, too, because I have been lucky enough to have been involved in town planning for the past twenty years, to see the town develop, to have left my mark here and there. I think we've had some successes; a town like Belfort is still a complicated town, with military, working-class, industrial aspects—not everything is magnificent.

DC
I find this public dimension providing urban developments with real quality is a real strong point in towns in Europe. I was rather surprised and a bit disappointed to find that, in comparison, there are very few public spaces in Tokyo.

EB
Yes—the cafés in blocks of flats are incredible! Elsewhere, in most large towns in America for example, it's the car that structures everything. European towns are often structured by politics: it's a feature of them caused by the importance of public facilities and the central position of some of these buildings; it's a certain affirmation of the power and place of politics, the agora, and also of particularly structuring public functions: universities, town halls, administrative offices, hospitals, and so on.

DC
Yes; we've already talked about places of education, but we could also mention places where therapy is provided, as they have an absolutely vital role to play in the functioning of a society. Nursing homes, retirement homes, hostels and centres for handicapped people, and so on. They are different publics, with specific needs, and the buildings are difficult in one sense, because they demand that special attention be paid to a whole dimension of comfort, little things, small spaces, mechanisms that need to be set up to receive these people. I remember one retirement home we delivered; the director congratulated us:

Patios and circulation areas
Retirement home
Pont-sur-Yonne, 2014

'It's incredible! The families all walk about in the corridors!' We had created a sort of route that opened onto planted patios, with natural light, and had altered the standard arrangements quite a bit in order to escape from the norms for a corridor. Everything had been thought out to encourage the residents to leave their rooms. I think that's extremely important: I want architecture to allow people to come and go all the time, with something to look at. Architecture should be organised in such a way as to allow life to continue. Everything that creates sectors should be banned, and places for gathering together should be placed strategically in the building. Work on the light, the orientation of the rooms, the relationship with the seasons—I think all these things are really important, particularly for the elderly. We're back to the idea of anchorage. We have no control over use, but we have to imagine an ergonomic use of the space: what do we do, for example, to make sure that people see and meet other people? The programmes for these places are often very dry and technical: the nursing station, the number of rooms, and all sorts of rules, including very strict fire safety rules since these are places where people sleep. How can we get away from all this technical paraphernalia and propose an improvement, something extra?

EB

These issues related to the diversity of users are indeed crucial—for a local councillor, they're on a different scale, and expressed in two ways: the population as a whole is the first and foremost concern of the mayor, it is the wealth of his town; the second thing involves asking *who* that population is. At the end of the 1990s the principle of social mix was brought into question again: I find it unbearable: 'Diversity isn't something you can decree,' they said. But it's something you can accompany, for heaven's sake! Diversity is inseparable from the republican ideal: there's nothing worse than compartmentalisation, social separatism, and an inward-looking attitude. A lot of people complain about communitarianism today, but it's largely our society that has produced communitarianism by excluding, relegating and segregating people. Some mayors would perhaps prefer to have more well-off people than working-class people. Personally, I feel that if a population includes ten thousand poor people and four thousand unemployed people, although it's necessary to accommodate managers and middle professions as well, what's essential is that all these populations should be able to live decently in the town. The policy we have implemented in Belfort, for example, has consisted of breaking up the concentration in the priority urban areas by scattering subsidised housing throughout the town.

So the problem isn't just about buildings; you have to ask yourself what old people do in the town, and how we can help them stay in their own homes for as long as possible. How we can create links between the generations. How we can produce that social mix. And that's where public commissions have a role to play. In an urban renovation project, for example, when we create a mixed development zone we try to promote access not only to home ownership but also to private and subsidised rental. My solution, even with thirty-five percent of subsidised housing, has never been to reduce the percentage: packing people off to nearby villages doesn't make the situation any better. Transport is in the town; the town includes fragile populations, and any population, whatever it is, is more of a wealth than a burden.

So how can this obsession be translated into an urban project? The offer of housing has to be balanced for all the town's residents, without forcing people to live in any particular neighbourhood: at one and the same time we have to retain Alstom's managers, the middle classes, and the working classes. The answer lies firstly in architectural operations, and secondly in bringing these populations into contact with each other, and that's where the public space comes in. How does mobility work? How can the town be made more accessible? How can public transport, cycling, and pleasant walkways for pedestrians be developed? Accessibility for handicapped people is particularly interesting in this respect, since it forces you to consider a different way of perceiving the town. What we do for these people benefits everyone, since we soften the violence of the routes in town: when we lower the level of a pavement, for instance, it's as helpful for someone with a suitcase as it is for someone who's handicapped. And of course these concerns for the quality of the public space—questions about paving stones and street profiles—also call for a certain frame of reference: the architect's perspective adds an aesthetic dimension—perhaps even an anthropological dimension—to the technical aspects. Highway engineers, gardeners—everyone has a role to play; but you also need someone to bring all this together.

And lastly you need to ensure real dialogue with the population. In 1989, for example, we revised the local land use plan for Belfort. We insisted that drawing up new plans should be a collective effort, because the revision didn't only concern owner-occupiers, and it represented much more than a purely legal document. We wanted to get the whole town involved in thinking about its status so that the final plan would reflect a real urban project—which was in fact what happened subsequently with the local town planning schemes and development projects, including sustainable development. We tried to make each of these a definite concerted event, to explain and recall what the town is. It was much more than an administrative event: it was a dialogue about a real issue, since we were going to define the legislation on town planning—on the town we wanted to build. The contribution of local architects was particularly interesting. We had previously been criticised for being too ready to call in outside architects for public commissions and it wasn't easy to organise, but the confrontation between 'outsiders' and the local architecture community made it possible to open up new areas of thinking. You always want the best for your town. You look for who could embody it.

DC

I think this mixing is in fact essential: when public commissioning runs out of funds, its demands must be even greater. What you were saying a moment ago about the social mix of populations brings to mind an old people's home that we're completing in a small village, Poissons, where there's also a problem with the school canteen; the mayor proposed that the children should come from the school to eat at the retirement home. So the children invade the retirement home four days a week. It represents a saving, obviously, because they have not had to build a separate canteen building, but it also provides an opportunity to get very different people to meet each other, and to make the children aware of a different type of vulnerability. And in return, the elderly people enjoy the youth and energy of the children. In Antwerp, where some communities don't always function very well, the mayor insisted that the town planners site a new group of schools at a point where a number of neighbourhoods meet, so that they wouldn't be the schools of any one particular neighbourhood, and it would perhaps be possible to get away from that segregation.

EB

There's real work to be done on the outskirts of towns— on the relations and exchanges in these areas. In Toulouse, the metro has done much more to open up the Mirail neighbourhood than all the urban operations that are still ongoing. What is at issue is not so much doing something original but rather extending the production of town planning by democratic, emancipatory architecture, and having procedures that correspond to this urban ideal. I say 'urban' rather than 'architectural' because I consider architecture to be one aspect of this urbanity: an autonomous aspect, it's true, but one that is only meaningful when it is combined with the urban fabric to make the town, to make a 'city' in the Athenian sense, in the political and philosophical meaning of the word: in the sense of a human community.

Local councillors have to learn to play the role of the person bringing all this together: the different departments of a town planning agency, for example, where there are issues involving sociology, aesthetics, geography, the economy. Without minimising the specific characteristics of everyone involved, you have to make sure that they are all fully aware of the culture of the others in order to produce an enriching, stimulating, forward-looking town. It also means that you have to manage, despite the constraints of all the procedures, to preserve a constant, vital dialogue between users, local councillors, the architect and the different trades. The responses, or the technical, political and democratic proposals, can then come from the experience gained at urban workshops, consultations, presentations and discussions on the projects. It's a whole: an urban project that's redefined every ten years combined with periods of consideration and research that nourish thinking in the town. It all contributes to creating a rich and stimulating culture of the town and architecture. It's as much about building up networks of design offices as about maintaining the town's heritage and being attentive to new artistic productions as merely passing on a feeling of beautiful things to the next generation.

DC
I'm very aware of these links, although as a practitioner I haven't come across many truly experimental projects. On the other hand, as a teacher, I always insist on dealing with architecture and town planning together. Transversal work is very important in my workshop—probably much more than it is in reality. There's probably a utopian aspect involved. The students work together on urban projects. At the moment, for example, we're studying a site in Rotterdam. The students, divided into three groups of ten, take one part of the plot and start by formulating an approach that is clear from the urban point of view. It is only thereafter that they take on the role of architects and develop part of their guiding plan. This creates a to-ing and fro-ing between seeking general coherency in the town and developing the architectural project, and the result is usually interesting. What needs to be unpacked? Which attitudes are possible, and which are untenable? Architecture must be put into perspective. It's more than a gesture or an intuition—it's an entire process.

EB
Quite so, although I think even the term 'process' is over-technical: what's needed is a word that conjures up an image of the alchemy that can only really occur if it is carried along by a real ambition, with no censure as to either the matter of the urban project or the time-frame and geographical situation. You have to be capable of both going beyond borders and making a form crystallise—although the form may be porous, malleable, open to the evolutions of society. The architectural phase is the exciting stage in the business: when town planning and architecture combine with the human project.

There is a whole range of tools available to users, from the neighbourhood council to the urban workshop, including projects within schools. In a project like that of the Conservatoire, the architect is included in these discussions as much as possible —and indeed you spoke at the community meeting. Research is also vitally important in public policy and social innovation: in these thoughtful stages you have to be able to rely on people whose work has explored and investigated the adjacent conceptual issues—a to-and-fro between concept and reality. In order to make a city beautiful and dynamic, you must first design it, think it through, project it.

I still have in my mind a number of operations that put this idea into action, I think, in an exemplary fashion. For example, my first operation, when I was deputy mayor with responsibility for young people and immigration. A housing agency consulted us to find out whether it should create adapted housing or share work out among the existing housing stock—I thought these ideas were absolutely fantastic because they meant we could express what we thought of the populations concerned. On the site there was a single type of detached house, and two blocks of four- and five-roomed flats. By the time we had finished the substantial renovation work the project involved, we had transformed these two alternatives into twelve different types of housing: that taught me it was possible to change the rules of the game.

Another operation I'm particularly proud of is the mosque in Belfort. There were already a number of places of worship for the different communities, but overall there was no real mosque. One of these places of worship was in a former hostel for immigrant workers in the town centre, inside the walls surrounding the castle and its fortifications. I used to live not far away, and one day I heard the muezzin's call carried on the west wind; at the time, France's National Front party was handing leaflets out all over the town and I fully expected a riot in the neighbourhood. But it all passed off calmly, and we were still looking for a plot of land for building a mosque, with enough space around it for Ramadan celebrations—and it suddenly struck me as being obvious: it was in this historic site that we ought to build the mosque.

In the first place it was a tribute to memory, since there are thousands of migrant workers in the background of Belfort's development, and some of them must have attended worship there. It made it possible to not banish the mosque to the outskirts of the town; also, there was already a car park, and there were no immediate neighbours. We were nevertheless aware that it would not be easy to get the choice accepted. So with Luc Vilan, the architect at the town planning agency, we did a lot of work on drafting the specifications and considering the plot of land in order to both respect the historic building and construct a decent mosque. It was only after that we opened the debate, and it was just as well we had done our homework first because our opponents were quick to wade in—there were some extremely lively demonstrations and reactions. But our project included real social and architectural thinking. Luc Vilan, who had worked in the Damascus area previously, was very well versed in Muslim architecture. We proposed a mosque without any cupolas, based on a hypostyle plan. It took two years of debate; there were appeals to the administrative tribunal to have the decision reversed. We ended up with a long-term lease, without selling the land, and eventually the mosque was built. Without this combination of a strong vision of the urban project, the backing of architectural intelligence, and consideration for social insertion, the sustainable aspect and the heritage dimension, I doubt the project would ever have come to anything.

DC

These are valuable concordances; they multiply the strength of a project. I don't think the ideal town or the ideal building actually exists—you could say that they are still to be built! But if I were to keep just one memory, a single architectural experience, it would be when I walked through the streets of La Quinta da Malagueira, the neighbourhood on the outskirts of the town of Evora in Portugal, designed by Álvaro Siza in the 1970s.[J] It's a project that involves architecture, town planning, and landscaping. Siza seems to have gathered up, interpreted and then recreated all the complexity of the place. It mainly consists of housing and small shops or facilities: a grocery shop, a restaurant, a neighbourhood centre, and so on. Relatively few elements, in fact, and it would have been inappropriate to go in for architectural prowess.

At certain road intersections, you come across a small open space: empty spaces that are created at the intersection of the angles of different geometries. Nothing seems to have been actually designed and yet it's all there. Certain situations appear to be suspended, waiting, as if they were incomplete. Great breezeblock aqueducts crisscross the neighbourhood, alternately running alongside and passing through the aligned houses in an anarchic gesture, as if by accident. The landscape is straightforward. Large empty spaces form air pockets between the different sectors. A stream flows into a lake at the lower end of the site, and right alongside an open-air theatre adds another strange touch to the place. The streets are silent in the harsh southern light. You feel the presence of architecture everywhere, although without

being able to put your finger on exactly where it is. The perfection of Siza's design connects with the vernacular—everything looks as if it is exactly where it should be.

1 The Europan biennial, the first edition of which was held in 1989 and 1990, is a competition for urban and architectural projects drawn up by young architects on a common theme with real situations, proposed by local authorities in respect of various European sites.

2 The SIAC, International Seminar on Contemporary Architecture, took place in Belfort in 1984 and brought together some thirty European participants on the theme of 'Ten days to remake Belfort'.

Complexity
Daniel Payot, Alexandra Pignol
Strasbourg, on 12 July 2018

'When I speak of complexity, I use the elementary Latin meaning of the word "complexus"—"that which is woven together". The constituent parts differ, but the overall effect is as in a tapestry. The real problem (with reforming thinking) is that we have learnt too well how to separate things. It would be better for us to learn how to bind things together. "Binding together" is more than creating an end-to-end connection: it means establishing a connection that forms a loop. Indeed in French the word for "binding together" *(relier)* includes the syllable *re*, meaning "return", which represents the loop turning back on itself. A loop is autoproductive. Life originates with the creation of a kind of loop, a kind of natural machinery that loops round on itself and produces increasingly diverse elements that make up a complex being that will be alive. The world auto-produced itself in an extremely mysterious fashion; knowledge today has to have instruments —fundamental concepts—that are necessary before any binding together can be possible.'[1]

I Architecture and complexity

AP
Edgar Morin's definition of complexity could serve as a good starting point.[2] The view of complexity that philosophy has is definitely not the same as the view architecture has. Perhaps you could start by giving your definition of complexity?

DC
For me, complexity is an approach, a method for producing a project. For centuries, architecture tried to eliminate complexity: it almost had the role of a simplifier. Architecture was expected to solve everything, and above all it was expected to provide simple answers to complex situations. Architecture used to set aside a whole series of arrangements in order to achieve this simplification, but I don't think that's the principle nowadays.

In both my teaching and my work, I consider the multiple parameters that face the architect to be elements that trigger the project. These parameters are sometimes contradictory, but they can sometimes provide the source of the architectural idea. Adopting this attitude makes it possible to envisage architecture that invents, or tries to invent, something: architecture that is not forced to adopt a pre-determined posture. It's a very interesting process because it's open, and thus enables us to explore ways of producing projects and situations that are more flexible.

I think one very contemporary question is the flow issue: traffic flows at a railway station, for example. The Dutch practice UNStudio recently completed the renovation of the railway station in Arnhem in the Netherlands. In their project, Ben van Berkel and Caroline Bos applied the principle of beginning work on the basis of flow diagrams, with the intention of the architecture accompanying the flows. The absence of an *a priori* geometric outline generates a particular degree of plasticity that would not have been achieved if the architects had not considered this parameter to be a decisive element in the project.

The complexity that I'm particularly fond of is the complexity that makes it possible to convoke and combine heterogeneous programmes, so that mono-functionality disappears, leaving room for something that is richer and more contradictory. What is interesting then is what occurs between the programmes: the relationships architecture is capable of creating, and which are able to produce places that are welcoming and strong in spatial terms. I am very keen on the spatial dimension of architecture.

It seems to me that complexity, for an architect, calls for a certain degree of flexibility. The architect is like a sponge, capable of absorbing very diverse data. When you are producing a project, it is impossible to foresee what data is going to form the basis for the architectural idea, so you have to consider all the data at the same time.

I often tell students that they really shouldn't try to ignore any of the existing parameters. It's a horizontal process, almost an interplay of many parallel pointers, and not a linear way of thinking. If we ignore what already exists, architecture becomes a bulldozer trying to make its own space, and that can be rather brutal: we put ourselves in a forced position where all dynamic disappears.

Architecture creates a relationship with the surrounding landscape, the climate, the use made of the buildings, the programme, the topography, the social context, and so on. The public buildings we work on are often in almost hopeless contexts. The theatre in Freyming-Merlebach, for example, is in a town where unemployment is running at almost twenty-five percent.[3] I am particularly keen that these buildings should look like jewels set down in the landscape. It's often what's expected of them: they become the witnesses of a kind of political resistance—mayors who make the decision to believe in the ability of their towns to achieve a makeover. In Freyming-Merlebach, with its brick houses, the idea as far as I was concerned was not to create a harmony between the building and its context but on the contrary to make the theatre stand out from the landscape, almost like a pearl. It is tall, white and bright, and the town is very proud of it. It's not always about blending in with the context; sometimes you have to accept the break.

AP

So architecture to some extent—and particularly in this case—has a monumental aspect?

DC

Yes. In this specific case, the theatre's stage house gave the building an unavoidable height. But as soon as it was necessary to design the square in front of the building, it also created a public space. The pétanque ground behind the building produces other uses. There is a link of some kind; although there is no obvious connection with the theatre, the different activities all have their place.

If we think of production as a game and try to work flexibly, then there is room for intuition to come into play. That's what I like about scale models: they add something tactile to the cerebral dimension. You can touch them, move them around, look at them, take them apart. These different parameters that I associate with complexity add to the game that is being invented. A game with rules that are vague and subject to change.

A few days ago I was at the conservatoire in Belfort. The director told me that the music teachers, particularly those who play the flute, are huge fans of the central staircase. The space creates a great acoustic, with reverberation similar to a church. Another place that wasn't included in the original programme, a sort of all-concrete agora with no particular acoustic finish (unlike the music rehearsal studios), has generated unexpected enthusiasm. I sometimes bump into a saxophonist who plays under a bridge in Strasbourg because that's where he finds the right reverberation. That's probably what I wanted to achieve, although I didn't put it into words. The architecture generated an unexpected situation that was appreciated by the users. These places are generous because they are vast, and have a particular ability to be welcoming. There are some currents in architecture that claim we should strive for neutrality, but I don't subscribe to that idea. I appreciate strong areas that enable events to happen.

DP

I've noticed two things in the way you define the notion of complexity. You are in fact very close to Edgar Morin with regard to complex thought, except that he talks about it in relation to the production of science while you refer to the production of spaces in architecture. You nevertheless have a good number of points in common, as well as some things that refer more specifically to architecture. Let's start with the similarities: Morin starts out from the intuition that science has always had to face complex situations, and that, in order to manage to say something about them, it has forged a method of simplification—as in Descartes, for example. It was legitimate and sensible, but it reached a turning point: because the method was produced in order to generate simplicity, simplicity was being projected onto the actual reality. Conventional science then embarked on what Morin calls 'the paradigm of simplification'—which is challenged nowadays because it has ceased to function, because reality itself shows that it does not fit into the scheme. You're saying something fairly similar, since you take the method as your starting point. By renouncing the paradigm of simplification, you take an interest in something that, in reality, is multiple and heterogeneous. This last word is extremely important—you used it as well. It all lies in knowing how to arrange the heterogeneity, how to deal and contend with heterogeneity, and how to produce unity in spite of everything—Morin sometimes even refers to 'totality'. How can unity be produced out of something heterogeneous? That's an eminently architecture-related question, a project-related question.

Then, in speaking about arranging heterogeneity, Morin frequently uses the metaphor of fabric. Would you also use similar fabric-related images to illustrate your work as an architect—a number of different threads woven together, perhaps? According to Morin, the fabric that is the final product is not merely the sum of all the threads—in a way, the whole is greater than the sum of its parts. And he also says that once the whole has been constituted, once the heterogeneous aspect has been incorporated, there are two issues that determine what the fabric is really like. Either the heterogeneous element disappears altogether and a type of unity that you call 'brutal' is produced. Or an attempt is made to continue to display this heterogeneity, making all the threads visible and preserving something of their differences. There is no magic formula: there is always some kind of compromise, and that is perhaps also true of science. Do you think it's the same in architecture? In the production of knowledge, there is always the temptation either to regardless reduce heterogeneity to a supposedly homogeneous totality, with the idea that grounding certain knowledge must necessarily involve disregarding the various separate elements, either to take an interest in these singular heterogeneous elements, with the risk of producing a very diffuse or scattered result, and being unable to arrange the whole. Arranging things in science is a kind of challenge; one is constantly torn between an excess of unity and an excess of heterogeneity—and that is perhaps the price to pay for the thirst for knowledge. Being torn is not a defect: on the contrary, it's positive motivation and an opportunity to be seized. In what you were saying a moment ago—including about the relational aspect—I think you were also talking about that moment and that intermediate space between brutal unity and the total heterogeneity of dispersion. And there, you were suggesting, is necessarily something other than a principle of unity.

At that moment and in that place, a number of materials, a number of elements, a number of principles are necessarily brought into play. As you say, it is not a matter of settling into a given vision but of analysing what already exists by observing that there are different expectations and constraints. You have to manage to think about all of that as a whole.

On two points, what you are saying seems to me to relate more specifically to architecture—although to some extent that's where we already are. Firstly, when you speak of what could be called 'the opportunity of context', you say, taking as an example the theatre you built in Freyming-Merlebach, that architecture is sometimes positioned in a reality that has a hopeless, or at the very least an extremely difficult, aspect, and that the architecture can then mean resistance to disintegration. Making it such is certainly an arduous task, since nowadays, as soon as it is a matter of a public space, we are necessarily confronted with perceptions, and sometimes even ideologies, that push us, sometimes very vehemently, towards simplification. It can't always be easy to impose complexity ... Even if you consider it as being close to reality, that doesn't prevent the complex reality often finding itself covered in political, economic, topical slogans that are witness to dichotomy, communications options and rigid achievements, obeying demands for spectacular or consumerist clarity. Could you develop this point a little more, from the architect's point of view? I feel there was a decisive point in what you were saying about this: how to get across this idea of resistance, this complexity that itself becomes the sign of a refusal, an alternative to resignation, hopelessness and disintegration.

Let's call the second point 'the surprise of uses'. You say that working for users you don't know can become very stressful, since it's not possible to reason in terms of *a priori* concordance between what is being asked for and the response to it; you can't just tell yourself, 'This is what they want, these are their needs, I have analysed them and I am meeting them satisfactorily.' Obviously you do analyse the users' needs, but never in a way that claims to be exhaustive: you analyse them and you respond to them in line with the logic of the project, but it may be that once the proposal has been formulated you realise that the user has other ways of reacting to what you have designed, like the flutists at the conservatoire in Belfort. A constructed space can be appropriated differently in this way—either in the use made of it or in the everyday perception that people have of it.

Something else Morin says about science, when he talks of incompleteness, is that from the moment we embrace complexity, we can no longer claim to have covered a question completely or totally, because we have become attentive to all requests, to all the heterogeneous elements. The possibility of an absolute synthesis ceases to exist. Morin finds that particularly interesting and positive; he doesn't see it as a limitation, but rather as an opportunity. That ties up with what you called the dynamic, open aspect—play is really the right word: we play and we produce, we produce starting out from play, on the basis of play, or with play. In the case of Edgar Morin, what is produced is science and knowledge. What you produce is spaces, uses, architecture: is it in fact the same gesture?

There remains a kind of margin where nothing is definitive. Perhaps time always postpones certainties, preventing them being absolute, but it is perhaps in this way that they can really become certainties. Because the work of the architect is truly to produce positivity—things that are real, consistent and eloquent. Morin says in a comparable sense that complex thinking doesn't eliminate simplicity, clarity, legibility, but incorporates them into a graduated functioning that pays attention to plurality and differences. That is perhaps also a question that architects ask themselves: how can I not renounce what is simple and legible, a use that is after all expected? How can I not renounce that, and still leave room for surprises and relationships that are all the more unforeseeable because the project lets them function as freely as possible? And the less you anticipate these relationships in absolute terms, the more you encourage them …

DC

Paradoxically, most people expect the architect to produce a synthesis, so that the final architecture achieves some kind of resolution of all the constraints. Architects often refer to constraints; some even explain their projects in terms of constraints. I don't like the word. We sometimes need almost a double language to be able to transmit relatively simple messages orally. The process of producing the project is always kept hidden away. We draft a text for competitions, of course, but it never touches on the process or any complexity, because that's not what's expected. It's like a trade secret: you never present the idea that underpins the project. It's true that some projects call for simple markers. When you want to fly somewhere, you don't want to get lost at the airport: the building needs a degree of clarity and spatial legibility, it needs to be restful and clear. It's necessary to be able to appreciate how far away the terminal is, to be able to see into the distance, to be able to understand the scale of the building. Nobody wants to miss their plane! But there are also some places where it's quite pleasant to get lost. The media library in Thionville for example, a 'third place'[4] you can go to for no particular purpose, just to wander about and see what's going on. There, the type of space authorises the use of meanders and more nuances. The playful dimension—perhaps the most noble dimension of architecture—is also interesting: how to offer welcoming places, places where you can just pass the time of day. The function of the space is its very lack of precision.

DP
You said quite rightly that the notion of complexity, which some people take to mean formal complication, or spatial ambiguity or ambivalence, is not like that at all, but opens up the possibility of multiple and varied experiences. Indeed complexity and complication are two very different things: a situation or a space can be complex without being complicated. And also, as you say, there is a wide diversity of spaces; some must be immediately simple and legible, while others, like this media library, by allowing other postures, make it possible to encourage experimentation, discovery, play, and so on. In a media library, there is a relationship with facts and knowledge, but it's not direct; you have to go towards what you're looking for, you hesitate, you make a mistake, you turn aside—all of that can also be incorporated into the programme.

That means you're looking for a type of architecture that encourages all that. Complexity is built up from the inside; it refers back to the multiplicity of experiences. That doesn't mean that the external form has to be complicated. That was rather like the dichotomous alternative laid down in the 1960s and 1970s by Venturi and some others. By wanting to combat what was called the 'puritanism' of the Modern Movement, the spaces that were created were sometimes extremely complicated. You follow up a different idea: to combat the simplicity which is, you say, a form of insult to our capacity for experiences, you try to find a form of architectural writing that allows a multiplicity of experiences, including, if it's appropriate, the experience of losing one's way.

Media library
Thionville, 2016

II Architecture and distraction: The infancy of uses

DC
There is often a lot to be learned from watching children. They have a different relationship with their bodies. They find it easy to roll on the ground, to adopt postures that are not like those of adults. Watching them move in a given space is like watching some enviable kind of demonstration of ergonomics. Children have an innate ability to adapt. Claude Bonnet, professor of cognitive psychology, has suggested that the reason children may be receptive to some spaces that adults wouldn't like is perhaps because they do not yet project any pre-established images. Places intended for use by children make interesting subjects, and they can be used for doing things differently. I visited the Montessori kindergarten that Tezuka Architects delivered in 2007 together with Kashiwa Sato in Japan, near Tokyo, where the children can get up onto the roof and slide down into the central garden.[K] It's a place intended for children, and it makes no attempt to constrain them. That also means that different teaching practices are applied. Architecture can sometimes produce new situations and accompany teaching practices. It has a great deal of power.

AP
Architecture also makes it possible to unravel the rules. When you go into a museum, which *a priori* is a rather solemn place, there is often a very long bench somewhere which children might appropriate for playing games and sliding about. Architecture sometimes makes it possible to bend the rules when faced with a pre-established use. It can and should generate, including among adults, a renewed attention to the space. We spend time in a lot of places in a very distracted fashion.

Architecture perhaps makes it possible to twist the conventional way of perceiving, setting up, practising and being in a use. Suddenly we have things we need to re-learn. Happily, architecture allows that. And that brings us back to what Daniel said just now: when people see the spaces you have been able to create, they are struck by their simplicity, in the ameliorative meaning of the word. It doesn't give the impression of something complicated, or verbose from a formal point of view. They are often relatively simple volumes, and when you are inside them, there is a kind of evidence in using the spaces, while at the same time it's full of nooks and crannies where you have to stoop a little, or perhaps return to the centre of gravity we had when we were small … I think you're allowing me to re-learn how to look at things and use them.

DP
Is that your aim, to take us back to childhood?

DC
Perhaps! I've always had trouble with rules. And there are an awful lot of rules when you're an architect. Perhaps architecture sometimes has the power to overturn them. For the court building in Montmorency, there is something soothing about the garden set out between the two courtrooms, with its oak tree and the flowers that the landscaper Bruno Kubler chose very carefully. I felt it was important to be able to look out at a garden from inside a courtroom where difficult situations are being acted out. You hear and you listen, but you can look at something else. Like in a train, when you watch the countryside go by.

DP
Not being restricted to a single function: we aren't unidimensional, and architecture can remind us of that. You're in a given situation, in a courtroom devoted to a very precise function, and at the same time you can escape, you can look somewhere else. Even without being aware of it, a multiplicity, a variety is introduced into our way of living. Architecture has a considerable role to play in this openness—or, on the contrary, in being able to keep us focused on a single function. At one point that was actually the rule: a single function that architecture had to adhere to totally, constantly reminding us unequivocally of what we were there for.

Regional court and industrial tribunal
Montmorency, 2013

DC
Alexandra, you mentioned just now a form of distraction in the public's experience of certain places. That distraction doesn't exist for the architect: it's part of our professional persona to look at everything in a building. Which is often very uncomfortable when visiting museums, for instance: we have difficulty concentrating on the works on display because we're looking at the plinths, the ventilation, the lighting. Things that not everyone looks at, which is just as well! In designing a project you have to be extremely precise, so that all the spaces are produced and controlled. As a result, the distracted user perceives an atmosphere, an atmosphere that has also been constructed. The ramp in Frank Lloyd Wright's Guggenheim Museum in New York was designed to the nearest millimetre.[L] Everybody is enthusiastic about the place: if you've ever been there you cannot forget it. What I think is important in the notion of space is the feeling of being surrounded. All the senses are mobilised, and the effect is particularly strongly felt in certain places. A swimming pool, for example. You feel more exposed in a swimming costume: sensitive to the ambient temperature, the humidity, the feel of the floor surface beneath your feet. There is more call on our senses there than in other types of building; there is more call on your senses than when you're wearing a thick skiing jacket, a hat and sunglasses.

DP
'Distraction' (in German, *Zerstreuung*) was the word used by Walter Benjamin in the 1930s. He said, *inter alia*, that we do not have the same rapport with architecture as with a painting. We stand in front of a painting and enter into it patiently, attentively, taking our time. Most non-architects don't have that rapport with architecture, that way of looking at it, the reflex action of standing in front of it to analyse it. They walk into it, they are inside it without thinking about it, without analysing it. They are assailed by a host of perceptions, impressions and sensations, but they all remain implicit: they aren't set out in black and white, they aren't conscious. The architect must somehow anticipate them and take them into account, and it's a difficulty that I can imagine is particularly motivating.

III Architectural idea and project: The explicit and the implicit

DP
Architecture is an art of the explicit. Once a building has been constructed, it's there—it's tangible, and unavoidable. But at the same time, I can understand that there is something going on in the background that's not at all explicit: you referred to a 'trade secret' just now, a process that can't really be talked about when speaking up for a project in the context of a competition or a public commission. When we say that the user appropriates the architecture, not with patient concentration but in an almost subconscious fashion, much is implied. Perhaps through notions such as complexity, you express the fact that this implicitness should not be seen as a constraint, as something prejudicial or frustrating, but on the contrary as a fringe area containing a host of possibilities, an area that can be opened up, and behind which there is potential to be found. Regarding the relationship to the body, when you design a swimming pool, do you personally sense the foot that is afraid of slipping, the different sensation of cold and heat, because you want to incorporate them in your project? But one might also be forgiven for thinking that some swimming pools have been designed without paying much attention to this implicit dimension of the relationship with the body—or at any

event without it being indicated anywhere on the architectural plans.

Seen from the outside, the relationship between explicit and implicit appears to constitute one of the conditions for producing an architectural project, and places perhaps a dual constraint on the project. You can see that I'm using the word 'constraint' now even though you said it's a word you don't like, but I can't find another word just at the moment to suggest the necessity of satisfying demands in terms of both precision and legibility at one and the same time as well as, within the legibility, keeping room for the implicit, even though that implicit is only controlled up to a certain point. That is perhaps one of the things that bring architecture close to other types of experiences, or even to thought: you try, but you never really know if you are getting it right. Do you think the words 'explicit' and 'implicit' are acceptable? Do they reflect something of how you see your experience as an architect?

DC
There are always several ways of 'reading' a building. I like it when certain things fall into place in a project without any rational explanation being necessary, because those elements that don't explain themselves can subsequently question and refer back to a more open interpretation process. That interests me because architecture is never a demonstration: as in a work of art, the arrangements are open to interpretation. You also have to make the strength that architecture can have speak out, and assume it, even if that's controversial. That is also its role, beyond that of utility.

DP
You said that an architectural space is not right or wrong in the mathematical sense, in the sense of 'true' or 'not true'. Do you ever use the word 'right' to mean anything else about a space—not because it would be appropriate according to some criterion of external truth, but because it is exactly what was needed at that time in that place?

DC
Le Corbusier used the term 'plastic acoustic' to mean, 'There—that's perfect!' We are sometimes able to say that a building is 'right' in the response it provides. The new building for the Centrale-Supélec in Saclay, for example. It was designed by OMA as a large rectangle crossed by a diagonal (like a street, with a central space). I feel there is something 'right' about this architectural response and its interpretation of the programme: creating places where all the students can meet up.[M] The other architects in the competition proposed separate buildings, while OMA thought up a large, well-lit and unpretentious space. There are blackboards on which people had chalked things that were incomprehensible but looked good—rather like music scores. Yes, there's something right about that. At an educational institution where everything is highly specialised, the architects went in the opposite direction, making it a place where dialogue is possible between the people being taught and their teachers. I've seen the director eating in the canteen with the students, carrying his own tray like everyone else. And I think that it's the architecture that made that possible.

DP
Or an architectural idea? When we hear the word 'idea' we immediately think of something abstract. Whereas an architectural idea should be both conceptual and have a material interference in the space itself. Here's the problem: how do we get to that point? At what point does that happen in the project process?

DC
It sometimes happens when you start listing all the things you *don't* want to do. By elimination, you do whatever's left. Seriously though, the site may suggest a lot of things, but the programme itself may do as well, by the relationships that you set up between its different elements: then it really is the architect who decides. I often quote the example of the old school of architecture in Strasbourg, where the administrative offices gave onto a terrace.

Obviously no-one ever dared go onto the terrace, so it was completely useless. I often used to ask my students to imagine putting the canteen where the offices were, or placing the library alongside the terrace: there were plenty of possibilities that could be imagined. The positioning of administrative offices—the people in control—is very important. At the school of architecture in Oporto, Álvaro Siza placed them to the north, alongside the road, to keep them out of the way. 'Out of the way' is the most unglamorous position: you're invisible and forgotten. But when you visit the school of architecture in Oporto, all you feel is the pleasure of seeing the teaching staff and the students. That's the power the architect has. The criminal[5] who managed to escape from prison recently—the programme came into that too. The programme isn't neutral!

DP
What I find really interesting in what you're saying is that the architectural idea and the project that develops that idea are somewhere between two interpretations. Firstly the interpretation of the programme: interpreting already means being active. You talk of 'reading': interpretation doesn't mean merely appropriating the programme; it means finding a meaning in it that it didn't necessarily have at the outset, or interrelating some of its elements. It's a decision; it's positive analysis. Then, once the project has been completed, there is the multiplicity of the interpretations of the users—and the interpretations of onlookers: as an architect, you analyse the work of your fellow architects (or your own work, a number of years later) and you sometimes project onto it a meaning that wasn't there at the start.

The idea of the project is doubly hermeneutic, doubly a matter of interpretation. And that is something that no-one really comments on—particularly not philosophers when they're talking about architecture. The image of architecture has for a long time been one of decision-making, of wielding power. Less emphasis has been placed on the fact that the undeniable architectural decision is constantly in relation to something other than the purely arbitrary. The programme-based argument has been advanced to explain this decision-making aspect. But you deny that as a constraint: it is an imposition, but it also leaves room for analysis and the possibility of connecting the constituent elements. Reading that may produce an idea.

DC
At any event, if the programme is well thought out, the result may go beyond the client's initial wishes. Rem Koolhaas is the best architect to demonstrate this point: he questions the programme, twists it around, transcends it. Coming back to your question, I think that there are some buildings we can call 'right': one example is the Pompidou Centre in Paris, by Renzo Piano and Richard Rogers, which is more than forty years old now.

AP
But it took some time for it to be perceived as 'right'. Some buildings are impossible to understand at first glance, and indeed it took me some time to find my way around the Pompidou Centre. Today it feels quite obvious to me, because I have been there often. You have to take the time to get to know architecture to be able to understand it: like something that is rather complicated (in a very good sense), when there is nothing obvious that you can read immediately. Often places that are obvious are also rather coercive. Both of you have frequently mentioned that fact that a programme may include a degree of brutality. In Saclay, the programme OMA started out with was perhaps coercive, with a blackboard somewhere in the classroom and students who only went up to it when they were asked a question. In the project, however, there is a non-violent appropriation of the programme, and that probably took some time as well. There is a question of temporality in all of that.

DC
Between 1997 and 2000, Richard Rogers refused to take part in the renovation of the Beaubourg building—which cost some four hundred million

French francs—partly because he felt the spirit of the building was being lost. It's true: the lobby isn't as good, the shops are very small, there's no free access to the roof any more because there's a top-class restaurant there now instead of the cafeteria. There used to be soft carpeting in the lobby—people used to sit on it, and even lie down on it. That lobby called up different attitudes from those you usually see in a museum. Visions shift with the passage of time; they become rigid. It doesn't take much: now that the floor is mineral, people stay standing, and everything is more conventional. The strong point of the project used to be that it was possible to go anywhere in the building without having to pay: it was a very generous idea, very 1970s.

AP
Can architecture—can a constructed space—allow access and re-appropriation without laying itself open to damage? In Saclay there is a kind of agreement—not everyone goes into the building, because it's the educational institution that it is. But I agree—I also have a problem with closed buildings. The idea of generosity, being able to walk around, being able to stroll up and down in the space—I think that's important, and not at all anecdotal. I'm thinking of the Arab World Institute in Paris, which was locked down from the outset, with security guards—all pretty dissuasive.

DC
In Saclay, all the buildings are open (I was surprised that it was like that). In Strasbourg too, there is free access to the university buildings. At the school of architecture in Strasbourg, on the other hand, there is a security guard, and I feel that changes the ambience. Being able to walk into a university building without being challenged is one of the advantages we have in Europe. I remember going to lectures at the Sorbonne when I lived in Paris. You just took a seat in the lecture hall—nobody asked you for anything. To be able to go and listen to a lecture in the United States, you have to be enrolled at that particular university.

AP
There is perhaps in Europe a way of doing architecture that has inherited those values: generosity, shared uses, and so on. I talked about this with a friend of mine who teaches at the University of Dallas. 'You think this European generosity is self-evident,' he told me, 'but in the United States everything is privately owned: things are designed as a private space or a space that will be used privately.' The dimension of a public space is more difficult to conceive, and not only because of present-day politics. There is perhaps indeed a European way of thinking about public spaces.

DP
On the historic university campus in Strasbourg, there's a low wall around a garden. You can go into the garden, and you can see through the wall, but it is there nevertheless. At the time it was impossible to create a space like that without something to delimit it. For the school of architecture and the Arab World Institute in Paris, these uses are related to what's going on in the world. The question is whether the architecture in itself should allow free entrance or if it should set up barriers, even if no security guards are present. Some types of architecture don't encourage anyone to enter: there's no need for security measures, because you just don't want to go there. Others really make you want to go in, even if there is a guard out front. What makes architecture welcoming? And indeed does it always have to be welcoming? Some programmes don't make that a requirement.

IV Architectural culture and public discourse: Architects and politicians

DP
There's a problem with talking about architecture, perhaps particularly in France. The culture of architecture is better integrated in other countries. This is perhaps partly because architecture in France doesn't have a long university tradition. Whatever the reason, as soon as you start talking about architecture, all the clichés start to pop up.

Sometimes it's seen as an attempt to be spectacular in the hope that the project will serve as a showpiece in the public space and demonstrate that the town in amazingly up to date. Or else everything is assessed in the light of personal minutiae, focusing on the tiniest details. Either way, architectural culture is often at an extremely low level.

I am often struck by the enormous gap between public discourse, which quite often has not incorporated architecture at all, and architectural discourse, which is—on the contrary—very attentive not only to the specific logic of the project but also to the context and everything it may give rise to in the way of practices and uses. I get the impression that one of the problems architects have to deal with is delimiting a space that provides some kind of mediation between these two antithetic discourses. I thought about that when you were saying that it was impossible to talk about the production of a project in front of a jury. It's obvious that the material a practice has to produce depends on the particular competition, and also that it's necessary to come up with compromises: it would be understandable if there were a genuine desire to understand the project, but that isn't always the case. There is a gap between the ideological indigence of public discourse and the demands you make of yourself as an architect. Because the architect's discourse is increasingly refined, plural, and complex. There are more and more parameters; heterogeneity proliferates. As an architect you take all that into account in a very refined fashion, while the public discourse often still clumps about in hobnail boots. But perhaps this is just a caricature, and your experience is rather more encouraging?

DC

I have very fond memories of the discussions I had with the mayor of La Courneuve—a passionate man. The budgets we are given are sometimes gigantic. There's a high level of complexity, calling for the integration of a large number of parameters. The vision must be right both at the time and in the long term. Some locally elected representatives do what they can, but you sometimes get the feeling they are incapable of talking about their towns. The city of Strasbourg missed out on a number of major occasions: Le Corbusier should have built the Music and Congress Centre—it was perhaps his best project.[6] N Rem Koolhaas lost three competitions there. The Museum of Modern Art could have been designed by the Japanese Arata Isozaki, the music conservatoire by the Spanish architect Enric Miralles, and the building occupied by the council of the Bas-Rhin *département* by Tschumi or Snozzi. It's valid to wonder how the city might have evolved with such emblems.

DP

In a dialogue situation, like we are in at the moment, we don't necessarily all think the same thing, but we always presuppose there is something we all have in common: language, certainly, but also certain representations. That is what enables us to understand each other, even if we are saying different things. I get the impression that between architects and public decision-makers there is no commonality of this kind. So how can ideas be got across? I think it's a shame to reach a situation in which, when an architect talks about the project to public decision-makers, he's not able to promote the actual architectural idea. Perhaps the situation is better in other countries, but it probably has something to do with actually working as an architect. Hence a host of misunderstandings: the architect's job has long been the butt of a great number of caricatures. In his *Dictionary of Accepted Ideas*, Flaubert deliberately provided an example that was as absurd as it gets: 'Architects. All idiots: they always forget to put in the stairs.'[7] What he wanted to show was precisely that public discourse always uses clichés. When there's a discussion among people who aren't architects about something that has just been built, a lot of their reactions are along the lines of 'I like …' or 'I don't like …' Gut reactions that are often negative take the place of what could be genuine architectural critique. That raises the problem of presuppositions that can be used as the starting point for real discussion.

It's perfectly possible to disagree with any given architectural choice, but how can you talk about it without some knowledge of the language? Those who share the language understand each other, but it takes them a great deal of effort to manage to convince anyone outside their circle.

DC
Another point is that architecture often becomes a political argument. Often it's a term of office that dictates the choice of programme—the new building needs to be inaugurated before the next person takes up office, so that it's the person commissioning the project who reaps the benefit. That results in a certain degree of rapidity, instrumentalisation, and an additional responsibility. The architecture the politician provides is paid for by the man in the street, so there's often a consensual aspect attached to the project. Frank Lloyd Wright used to say that he never took part in competitions because the final choice was always somewhere in the middle. Patrick Bouchain also refuses to take part in competitions. At the Venice Biennale, he explained that he had won the contract for the *Lieu Unique* project in Nantes by reading a text: he had drawn nothing, but had merely explained what his working method would be. We always feel it's a shame we don't get the chance to communicate on that phase in the project.

DP
Do you think it's possible to improve the architectural culture of non-architects? There are many initiatives, but there is no way of knowing if they really work.

DC
Yes, by talking more about the history of art and architecture. The school system in France teaches history through politics and wars, but in Italy pupils are taught the history of architecture.

DP
Learning how to read a building would give them some idea for a start, as long as the emphasis wasn't only on the static aspect—there needs to be reference to the movement, poetry and dynamic of the work. Active approaches of this kind have become evident with regard to painting, but not yet for architecture.

AP
I agree. There is very little integration of the historical dimension of architecture—when I was a student the main emphasis was on the political dimension of architecture: when and why the building had been constructed. But nothing about how it had been built, even if we visited the site. I remember the Reichstag building in Berlin: we had to look at the display devoted to its history and the fire in 1933, but nobody ever told us about the building itself, even though we were actually inside it! Why don't we look at the actual space occupied by a museum, even if we would sometimes have to take the works on display off the walls? In the early twentieth century, the avant-garde movement attempted to hybridise art, literature, philosophy and architecture. They are all connected, and make it possible to create meaning for society.

V Teaching architecture

DP
When you define complexity as we have done as the arrangement of a number of heterogeneous elements, the thought arises that it must be very difficult to teach architecture. How should one go about it? If students are immediately placed in the presence of these heterogeneous elements, are they taught how to arrange them? If all the emphasis is on their arrangement, do they have an awareness of the heterogeneous nature of the elements? It seems to me there is a problem in this. How do you go about it?

DC
The way we teach is not neutral. I'm obsessed with teaching without impressing my 'brand' on the students. Students often have to deal with teachers with strong personalities, and they eventually

escape the hold such teachers have on them and become autonomous. But it's no easy task: there comes a point when you have to contradict your teacher. Some students never do, and stay 'former pupils of', dragging the process out. I'm against that: I don't think there's any reason to impose your own vision on a student. So what do we do? What do we teach if we don't want to impose anything? Should we use one or several methods? What do we have to do for students to be able to find their own path, their own way of writing? Being lenient doesn't work either: such teachers transmit nothing, they merely supervise their students. It shouldn't happen, but sometimes it does —the student becomes a sort of collaborator who turns up with his project and the teacher does no more than provide a little guidance to improve it. I always try, in the first instance, to get my students to understand that there are multiple types of architecture. Our master's degree workshop is particularly tuned in to the international aspect. Travel shows you that there are different types of architecture. The architecture in Brazil is not the same as in Europe. Certain elements are similar, but it's obvious that it's different: there's a more deliberate aspect to it, and the climate has produced another architecture. Travel also makes you understand that architecture has a local aspect as well. It relates to local culture; it's impossible to have a single vision and apply it everywhere.

With regard to the 'Architecture and Complexity' workshop, we are trying to deal with very difficult situations in which it's necessary to decode everything that's going on and everything that we can see. It starts with finding out something about the site, about cultures that are unknown to us, about the climate, and so on. The architect becomes an investigator. He has to decipher the local situation: what can you see, why are we there, what's going on? Often, in reaction to these situations, students adopt a particular posture. In California, for example, we saw that it was impossible to ignore the car. In Los Angeles, there are car parks everywhere. They are often nearly empty, as if it were essential that anyone in California should be able to find a parking space immediately. Conversely, in Paris, everyone who hasn't already given up owning a car spends all their time looking for a parking space. We discussed this in the workshop: do we arrive on the scene with our European attitude that cars are ugly? Or do we invert our position, as did one group of students that worked on a huge car park. Other elements were subsequently added to it, but the project was first and foremost that of a car park. The architecture the project produced was strange, but it was the result of how the situation had been diagnosed.

So much for the methods and the way we can define them up to the point when the project becomes a demonstration of the issue raised initially. The architect is then no longer merely someone who is knowledgeable or a technician, but an intellectual who is capable of gathering ideas together and adopting positions upstream of the project. In other words, the project becomes anecdotal. It needs to be firmly grounded, and that involves constructing a substantiated discourse that is independent of the project but essential to its strength.

AP

Paradoxically (the paradox should be seen as something positive in this case), the discourse, at least in the project workshop, must often be the formulation of a simple idea in the face of an extremely dense and complex context. It has to be fluid without being solemn or bombastic. The relationship between a simple idea and a dense context makes things interesting: it needs to be possible to talk about it in simple terms even though there is a quantity of very varied parameters, parameters that are different for each project.

DC

After a trip to Brazil with my students, I asked them to design a project to be located in either São Paulo or Rio de Janeiro. They had one week to come up with something, and one single constraint: the project had to be radical. Because Brazilian architecture, in these cities, *is* radical: radical in the sense of simple or obvious. There is a risk in some projects of getting lost in analysis: at some point you have to bring together and condense everything you know into some kind of intuitive response. Intuition is an integral part of drawing up a project —then come the more difficult, but obviously extremely important, mechanisms of design and checking the project's architectural relevance. But the way in which we prepare and understand a situation is also specific to the 'Architecture and Complexity' workshop: the architect does not restrict himself to what he is asked to do—he adopts a point of view, gets involved, takes risks (not without a degree of pride connected with the underlying issues). The architect says something through his project.

DP
In your mind, has there always been a link between working as an architect and teaching?

DC
Yes—always.

DP
Do you get the impression that the fact of teaching influences your own projects?

DC
Definitely. Teaching takes up a lot of time, but I don't see it as a hindrance. Teaching also means explaining, whereas within the practice it's possible to produce something without explaining: the two aspects are complementary. When Paul Chemetov went to see Le Corbusier as soon as he got out of his plane to ask him for lessons, he's reported as having said, 'You just need to look at what I do.' Le Corbusier nevertheless did produce a book of discussions with architecture students, *Entretien avec les étudiants des écoles d'architecture*,[8] that I bought when I was a teenager still at school, at the point when I didn't yet know whether I wanted to become an architect. I think he also gave a number of lectures.

DP
He was mainly interested in lecturing to other architects, because he hoped that his way of thinking could influence them. He returned to the basics in a very educational fashion. But that's not the same thing, because anything Le Corbusier said was the word of a master. As soon as you mentioned the subject of teaching, you referred to the otherness of the student: how important it was that students should not become clones, their personality, your role in helping students reveal their own personalities without merely working 'in the style of'. As soon as there is that gap between the student and you, as soon as there is that respect for his otherness, you create a situation that is totally different from imposing your way of looking at things on him. You give him a lot—details about conceptualisation, techniques and so on—but you also put him in the situation of interpretation that we were talking about just now in a different context.

DC
Yes, this notion of 'master' that is often used is rather heavy-handed. There are discussions about it within schools of architecture. Some teachers still have a completely different way of looking at things: 'There's only one way of doing this and that's the way you have to do it.'

DP
But that's how architecture was taught for centuries. This brings us back to the problem you were talking about, because it's not possible to be lenient either, otherwise you contribute nothing. So there is even so a contribution, a gift, something that is passed on by transmission from the teacher to the student. The problem is probably particularly difficult when you teach constructive practices and not just ideas. In philosophy, you can teach a class on an author knowing full well that it is more than likely that the students and the author in question have completely different mindsets. Whereas you are teaching your students practices as well—the temptation of identification is perhaps greater. That's what you manage to get round, at least partly.

DC
Teaching a doctrine looks easier, but I'm not sure that all students are subsequently in a position of being able to say 'we've learned that, so now we are free'. I think some people must stay heavily marked by what they have undergone or followed ...

AP
You get round it perhaps through the tools that you transmit. The use of scale models, for instance, is a major feature in your workshop. It's even an instant association: model and Coulon's project workshop. I think that's how you avoid the master/disciple relationship, even if there are bound to be ways of making scale models that are specific to your workshop.

DC
It's funny, because I never really ask them to make scale models. It's only at the end of the semester, when I ask them to bring them all in, that I realise just how many models they have produced. When I discuss their models with the students, I look at them closely: they aren't just left there in front of me. The students can see that that's where space is constructed, and that makes them want to go and make another model. But I never say to them, 'You're going to make at least five scale models during this workshop.' The scale model has an enemy: the software called SketchUp, which students tend to use rather frenetically. When they work on it, not only is it quick, but they really have the impression that they are 'making' their own work—they find everything very easy, and that can be very deceptive. Whenever possible you have to use a range of tools, because that's what makes it possible to pin the project down.

In my approach I also ask the students to tell a story: What's going to happen? What are we going to see? There's a lot of work to be done on words surrounding the project. I very rarely use tracing paper for design work, because there's too much of a risk that ideas will 'set'. Talking about possible arrangements makes it possible to keep things more open: with words, there can be a host of interpretations. Otherwise things become confined.

DP
We've come back once again to the idea of reading and interpretation. That's where it happens.

DC
Another good thing is interventions by specialists who contribute a different viewpoint. The botanist Philippe Obliger, for example, manages to get students to understand that the landscape is important too: they aren't just designing a building, but a building in a landscape, in an environment. It's a way of stepping back. Or the structural engineer Akio Sassa, who makes grand gestures, moves about in space, leans on their hands: he makes them feel the structure physically, which works much better with students than a load of calculations. I remember the portfolio he sent us when he applied for the post of associate professor. During a workshop he had taken photographs of soap bubbles to visualise forces and formations intuitively. Structure isn't just something for engineers, it's something anyone can grasp and understand. The contributions of these people make the class more dynamic, more cheerful, even.

Also, since it's not always easy to hold the students' attention, what I do is get them to move about. We go out onto the terrace, for instance. Since the tables there are no good at all, we all end up squashed together like sardines and they listen properly. Then we go back inside because it's too hot, then we go somewhere else, and so on. I try to do that to create an arrhythmia in the classes—and it's one way of escaping the screen.

VI Architecture and philosophy

AP
What does philosophy bring to architecture? There is sometimes the impression of trying to extract thought from architecture, but it could perhaps be more reciprocal than that? I regularly warn my students about that: there comes a

point when the very specific view philosophy has of architecture must be able to be transformed into actual practice. Daniel, you have your own particular experience of the relationship between philosophy and architecture.

DP

I got interested in the idea of architecture before I knew anything about architecture itself. I had noticed that several philosophers, starting with Aristotle, compared themselves with architects. I began to wonder what ideas they might have of architecture and the work of an architect that would explain this. I came up with different answers for the different philosophers. That's how my deconstruction thought process works: questioning the philosophical text to see how it is constructed and what tricks it uses. It was by working on this that I came into contact with architects and schools of architecture.

At the time (in the early 1980s), there was some sort of demand for this connection between architecture and philosophy. Immediately after the creation of schools of architecture, the social sciences were the main representatives of the human sciences. Philosophy was less present, except in a few cases. It was difficult to make out the scale of demand, since basically architects have no immediate need for any philosophical input in their work. The meeting happened in a kind of third place, neither truly to talk about architecture, nor to analyse philosophical references; nevertheless there does seem to be an area of common ground where they can meet. It was as if architects needed to evoke the meaning of what they do, and philosophers needed to know whether their concepts and ideas could have material, physical effects—spatial effects, for instance—which is something they are never sure about. It's perhaps around this question of idea and meaning that their meeting took place. Thereafter there were many ways of meeting, and networks developed: they have added considerably to this meeting-point, in an interesting way. What is essential for me is that neither of the two requires a definitive response from the other. Some philosophers perhaps consider that if the concepts are under control, everything is under control. Conversely, the philosophical currents Alexandra and I are from are wary of that pretension. The concept is essential, but it is essential because it is positioned in a specific context, in an issue, in a *textuality* that can be read in an infinite number of ways. There is no last word to be had.

In what you've been saying, I felt particularly concerned when you showed this dimension not of unfinishedness but of incompleteness: architecture isn't the production of a system, it's not a matter of partitioning its singularities within a systematic totality. On the contrary: it's something that is alive, where there is leeway, gaps, space—spacing. It's perhaps on these points that we converge. So it would be dishonest of philosophers to turn up at schools of architecture saying, 'Here you are—we've brought you some truths.' What they are able to teach is more the unfinished aspect of meaning. From this point of view, we come back totally to what you were saying about interpretation and reading. That gives the philosopher a role that lets him liberate himself from all the caricatures: the distracted person who falls down a well, or the person who turns up convinced that he is in possession of absolute truth and says, 'This is what has to be done from now on.' Both attitudes are mocked—legitimately—because of the divergence between their initial pretension and their lack of productivity. By escaping from it, you are at the very least forced to become more receptive.

The thinking process is an incessant confrontation: what do we do with what we receive? We receive things, we arrange the material gathered, but we're never sure that that particular arrangement is the right one, so we rearrange things, we read the situation differently … I think that there's a connection with your projects there.

DC

What has always impressed me about philosophers is their ability to question things. Questions are never self-evident. There is indeed a link with architecture, whose aim is to move things about and not repeat them. Precision in manipulating the terms used and the weight given to the question of meaning seem to me to be particularly important. In your philosophy classes you manage to show the responsibility induced by architecture. The decisions that are made are not insignificant: they have meaning, or not. Philosophy was a great help to me when I was a student.

AP
It's the ability to understand and to try to put words to things that appear obvious but that we tend to not question. There's the rather annoying repetition of the question 'But why?' and a desire to understand that I feel comes with the job, so to speak: the inability to be satisfied with what is there, with what already exists. It seems to me that architecture has the same process of incessant questioning. You were talking about what feeds the project, but it is perhaps also a matter of questioning the actual process, and that is perhaps where philosophy can be of assistance (not in providing a truth, but for finding the right words to use in the questioning).

DC
That brings to mind the research studio of the Dutch architect Winy Maas at Delft University of Technology,[9] which he called 'The Why Factory'. One day when he was passing through Strasbourg, I asked a student to present his diploma project to the man. The student got a good mark and was quite pleased, but Winy Maas kept on asking him, 'Why? Why did you do that?' It rattled the student a bit, because some of the things weren't all that obvious.

DP
At the same time it's a test, being questioned. But our common enemy remains the answer 'that's the way it is'. The question 'why?' is essential. Not sufficient on its own, because it is by definition non-productive, but necessary. There is always a negative stage in the thought process, whether it is content with the concepts or moves into action through the project: it's the rejection of what seems at first glance to be obvious. Otherwise you just repeat, you risk hanging on to presuppositions, clichés, conventions. Behind all that there is a real question in the present-day world which I have the impression pays more attention to the obvious and the 'that's how it is'. I find it increasingly difficult to follow public debates on television or the radio —even though I'm convinced of their necessity— because they very quickly auto-regulate themselves into a battle of the obvious. It's a complicated situation that isn't quite dogmatism, but in which public speaking is so programmed that it is basically already prescribed—pre-scribed, written in advance. Then, within that prescription, the speakers adopt one or the other position. Even the total rebel has his role written in advance for the debate. And then we get stuck. You were talking about 'resistance' just now: in the discourse, in the project, you have to manage to divert, turn away from, liberate yourself from the pre-written, pre-scribed word. It may be possible in architecture; it's certainly possible in philosophy. Perhaps less so in politics …

DC
The word 'resistance' is interesting, but I'm not entirely happy about its immobility. It's a word I hardly ever use. I wonder more how to convert certain arrangements, how to embrace situations and twist them around. How to translate them differently. I prefer the more dynamic image of the judoka channelling his opponent's force to add to his own momentum. What always surprises me is the type of person who says one thing and does exactly the opposite. I feel that the architect, with his sense of discipline, really can't do that. He can't cheat. A philosopher can't either, I suppose.

DP
Except for Sophists, but they had an important role: bringing questions to the table. Saying, 'We're not indifferent; there are things at stake here.'

AP
The function of the Sophists was to dramatise the situation, something that other philosophers

were not always very quick to do. They conducted a debate, expressing themselves in a way that was sometimes more clever than honest, whereas the philosopher was supposed to be the bearer of some kind of truth. But the two are no doubt complementary.

DP
We are also dependent on the narrative that philosophy has expressed about itself. It's something that we can challenge, because during its history philosophy has often remained firmly attached to an established way of thinking in which it has assigned itself the leading role. From the nineteenth century onwards, philosophy has participated actively in a comprehensive rethinking of the very authority of the word. The philosophers who contributed to this critical undertaking found themselves in the position of shifting, questioning, and undermining discourse in general and philosophical discourse in particular. It was not a matter of renouncing a concept or an idea, but of saying that the concepts and ideas had to be forged and invented without relying on any *a priori* authority. The discourse then necessarily has to face up to related discourses, to the otherness of what is being said and done elsewhere. And we then find ourselves in the same situation of complexity that we were in at the outset.

Vitruvius expected the architect to be omniscient. Leonardo da Vinci said, 'I am a true philosopher: not only do I invent ideas and concepts —I also make them real.' In a way, Vitruvius was as much a philosopher as an architect. But his conception of philosophy was that of omniscience, the 'knowing-everything' stated at the beginning of his treatise,[10] in which he drew up a long list of all the disciplines the architect had to master. That would be inconceivable nowadays. Morin states it clearly: demanding omniscience would be a mistake. We are now completely distanced from both the illusion that there is a single simple principle that governs everything and the illusion that it is possible to manage to control all phenomena and their meanings.

Philosophers could perhaps learn from the architect what a project is, with the methods and procedures it calls for, the adventures of design, compilation and *effectuation* that it supposes. For centuries past we have probably not paid enough attention to the fact that writing a text also involves the same kind of procedures and adventures. We too are faced with heterogeneity, we too try to organise the ways things are arranged; the routes we take are both determined and hesitant, as yours are.

AP
The idea of a pre-project, a construction, an 'unravelling' in certain places and then reconstruction, in order to achieve a degree of consistency even if we know that such consistency, without being fake, is somewhat forced. There are times when you know full well that two things that you have juxtaposed probably wouldn't function in the same way in a different context.

DP
Yes, and the process of arranging things can be repeated immediately afterwards in a completely different way. That's the really exciting aspect of writing, and it is what brings architects and philosophers together. Indeed we refer to 'architectural writing': writing is the right word to use precisely because it is not merely the application of regulations, nor the juxtaposition of a few ideas or parcels of space. But nor is it composition in the conventional sense, where everything has to have a defined place. The project idea doesn't induce a one-way movement; it associates the fact of solidly establishing, founding, constructing with a dimension of temporality that can't be stopped, rigidified, or arbitrarily suspended. There comes a point in time when you do stop, of course, when you say that the project has reached its definitive form, but even that's not entirely true: it carries on, as we've seen, through interpretation, use, the mainly unforeseeable random events that will subsequently affect what you have built ... It is only in this posterity that the project will be sanctioned, and even then not always unilaterally or in a settled

fashion: when its qualities and its defects will emerge, as if it were written in an invisible ink that is revealed with the passage of time. The same is true, albeit probably in a different way, of writing and buildings. In a different way because philosophical writings, although some may have had serious consequences in real life, seem to be more volatile than buildings and monuments which, once they have been built, become very real objects.

VII Architecture revealing spaces: Structure, singularities and interpretation

DC
Architects are capable of making mistakes too: we often remove an empty space, we take the place of something else, we shape the landscape. That's perhaps why architects are either loathed or envied. It's not at all straightforward. One of my teachers in Paris used to tell us, 'Without architecture, Mont Saint-Michel would be no more than a boring rock.' And he was quite right: it's thanks to architecture that the site exists.

DP
Whereas we are often asked to make architecture invisible! To 'integrate' it. As if there weren't buildings that people are pleased to see. As if significance couldn't sometimes just mean being different, contrasting with the surroundings, making the object truly visible.

DC
We can't prevent situations sometimes creating something uninteresting in the town, like the temporary module we can see out of the window here. However, between the two university buildings opposite (occupied by Strasbourg's museums of mineralogy and zoology), there is a wonderful empty space with a sign indicating that it's covered by a building permit: shouldn't the empty space be left as it is? I think it should be. It's a question that always comes up.

DP
If we consider the relationship between things to be the most important thing about them, then things can't all be solid. As Hannah Arendt says, we manage to speak to one another because there is an empty space between us. Like this table in front of us here, that no-one is occupying totally: it's because there is this interval that we are able, over the top of it, crossing it, to talk to each other. Arendt compares totalitarianism to a situation in which the table disappears: people stumble up against each other, and because there's no gap between them they cease to be able to speak to each other. There are times and places when it's necessary to keep that interval. The way some architects deal with gaps is extremely interesting. It that a concern you would express in the same words? I'm thinking particularly of Japanese architects who have worked a lot on that, as if there were potential for revealing something within the actual gap.

DC
Toyo Ito said at a conference once that the concept of space was different in Japanese architecture. For a Western architect, an empty space is something that has been hollowed out. For a Japanese architect, it's more of an absence. I think that's reflected in their architecture: in some structures there is almost nothing, just a rather diaphanous sort of set-up. In a jointly-owned building, the individual owners only own empty spaces: the walls belong to them jointly. That empty space is what we produce.

DP
An empty space can also be a transition. Some empty spaces are totally inert—nothing happens there. But in architecture, the empty space is also there to create possibilities for circulation or standing still, gaps, breathing spaces.

AP
Thinking of things that already exist: your book is almost all about projects for new buildings. I was wondering, have you ever done any conversion

or renovation work? Does that call for a totally different approach?

DC
Totally different, yet exactly the same. I believe you have to accompany the building rather than enter into conflict with it—a conflict that is often extremely expensive. If you've ever knocked down a partition wall, you know how long it takes and the huge quantity of rubble it generates. You have to like what's already there, understand its logic, accompany it, rather than fight against it. With conversion work, you start out with the plans for what is already there. Then the programme falls into place, and in the end—since it all takes place very quickly on a computer—you remove a wall without paying much attention, just because it's in the way, to be able to do something else with the space. But that wall actually exists, and demolishing it is very expensive.

Some years ago, we reorganised the offices in the Administrative Centre in Strasbourg. There was a straight route, followed by something a bit odd that we began to straighten out. I asked the engineer to take a look at it, even so, because we couldn't understand why it was twisted. He decided to do some destructive tests—involving a bit of breakage to be able see what's going on—just at the point when I said to myself: this is absurd. Why remove this oddity? In the end we turned it into a colourful tunnel. It has become an event, without the need to break the structure, and that's much more fun. When something already exists you really need to have a good reason to change it. Buildings that have been converted are often beautiful places. If they haven't been demolished it's because they have a quality, there is something about them, an atmosphere. It's often worth not razing things to the ground.

DP
Your example of the Administrative Centre shows that there are several logics that may stand in for each other, or try to coexist peaceably. The important thing is to manage to make an 'idea'

Restructuring of the Administrative Centre
Strasbourg, 2007

out of something that seems at first sight to be rather accidental. Even during the period from the 1960s to the 1980s, many people wanted to create something clean, smooth, new, and were very dismissive of traditional materials, as if it were important to remove all trace of the past. We are more open-minded about that sort of thing these days.

DC
Yes, absolutely. Lacaton and Vassal rebuilt the Tokyo Palace in Paris: it had been built during the Universal Exposition in 1937 as a symmetrical building with two wings, one housing the Tokyo Palace and the other the modern art museum of the City of Paris. Plaster columns, moulded ceilings, and so on. Lacaton and Vassal ripped it all out: the moulding was only decorative, so they revealed the structure. To start with I thought it was a waste. Today I find it a very attractive place that works well—the other wing hasn't been touched— but even so: it's not neutral to demolish all that work. I think I would have tried to keep a bit more of it, working with the old and the new. o

DP
That's a genuinely philosophical question: revealing the structure was truly progressive, because they removed the decoration, the futile ornamentation, the fake wealth. But once that had been done, you realise that elevating that line of thought to a dogma doesn't work either. In a lecture on functionalism in the mid-1960s, Theodor W. Adorno quoted Adolf Loos and compared him to the musicians of the Second Viennese School—Schoenberg, Berg, Webern—who were close friends of Adorno, precisely on that point: removing all the flourishes and staying close to the structure, since they thought that revealing structure was a form of truth.
But he also said, in the second part of his lecture, that there is a kind of naivety in wanting to refuse symbols and ornamentation, since architecture can only be 'symbolic'. That doesn't mean that you have to keep adding layers—on the contrary, he was more in favour of paring down and making the actual structure visible—but he did say, when talking about functionalism, that in fact keeping strictly to the structure and claiming that it made everything legible wasn't right either. How can we keep or re-establish meaning without applying the lie or 'crime' of ornamentation?

DC
With this discourse in the debate on architecture, some architects consider the structure to be the 'true' and 'pure' part of the project. Personally, I think it also constitutes a closing-in.

DP
Does it mean structural mannerism?

DC
In a way, yes: talking about structure in the language of architects often leads to a rationality that mentally creates a sort of spatial straightjacket. A grid creates a division, and a tendency to determine compulsory positions. Students often do that. They position the structure, and then put themselves in the middle. Everything becomes very static. Personally, I like things to be as un-static as possible or, if they do become rigidified, that it should be for a good reason. Structure is not the same as architecture. Behind that there is a very serious, grim attitude.

Take, for instance, Le Corbusier's La Tourette convent. The monks' cells are all identical (which makes sense for monks). But some architects do the same thing for—for example—the design for a school, with a row of classrooms in a line. At the corners, the architect could, for example, offer wonderful views of the side of the building. Instead of which he reproduces exactly the same classroom. It's a vision of architecture that I don't share: if there is a particular situation, you make it into something particular. That's how you create diversity.

In the group of schools we did in Montpellier, one classroom opened onto a patio: it had three sides on the outside but no view of the distance, and I thought that it probably wouldn't be appreciated as much as the other classrooms. It was quite the opposite: the teachers had to draw lots for it —they all wanted it, because it was the odd one out.

DP
When there is something particular about a space, you ask yourself straight away how you could convert it into an architectural idea. Deleuze said that architecture was the art of providing a frame. It's not only visual; when you frame something, the thing that is framed opens into something else again. That's where architecture develops its fullest potential: when it has full knowledge of the language it speaks, but uses that language to show something else—something alongside, a particular space. Emphasising the importance of what is already there, as you said just now. It's not possible to turn up with a ready-made plan: the idea develops as the programme and the thing itself, its reality, is interpreted. Architecture is an interpretative art.

1 Edgar Morin, 'La stratégie de reliance pour l'intelligence de la complexité', in *Revue Internationale de Systémique*, vol. 9, nº 2, 1995 (quotation translated for the purposes of the present publication).

2 Cf. Bernard Dagenais, 'Edgar Morin et la pensée complexe', in *Hermès, La Revue*, 2007/2, nº 48, pp. 179–84, Paris: CNRS.

3 According to the French national statistics office INSEE, the unemployment rate was 22.5% among 15- to 64-year-olds in Freyming-Merlebach in 2015.

4 A 'third place'—a notion that emerged in the United States in the early 1980s in the work of the sociologist Ray Oldenburg —is a space separate from but complementary to the 'first place' (the home) and the 'second place' (the workplace)—an informal area for socialising and interacting. Cf. Conversation with Luca Merlini, p. 80, note 5.

5 On 1 July 2018, the convicted thief Redoine Faïd escaped by helicopter from the courtyard of the prison in Réau.

6 Le Corbusier (in an extract from W. Bœsiger [ed.], *Le Corbusier, Oeuvre complète*, Volume 7: 1957–1965, Basel: Birkhäuser, 1995, p. 152) described in these terms his project for the Palais des Congrès in Strasbourg: '"Mr. Pflimlin, the lord-mayor and the excellent administrators of the city had conceived a perfect program. / Under such favourable conditions an architect can say that he works as if for God: with conscientiousness, integrity, loyalty. / Then only can one appreciate the fact that architecture is of passion ..." / The square block of buildings with the adjoining ramps along the north is to be carried out in exposed concrete. / Symbols, in the form of reliefs, are to be cast into the wall surfaces, as in the stadium of Firminy. / Particular attention will be paid to the sound insulation between floors and halls, as well as to the acoustic of the conference rooms.'

7 Original title '*Dictionnaire des Idées Reçues*'; translated into English by Jacques Barzun, New York: New Directions, second edition, 1968)

8 Le Corbusier, *Entretien avec les étudiants des écoles d'architecture*, Paris, Les Éditions de Minuit (1957); in French.

9 *Technische Universiteit Delft*, top public university in the Netherlands.

10 In about 151 BCE, Vitruvius wrote a treatise on architecture dedicated to the Emperor Augustus entitled *De Architectura.*

J Álvaro Siza Vieira, Quinta da Malagueira, 1977–1995. K Tezuka Architects, Fuji Kindergarten, Tokyo, 2007.
L Frank Lloyd Wright, *Guggenheim Museum*, 1959. M OMA, CentraleSupélec, 2017.
N Le Corbusier, *Le Palais des Congrès de Strasbourg*, 1964. O Palais de Tokyo, 1937.

J

K

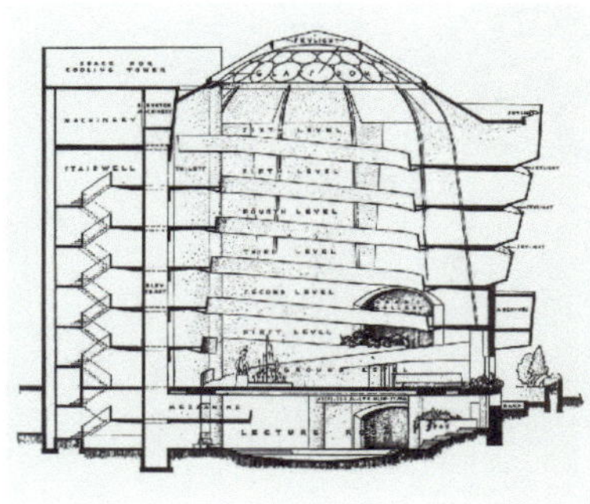

L

M

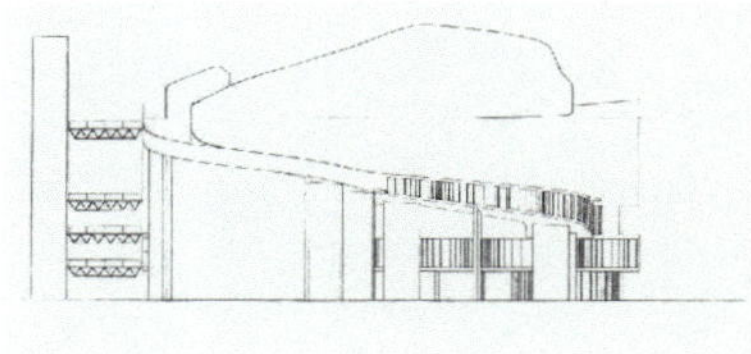

N

O

Buhl

Sharing —— Marking the entrance to a little Alsatian village that is lodged in the hollow of a valley in the Ballons des Vosges Regional Natural Park, this toddlers' day-care centre is a question of both people and landscape. The first issue we had to address was that of the plot boundary, since the site, in a rural mountainside location, is too big for the programme. We took the decision to leave it open to the surrounding landscape, the unused space becoming common land, accessible to everyone, and planted with sixty-eight apple trees of different local heirloom species. Above the site rise the ruins of the Hugstein Castle, whose origins go back to the early thirteenth century; the square plan of the school, its successive thicknesses and its massive, crenellated proportions echo its ancient neighbour, as do the round holes in the concrete curtain wall, which form a series of distinctly inoffensive arrow slits. Without a fence to keep it at a distance, the building poses its own limits: sheltered at the heart of the orchard, it consists in a succession of rings that converge around its heart, the central vestibule, which doubles up as an indoor playground in winter. Views through the complex allow the building's depth to be discerned, while the ring system eliminates corridors. The heart of the compact plan features tall glazed bays that let in abundant light, which is immediately reflected back by the double-height walls. Matte or glossy, in a range running from pink to red, colours fragment the space into a mosaic of surfaces; but overall the palette of similar tones resonates as one, tinting the air with a homogeneous hue. From the central foyer, access to the various day-care spaces is gained, where the children take their meals or naps and undertake all sorts of activities in between. Here a discreet shade of grey clothes the walls, while the generously glazed façades let in touches of colour. A few paces further and we arrive in the outdoor playground, from which can be glimpsed, through the apertures in the walls, the undulating silhouette of the Vosges.

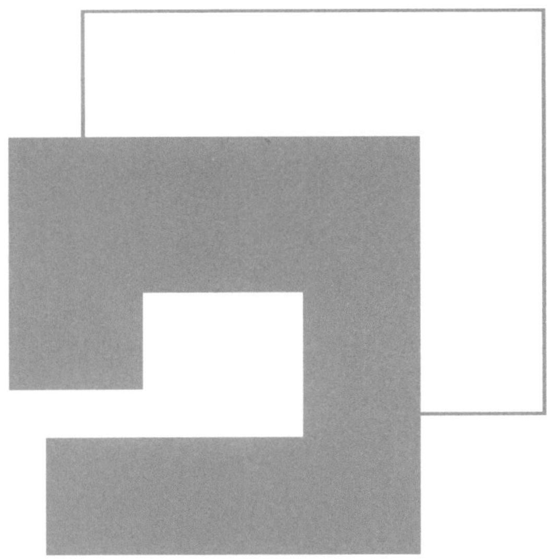

Outdoor playgrounds and day-care spaces form a ring around the building's heart.

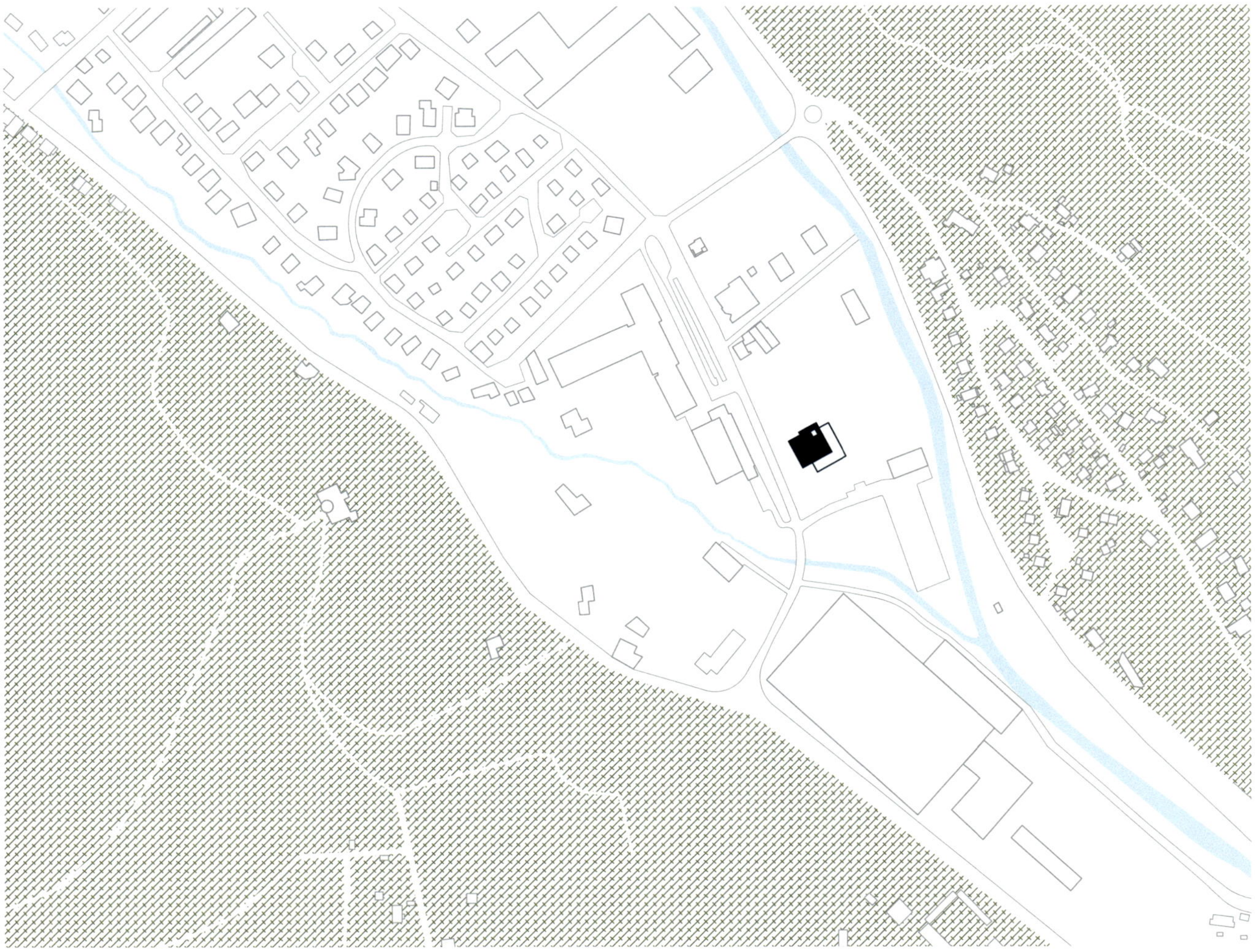

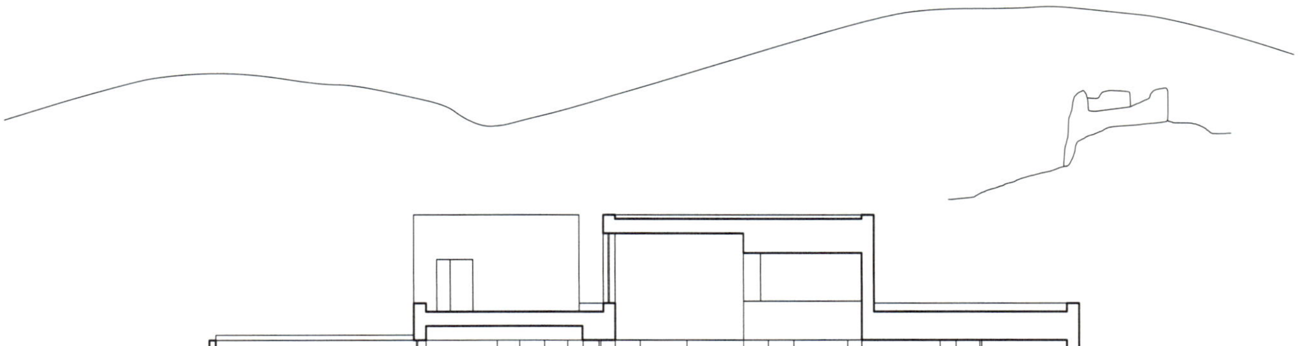

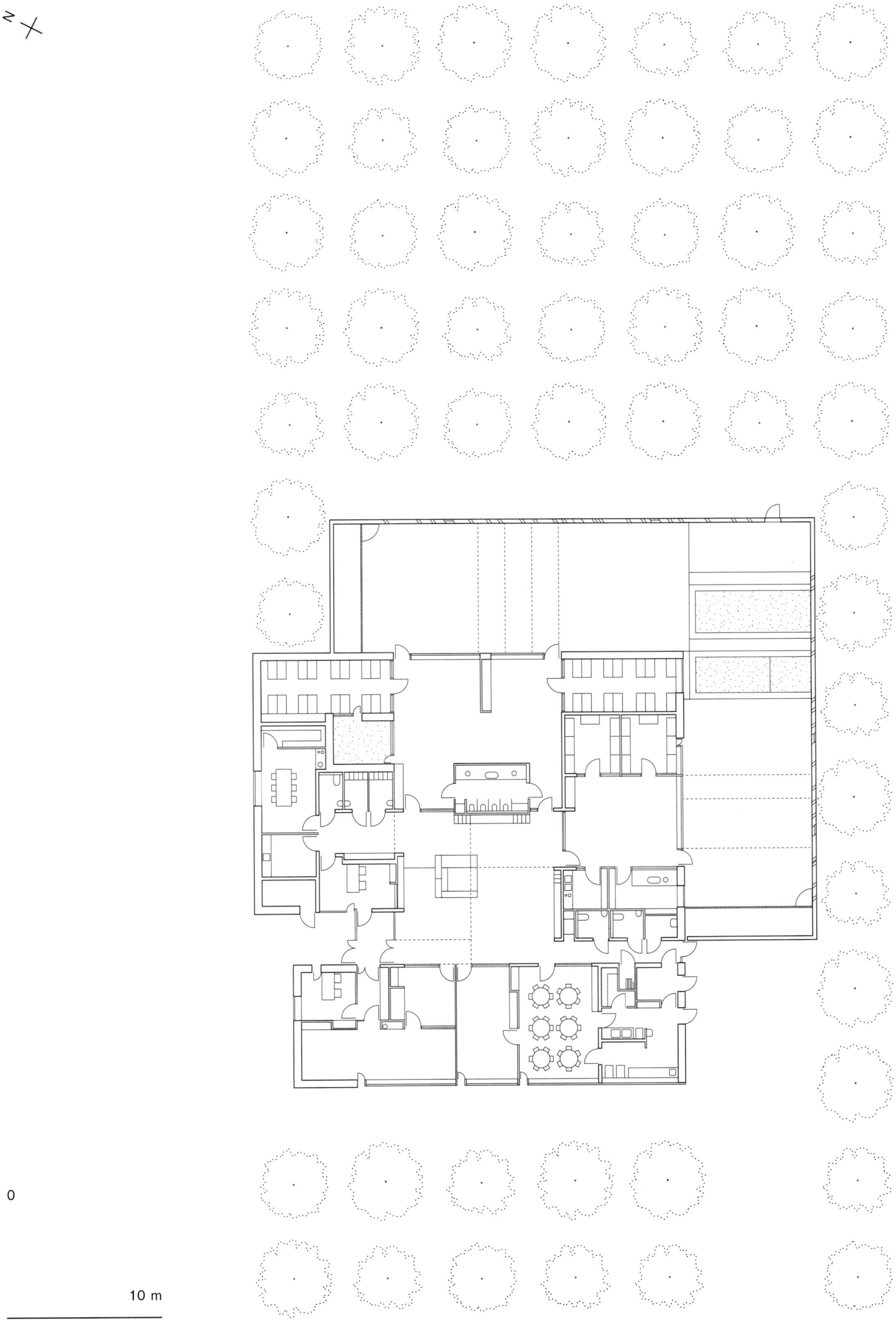
N
0
10 m

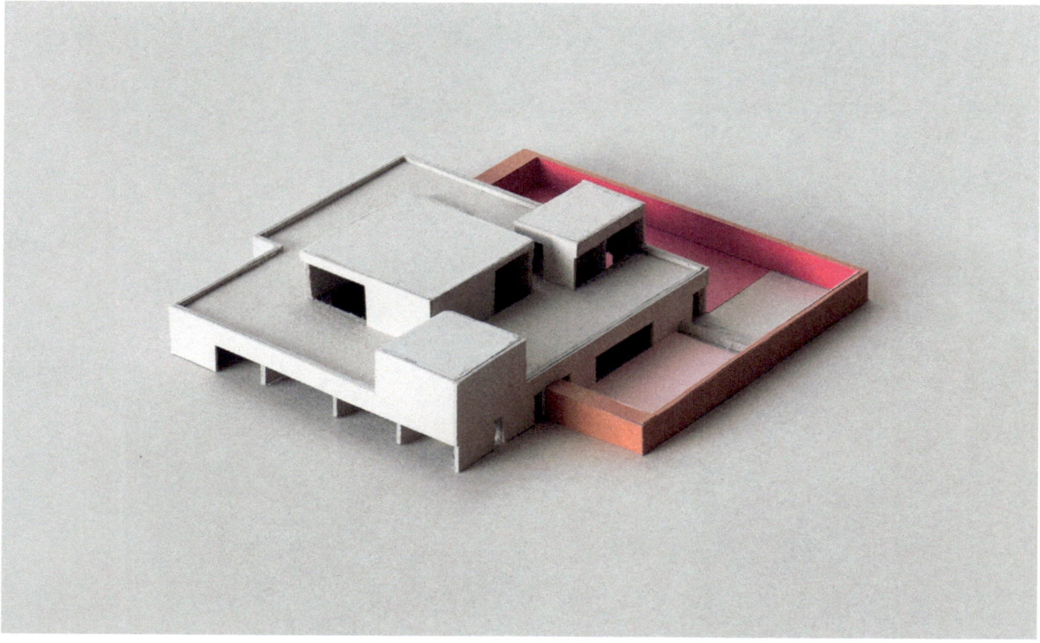

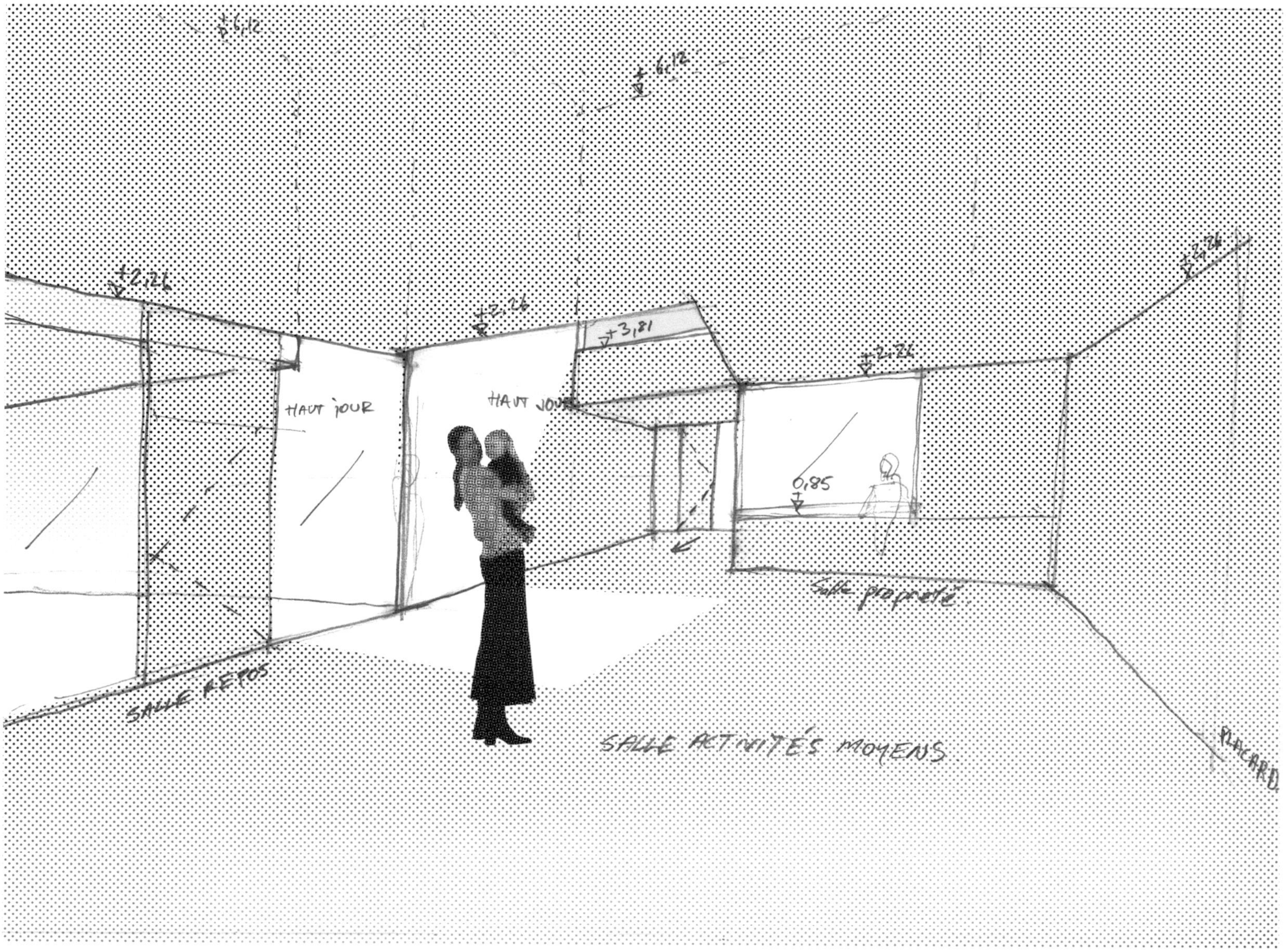

+6,12
+6,12
+2,26
+2,26
+3,81
+2,26
+2,26
HAUT JOUR
HAUT JOUR
0,85
Salle propreté
SALLE REPOS
SALLE ACTIVITÉS MOYENS
PLACARD

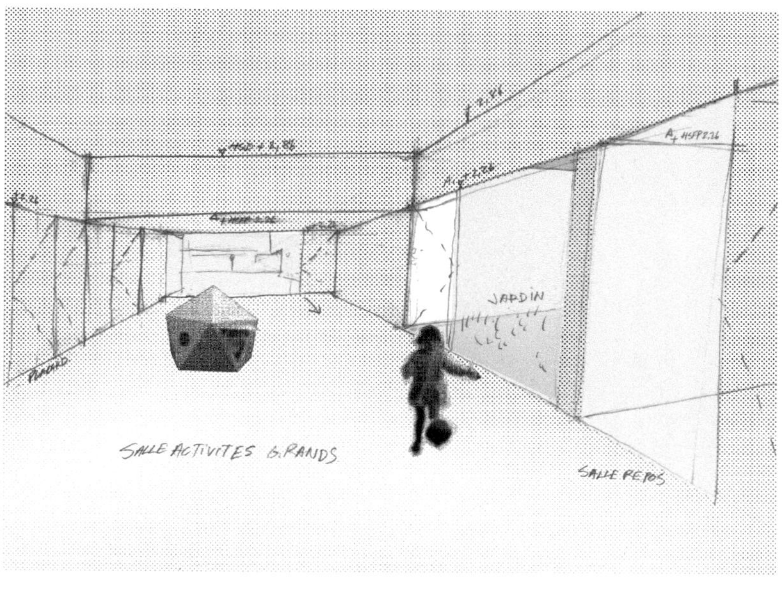

JARDIN
SALLE ACTIVITES GRANDS
SALLE REPOS

+6,12
+3,81
+2,26
GRANDS
±0,00
Hall d'arrivé
2 3 MAI 2013

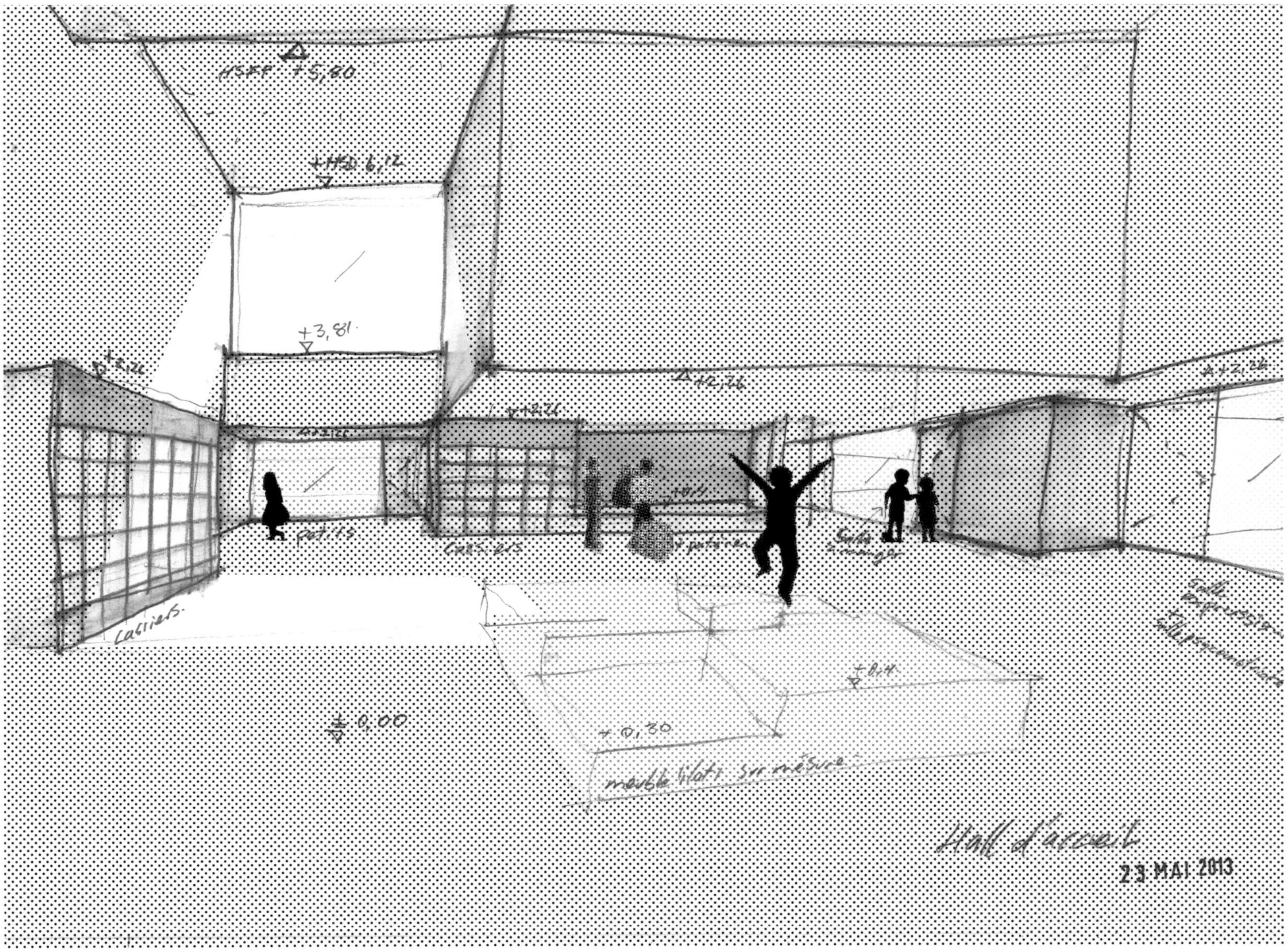
+3,81
Casiers.
+0,00
+0,30
Hall d'accueil
23 MAI 2013

VESTIAIRE
HOMME
SALLE
D'ACTIVITES

SALLE
D'ACTIVITES

2015
School complex

Montpellier

5 m

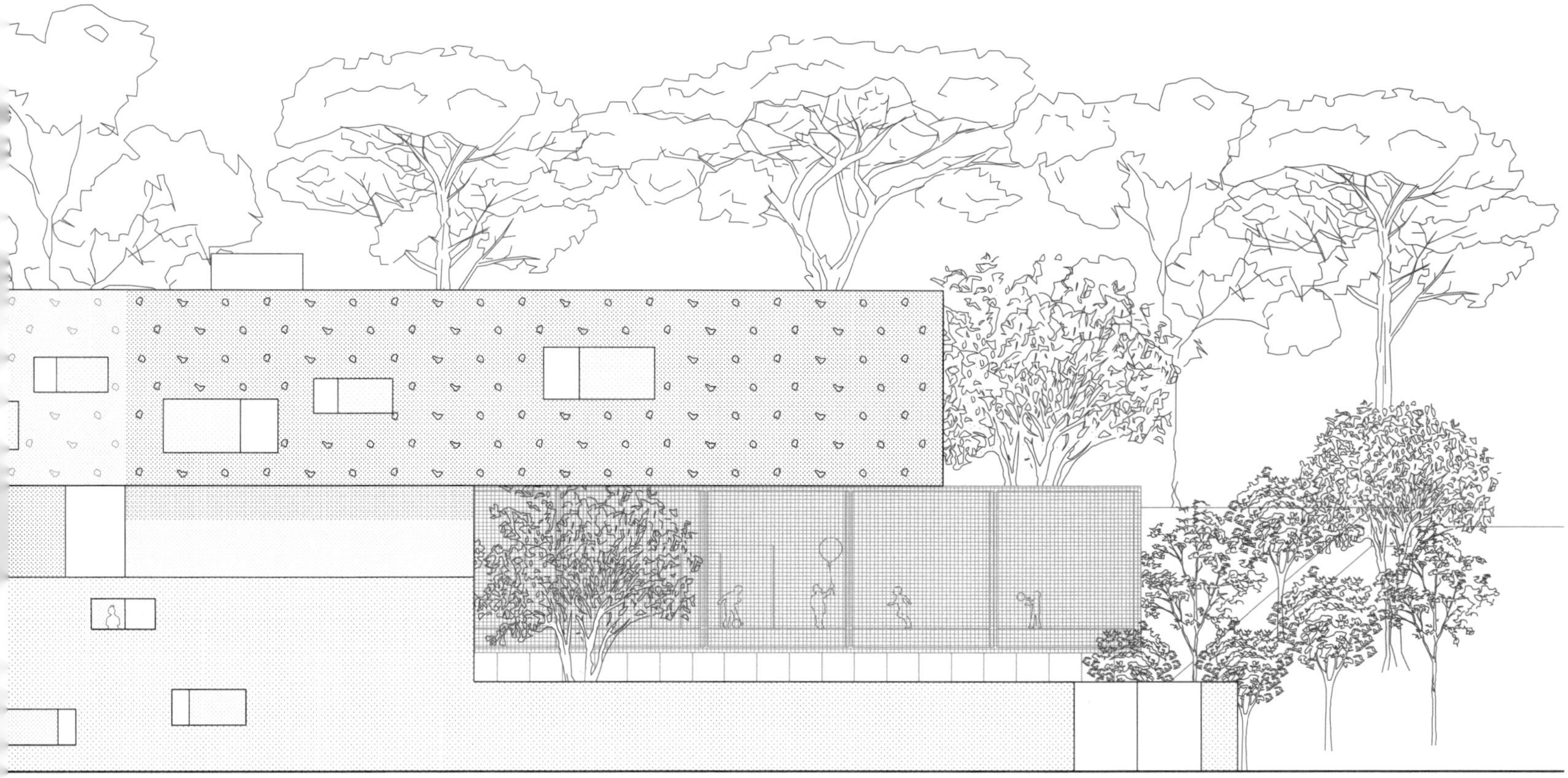

la mer comme monde

simple
comme ciel
la
le

la mer comme monde

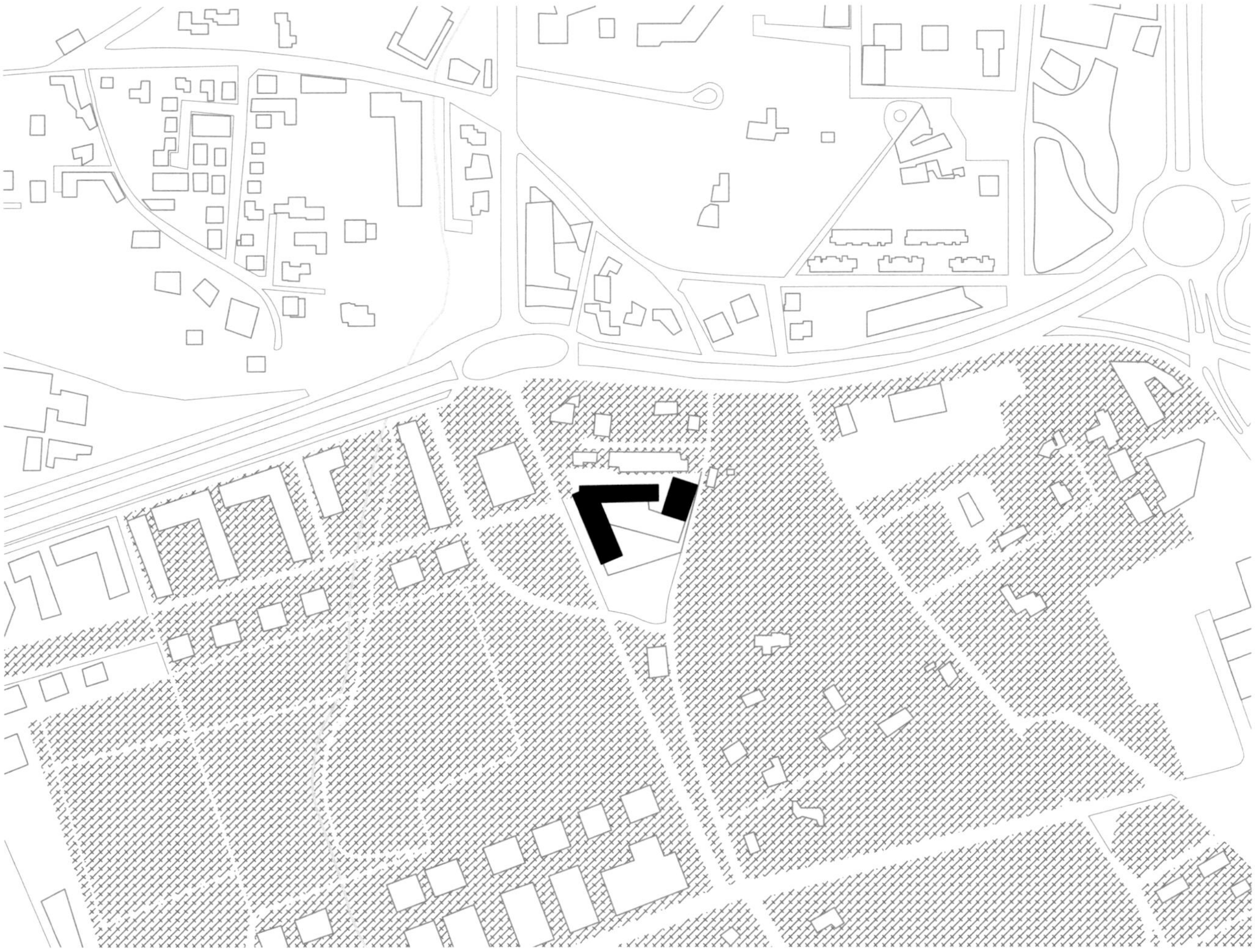

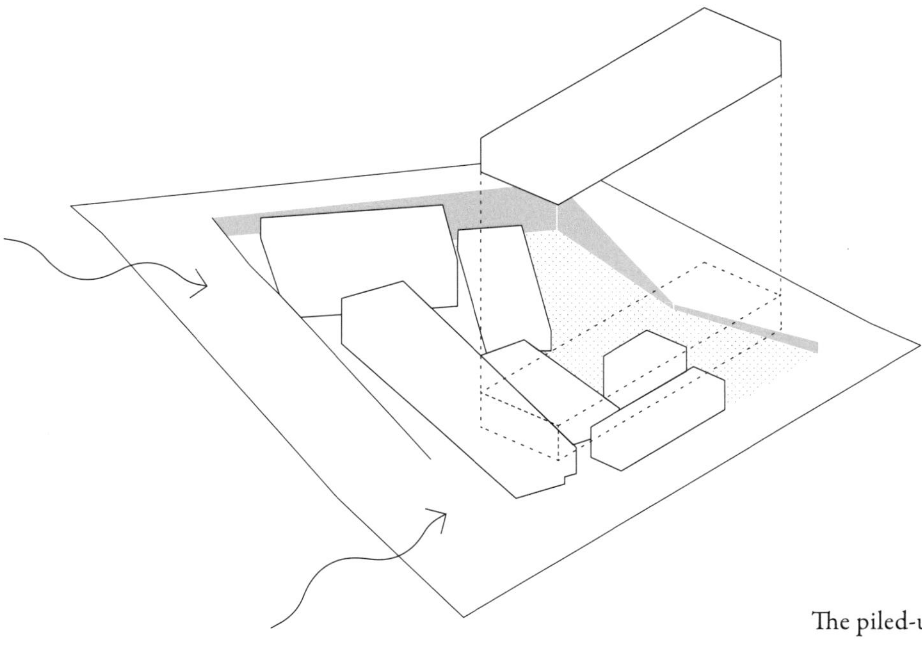

The piled-up volumes protect the playgrounds from the winds.

Breakaway —— Enjoying exceptional demographic and economic growth since the 1980s, Montpellier is rushing headlong towards the sea. New housing operations are sprouting one after the other, sometimes accompanied by neighbourhood facilities. It was in the context of this effervescence that we were asked to intervene on a strangely shaped, sloping site—an incongruous situation that led us to think somewhat differently. Our design consists in a piling up of autonomous vocabularies in the landscape, not without a certain amount of risk-taking resulting from the desire to escape the bland sameness of the new residential neighbourhoods. Each part of the programme is identified by a volume that is placed on the others with no apparent logic, the strong Mediterranean light accentuating the contrasts between the different colours and materials of the various façades. The afterschool spaces and the infant school occupy the ground floor, while the primary school is located in the storeys above; the infant school's roof becomes the primary school's playground, which is directly accessed from the first-floor classrooms. The building is a machine for producing shade, each cantilever creating a space that is sheltered from the sun, while to the north its volumes protect the playgrounds from the mistral and tramontane winds. Rather unusual in the office's oeuvre, this building emits a slightly offbeat energy that plays off the climate and the ever-blue sky and seeks to escape the grip of the surrounding urbanity: its shifting volumes open up a void that creates a breath of air in the closed figure of the triangle and, by establishing a special relationship with its surroundings, the school eludes the townscape so as to come closer to the characteristic atmosphere of the Mediterranean countryside.

N

1

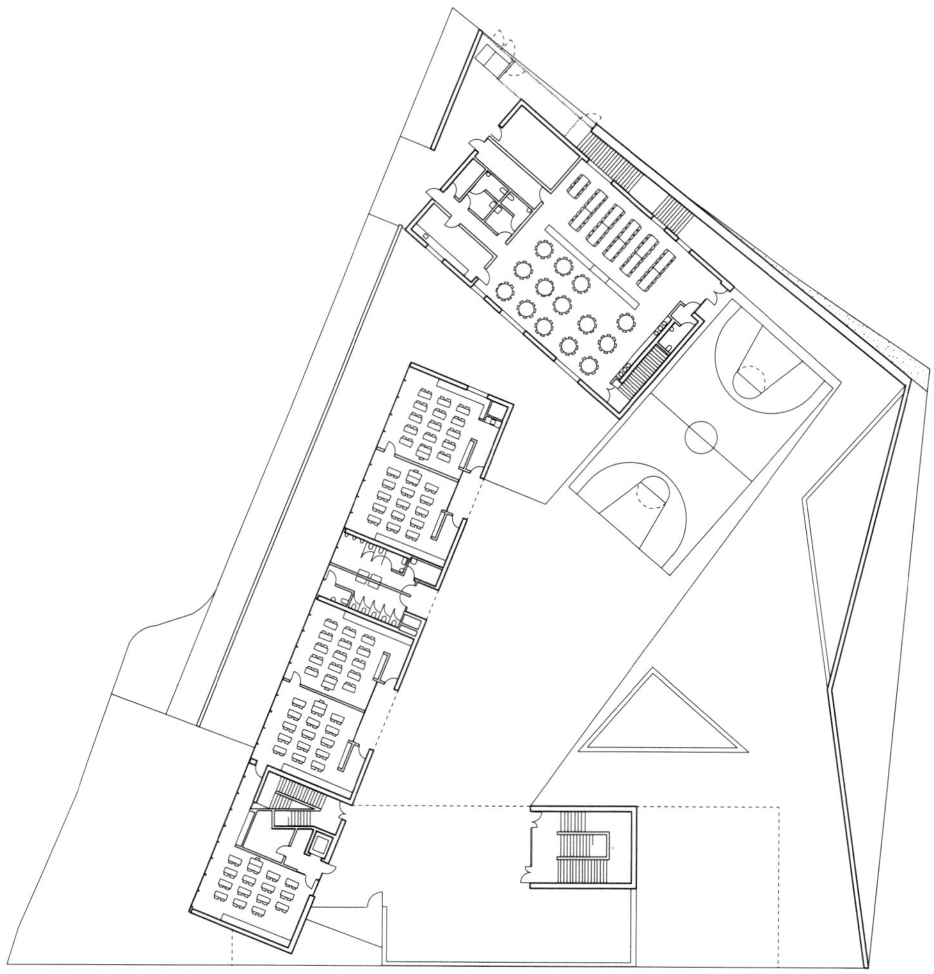

0

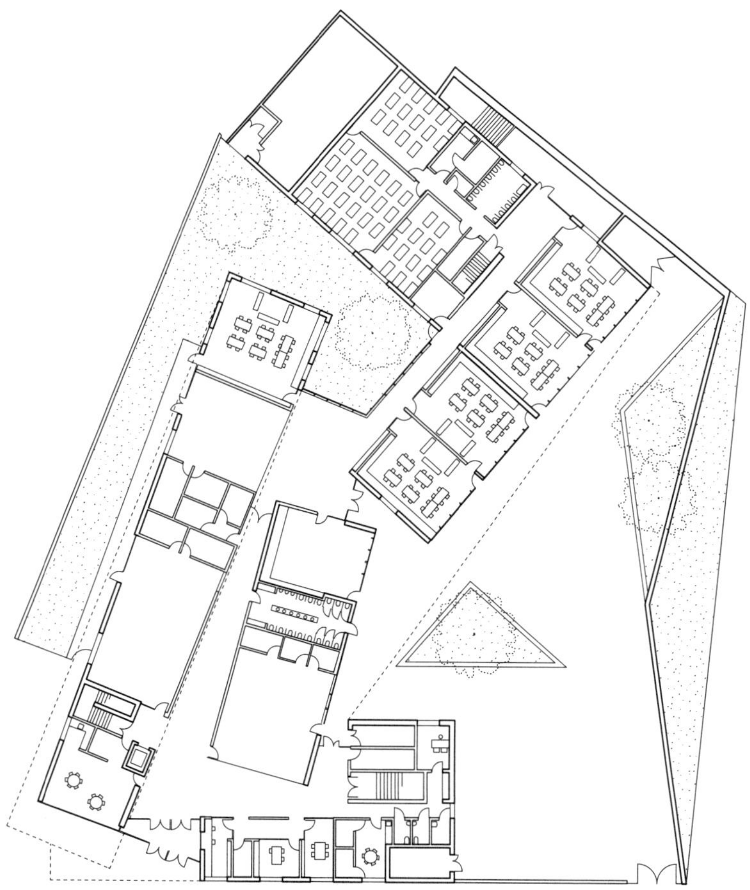

10 m

2

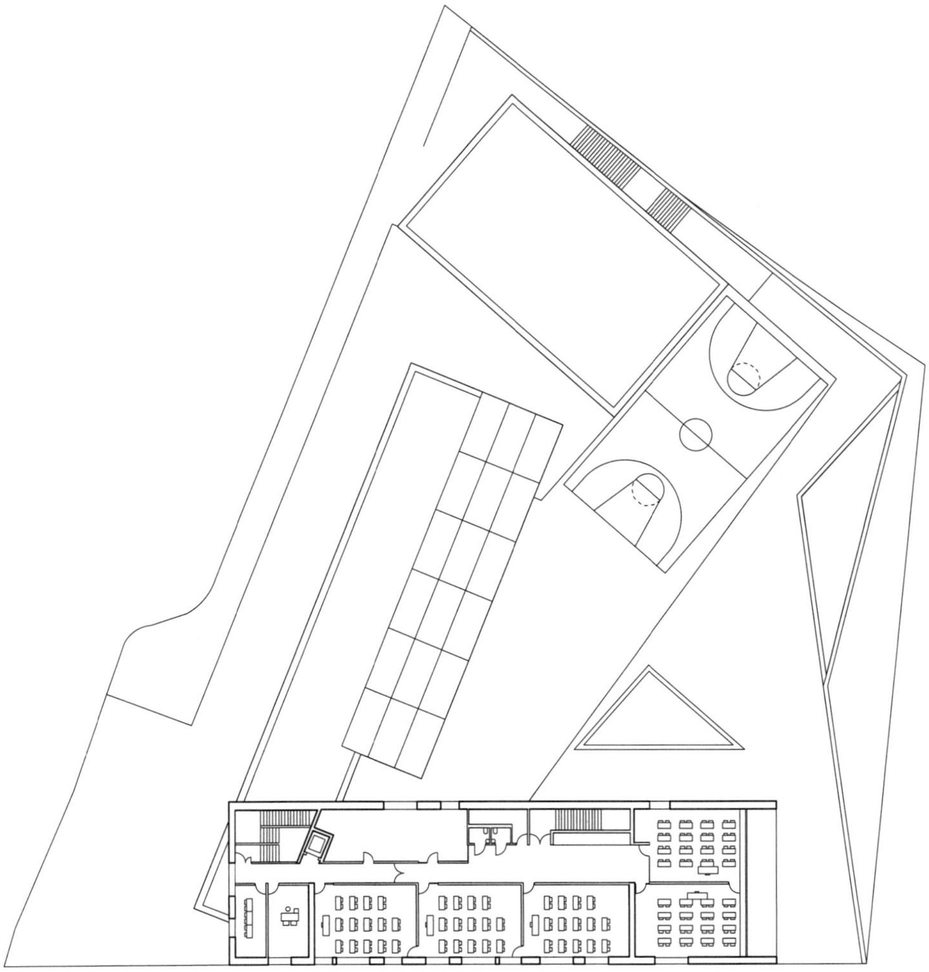

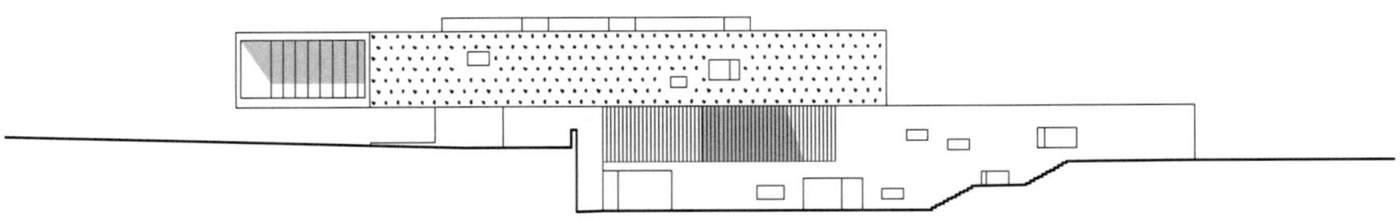

la mer
aurait
André

"Le monde aurait pu être simple comme le ciel et la mer" André Malraux

2015
Conservatoire

Belfort

administration
salle 07
auditorium
accueil

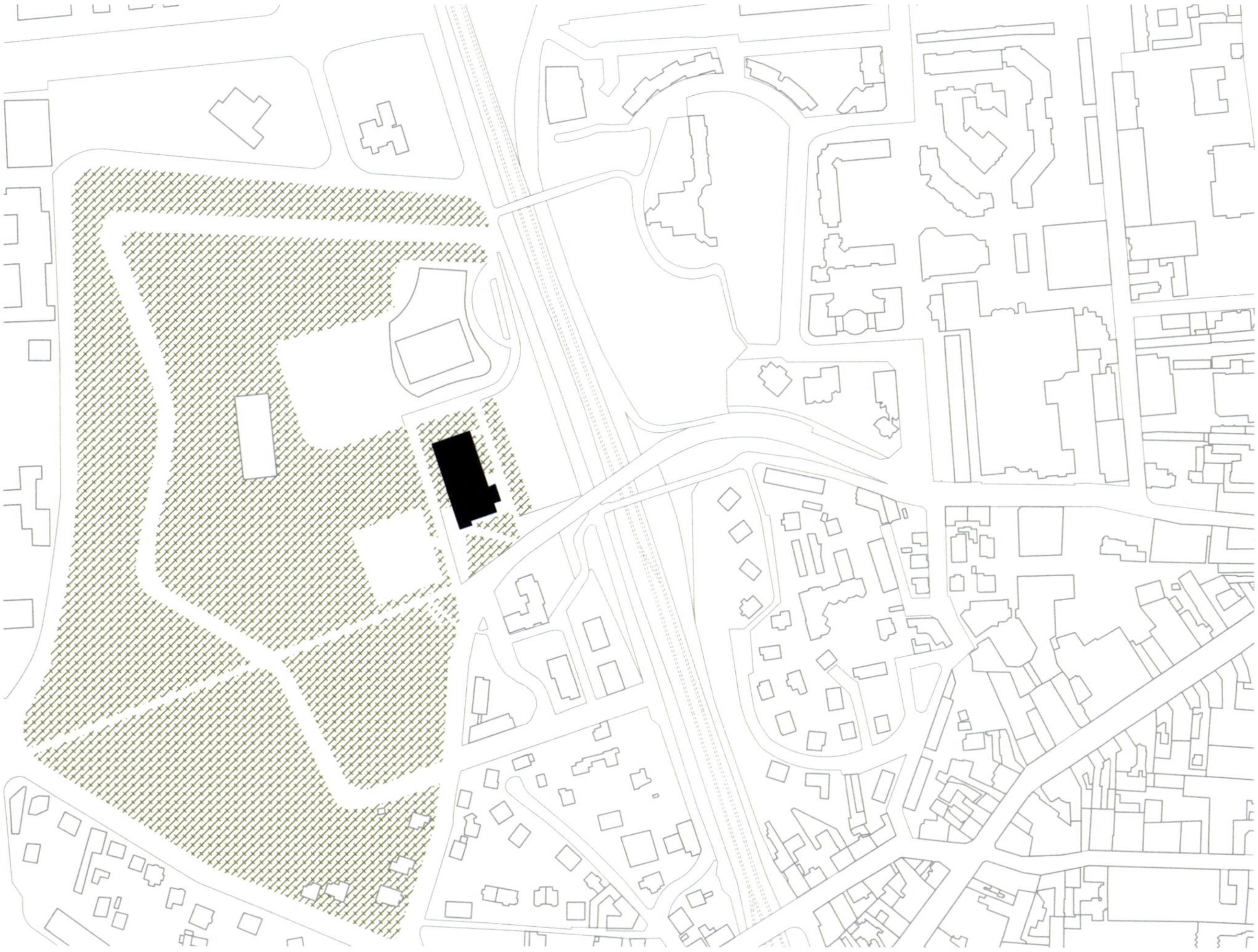

Resonance —— Backing onto the Bois d'Essert, in the heights of Belfort, this music and dance conservatoire looks towards Bartholdi's famous statue of a lion which defends Vauban's citadel. In the context of this intimidating face-off, the building stoically deploys the opaque mass of its light-grey concrete. Behind a row of pines, the façade is covered in a strange veining —the result of a dripping painting technique that mixes pale and dark blue, bringing a certain depth and thickness to the building's skin. Light makes the surfaces vibrate, animating the building, which, with its openings hidden and protected by the trees, takes on an enigmatic air. The programme required volumes with very different massing: two auditoriums, a theatre, a large dance rehearsal hall, a library, classrooms, administration spaces, and a multitude of variously sized studios, each one with an acoustic adapted to a specific type of instrument. Spaces nest among each other, with interstitial voids that link the floors; the entrance hall takes on an unexpected amplitude in which the concrete wall of the library, rising above the grand staircase, functions as a giant reflector. A dark and compact central patio reverses, with its white on midnight blue, the dripping finish of the façade. Surmounting all the others, the mass of the dance rehearsal hall is the only one that opens explicitly onto the landscape. Since each constituent mass required a specific design, the ideas of repetition and versatility disappear. The entrance hall and the patio offer a counterweight to this ultimate form of specificity: collective spaces, they constitute a stage, so to speak, for the proliferation of all the others around them.

2ème étage
salles 201 à 219
studios de travail 1 à 4
studio de danse
art dramatique
médiathèque
salle de convivialité
1er étage
salles 101 à 119
RDC
salles 01 à 07
administration
amphithéâtre
auditorium

N

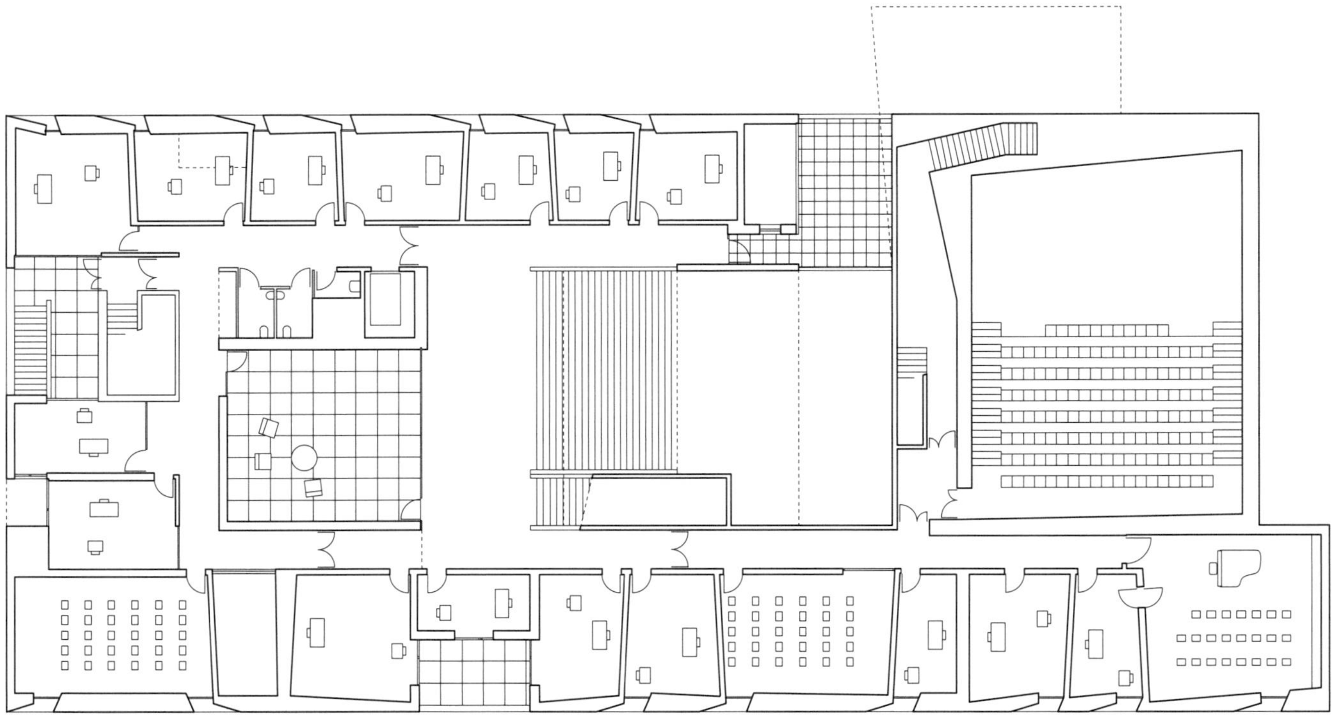

1

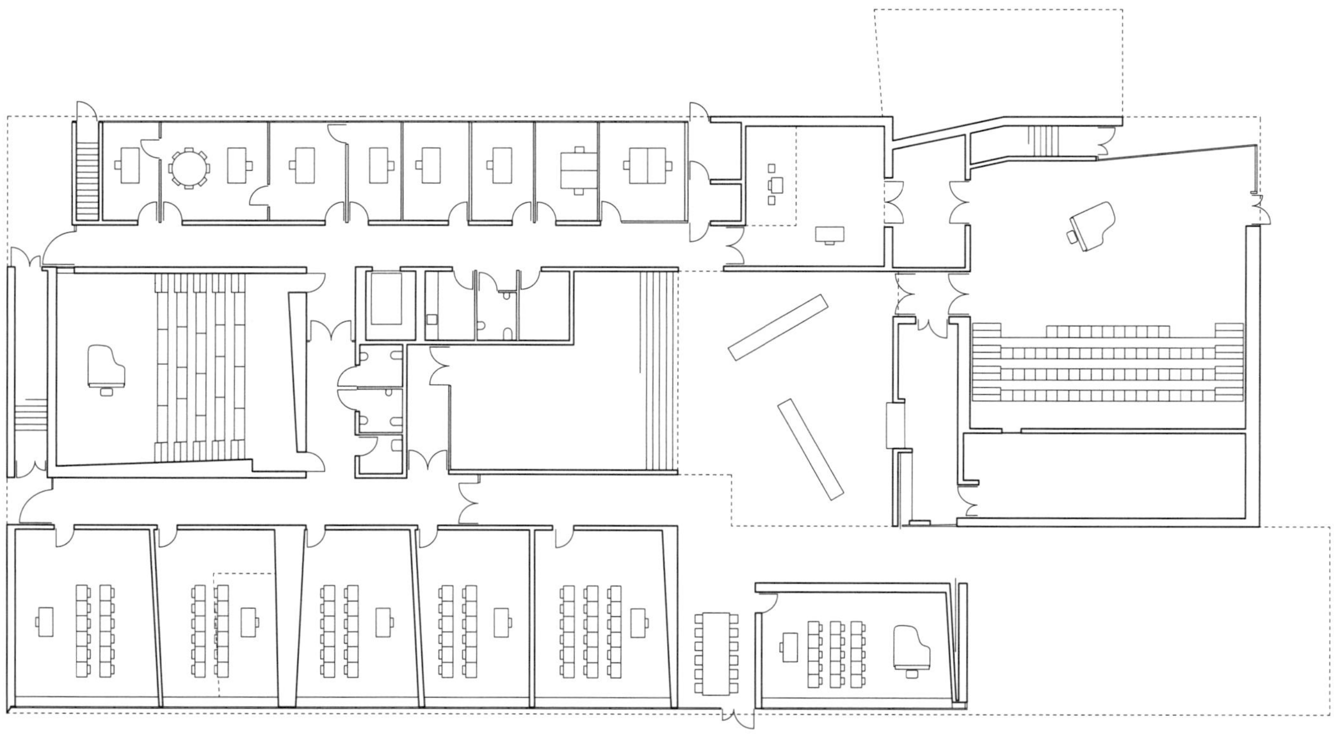

0

10 m

2

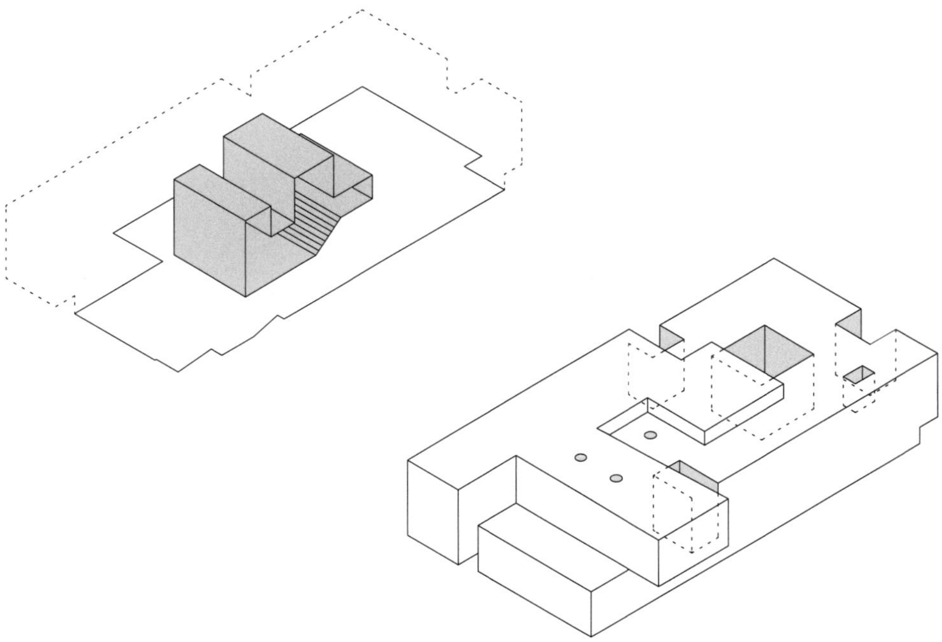

Void sculpture in the building: stairway, central patio and hollows in the façade.

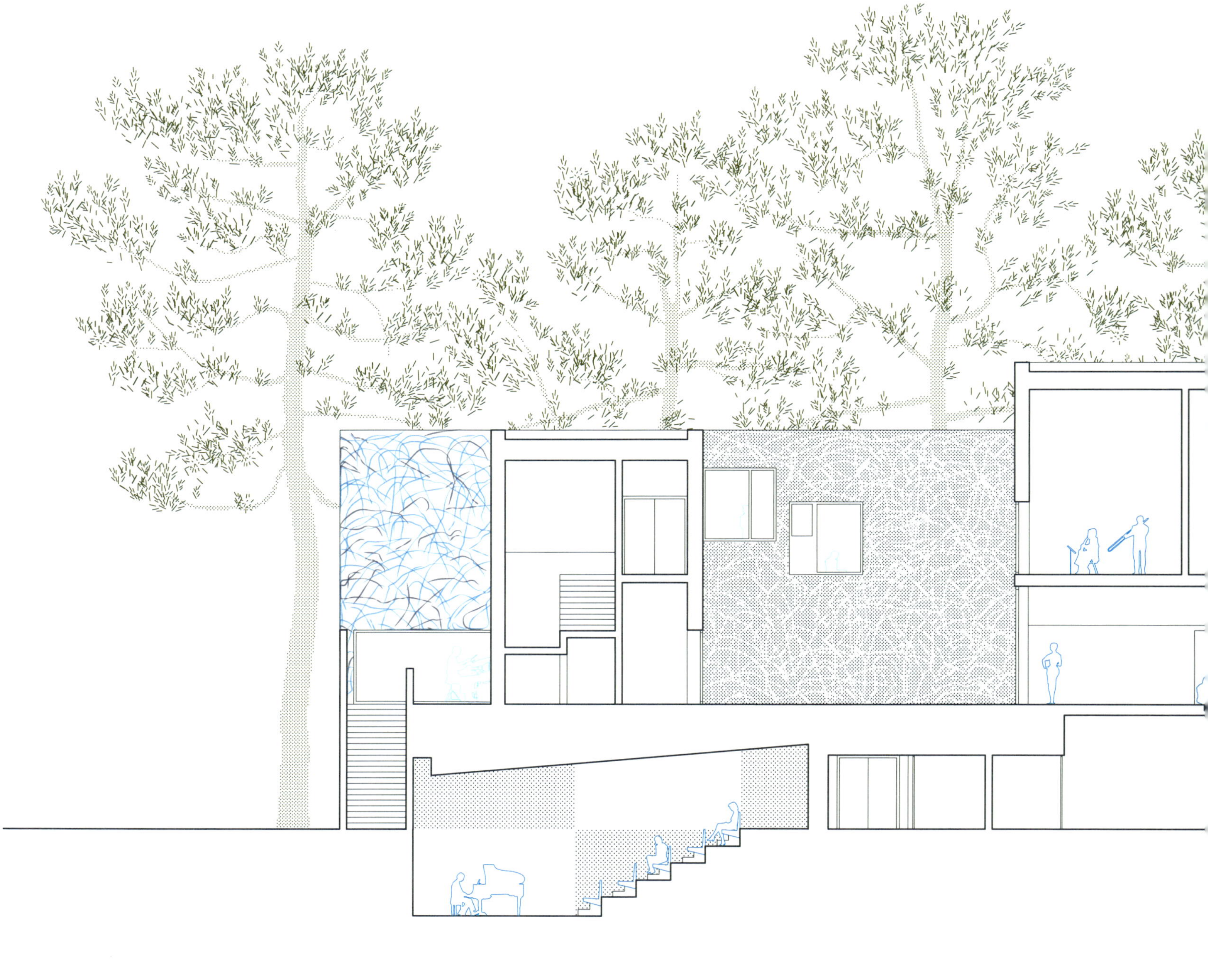

5 m

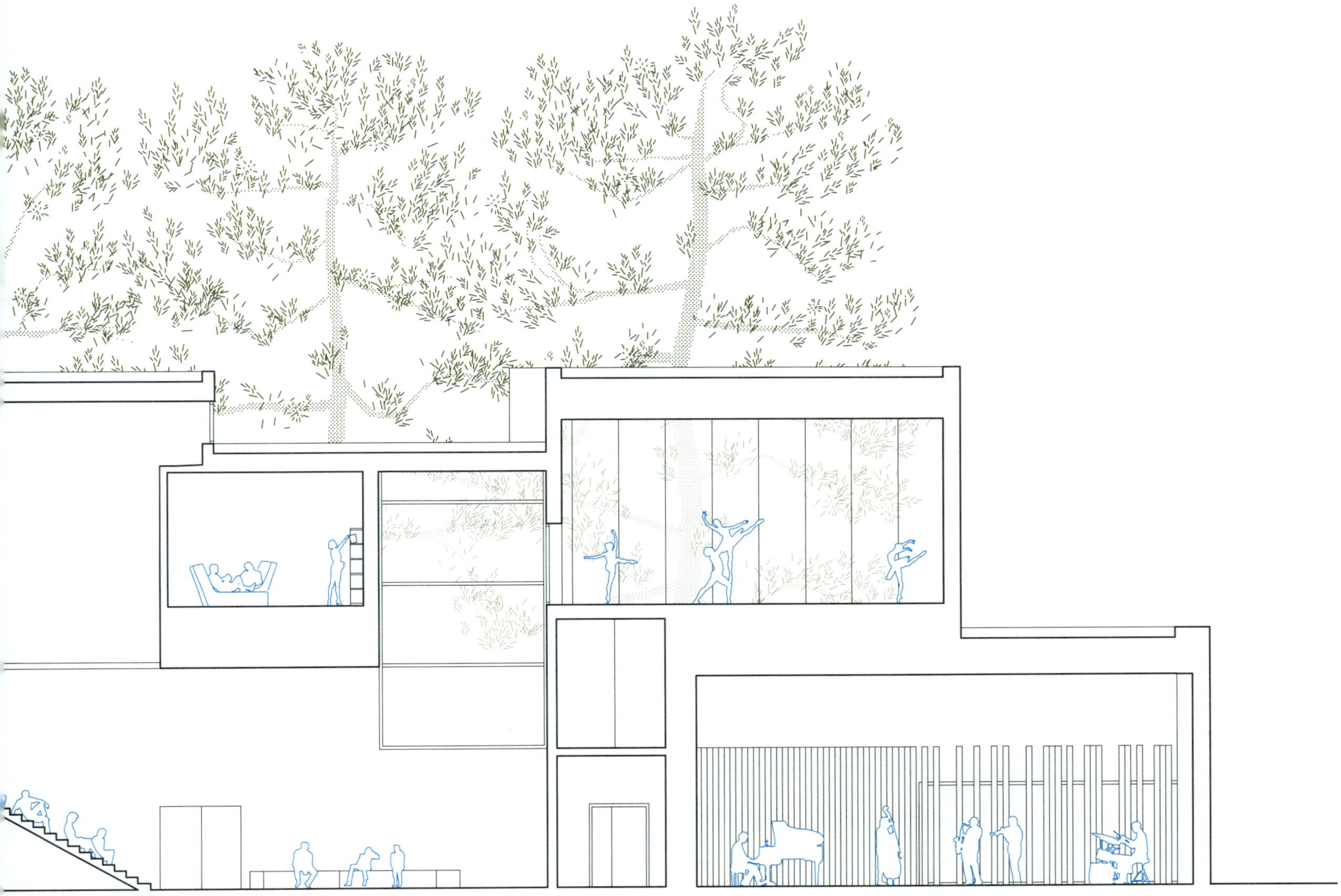

2014
Swimming pool

Bagneux

Metamorphosis —— Set in a Modernist post-war development in Paris's southern suburbs, this restructuring and extension of Bagneux's municipal swimming pool operates a radical transformation. The original and the additional blend together to form a new ensemble that is defined by its mineral materiality, from the extension's light-grey concrete to the cement rendering of the existing building—which has been insulated from the outside—, right down to the crazy paving of the entrance hall, realised in quartzite from Luzern. Strange and monumental, its head held high in the face of the apartment blocks opposite, the new swimming pool asserts its presence in the urban landscape. To the east, micro-beads in the bluish render mimic watery reflections, while beneath large vertical and horizontal blades, which provide a constant play of shadow and light, the terrace and the adjacent forecourt open up a generous quantity of public space, despite the small size of the building plot. Within its brise-soleils, the pool operates a suspension of time. The structure of the original volume has been preserved, with its oblique struts that complement the roof's incline. A radical use of colour divides up the space, while the toddlers' pool, flooded with sunlight from a large vertical bay, is more like a cocoon whose curves attenuate sound—a place where the imagination can wander. Soft light and fluid paths create marked atmospheres; a porthole in the ceiling beneath the paddling pool sends undulating blue light into the entrance hall, while, in the double-height rest room, another window with an organic contour gives onto a small garden. Outside, the large wooden terrace opens up in the middle of the surrounding apartment buildings. Tall barriers preserve swimmers' privacy, while the concrete blades of the brise-soleils, along with the layout of the corridors, offer a multitude of nooks, crannies and passages. Both open and protective, this place of awakening lets the body discover uses for it.

1

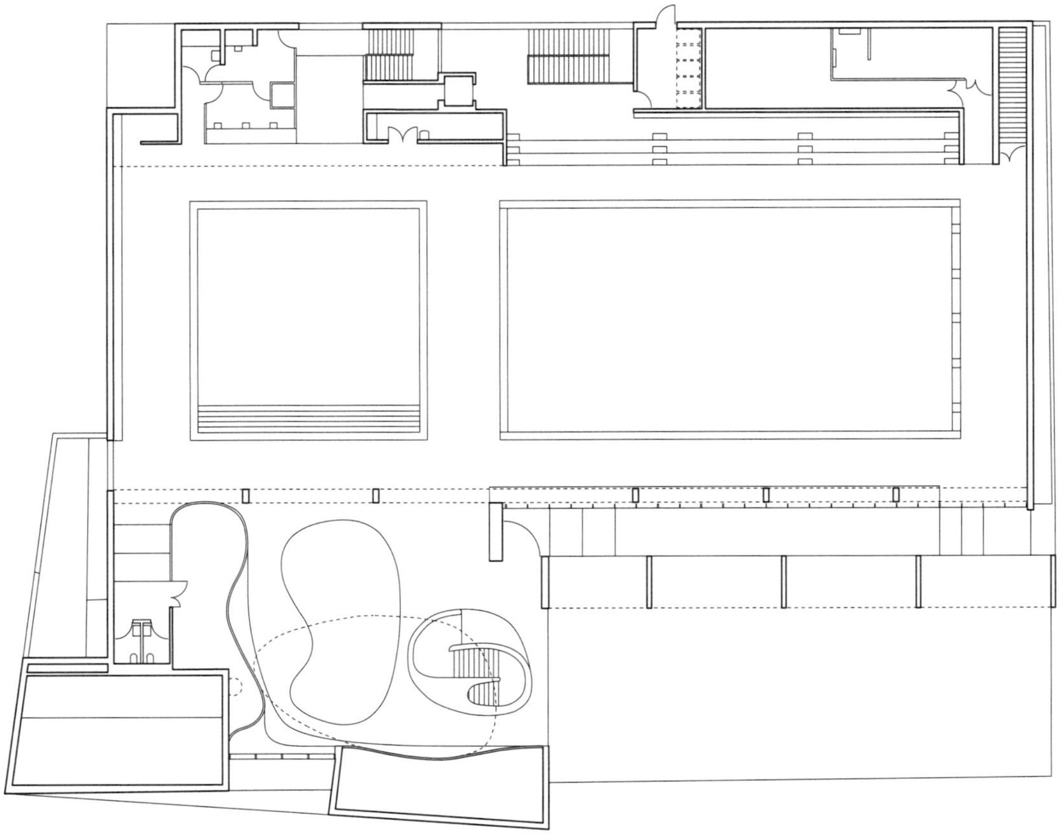

0

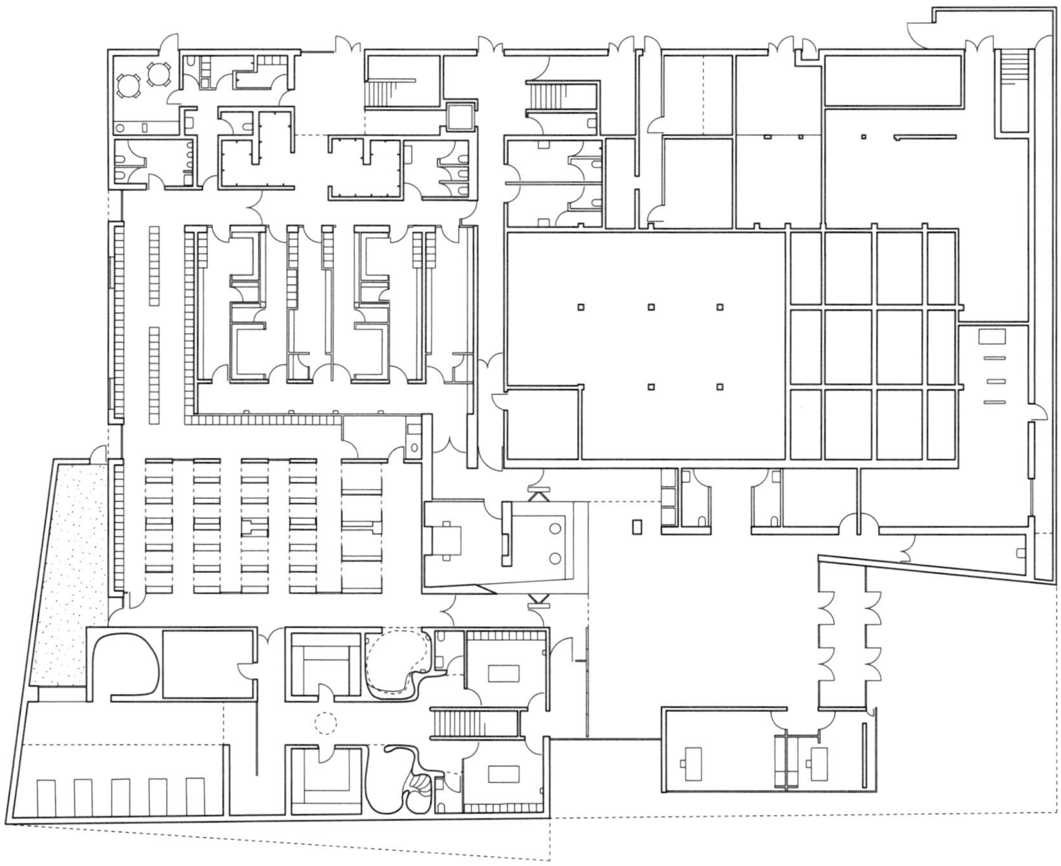

10 m

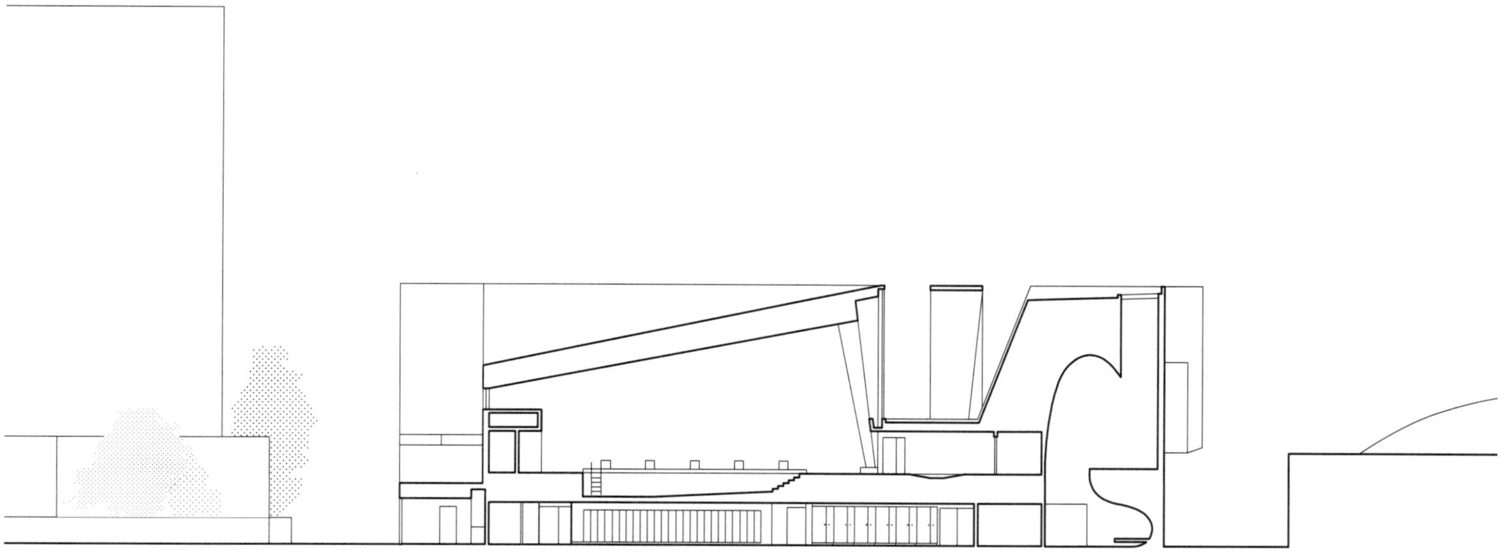

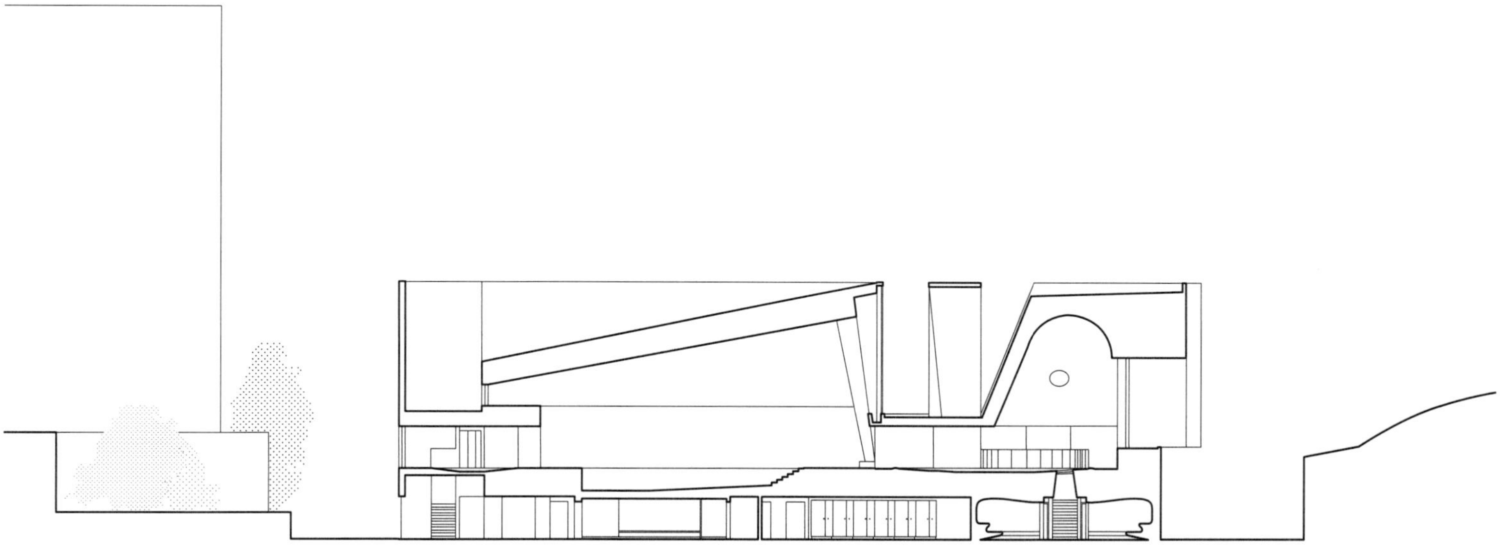

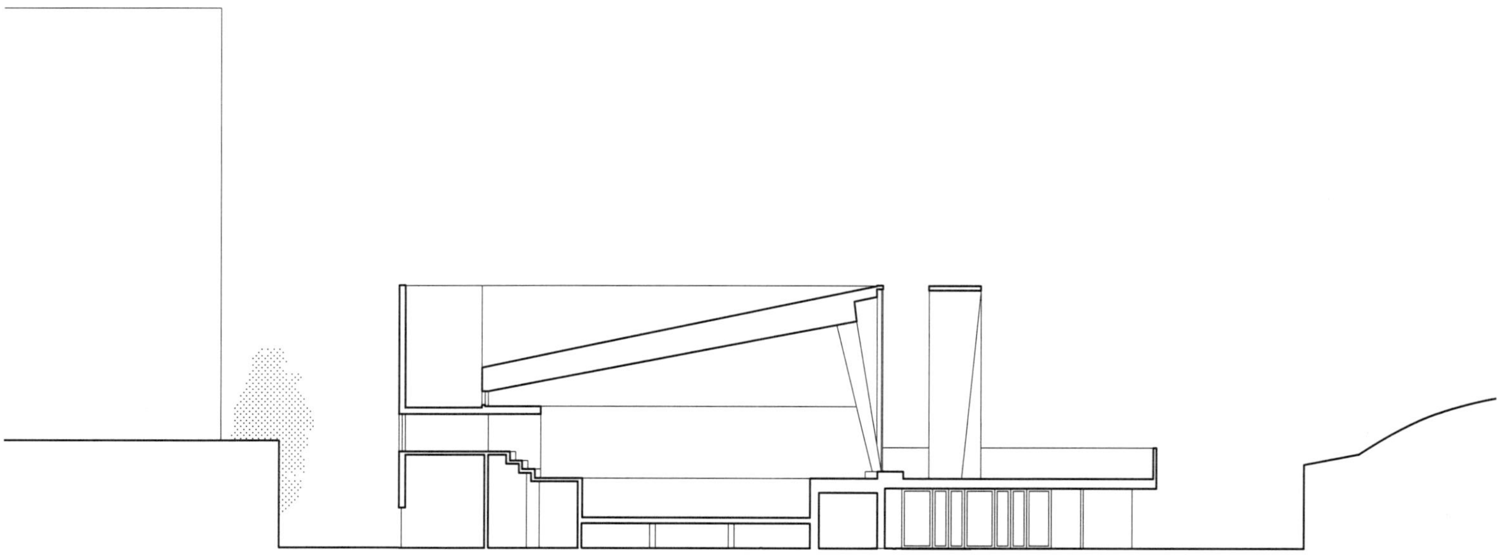

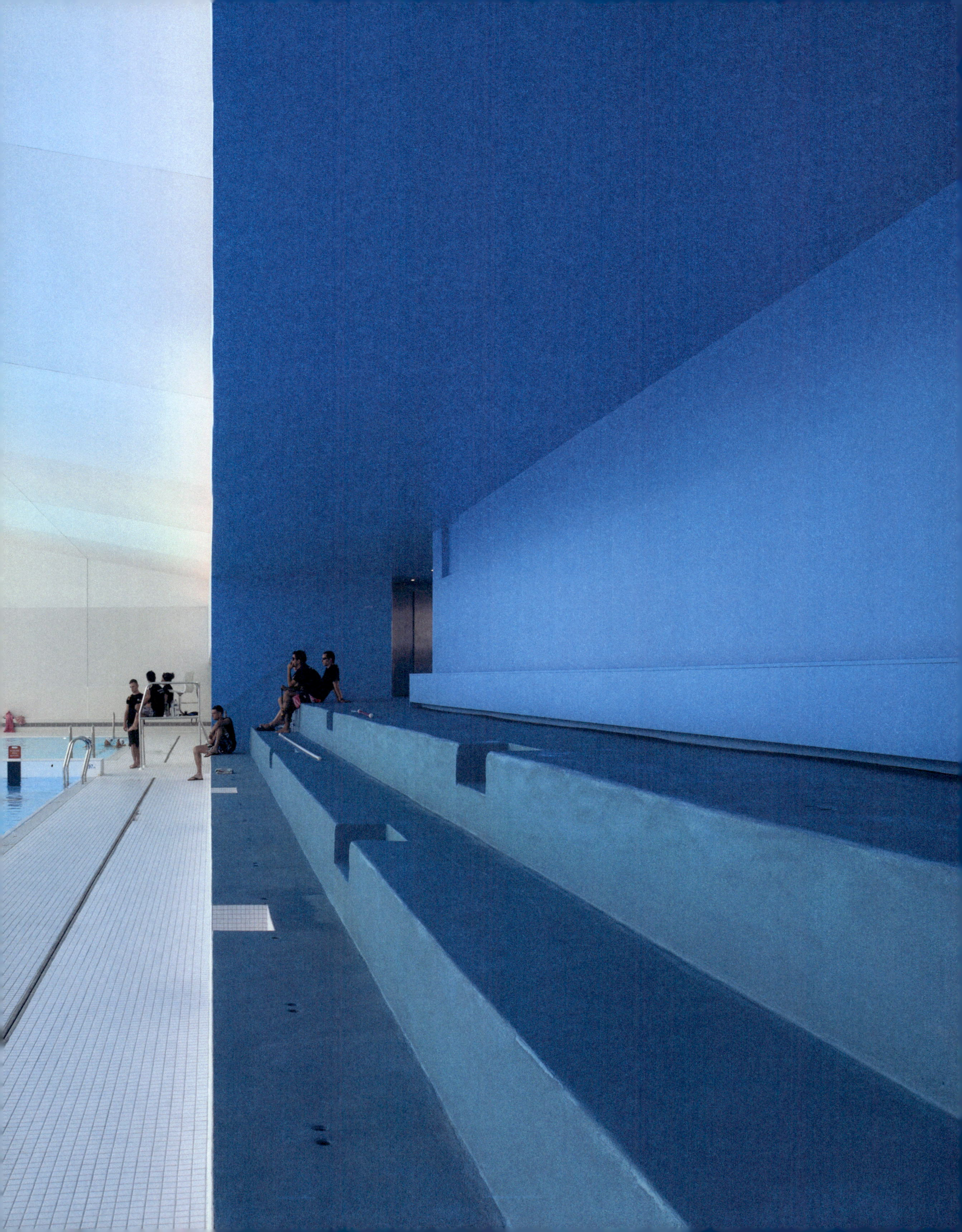

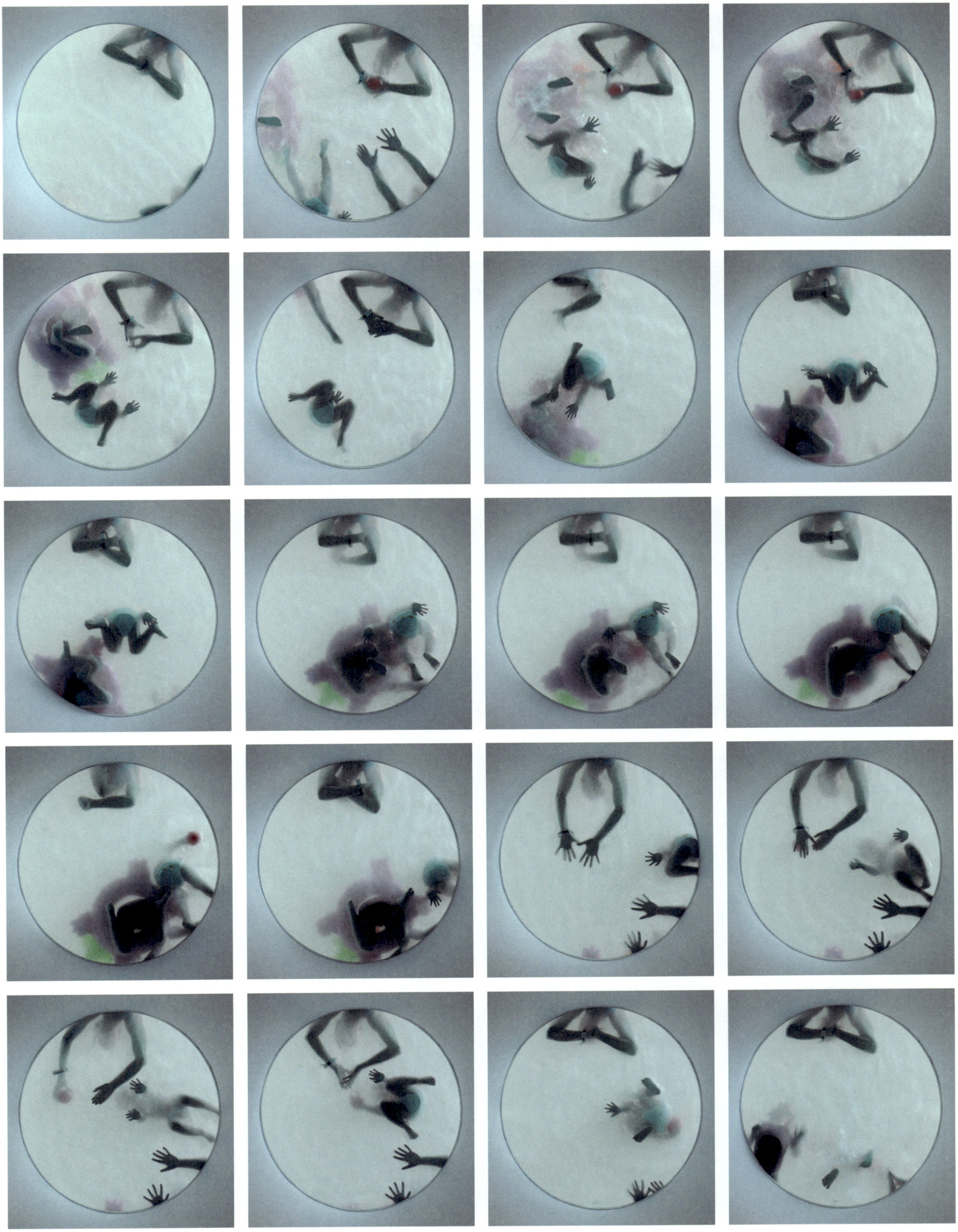

2016
Media library

Thionville

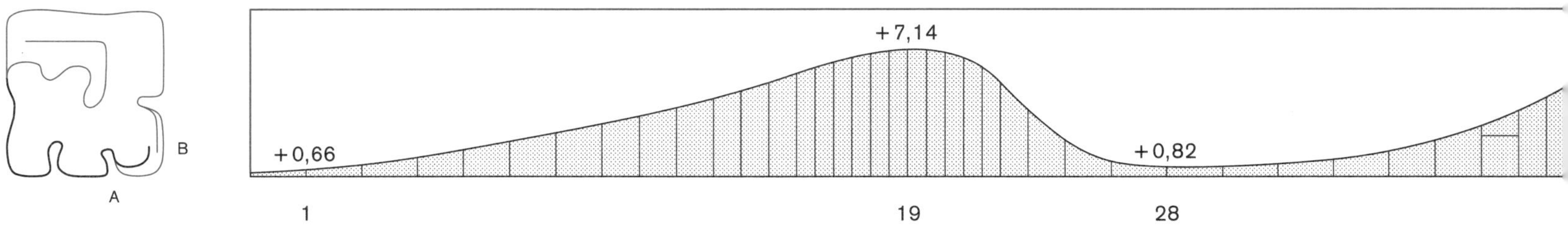
B
A
+0,66
+7,14
+0,82
1
19
28

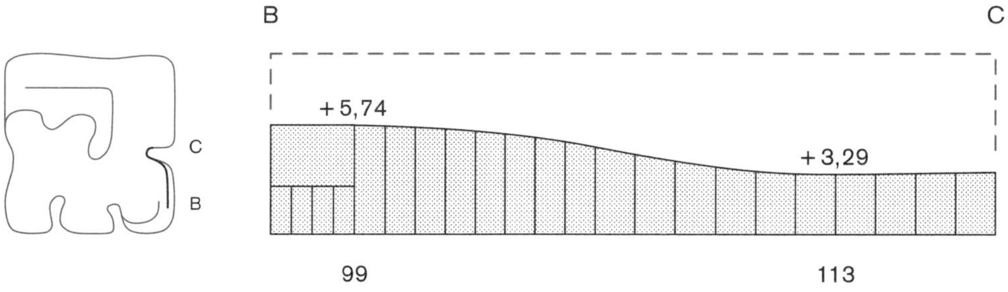
B
C
C
B
+5,74
+3,29
99
113

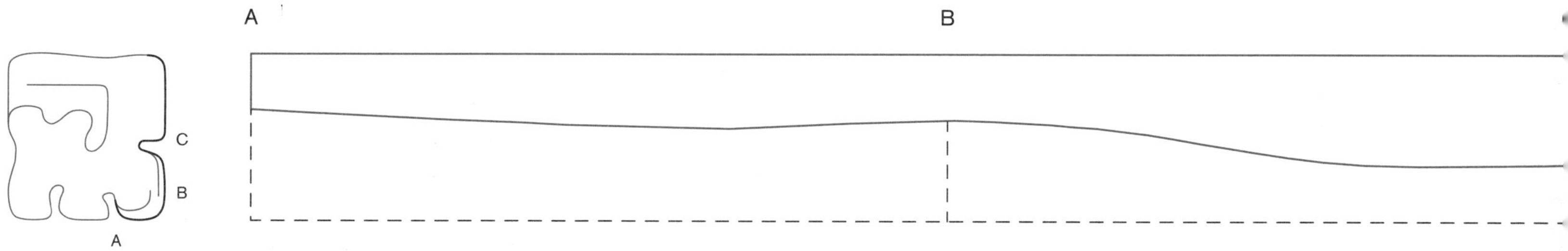
A
B
C
B
A

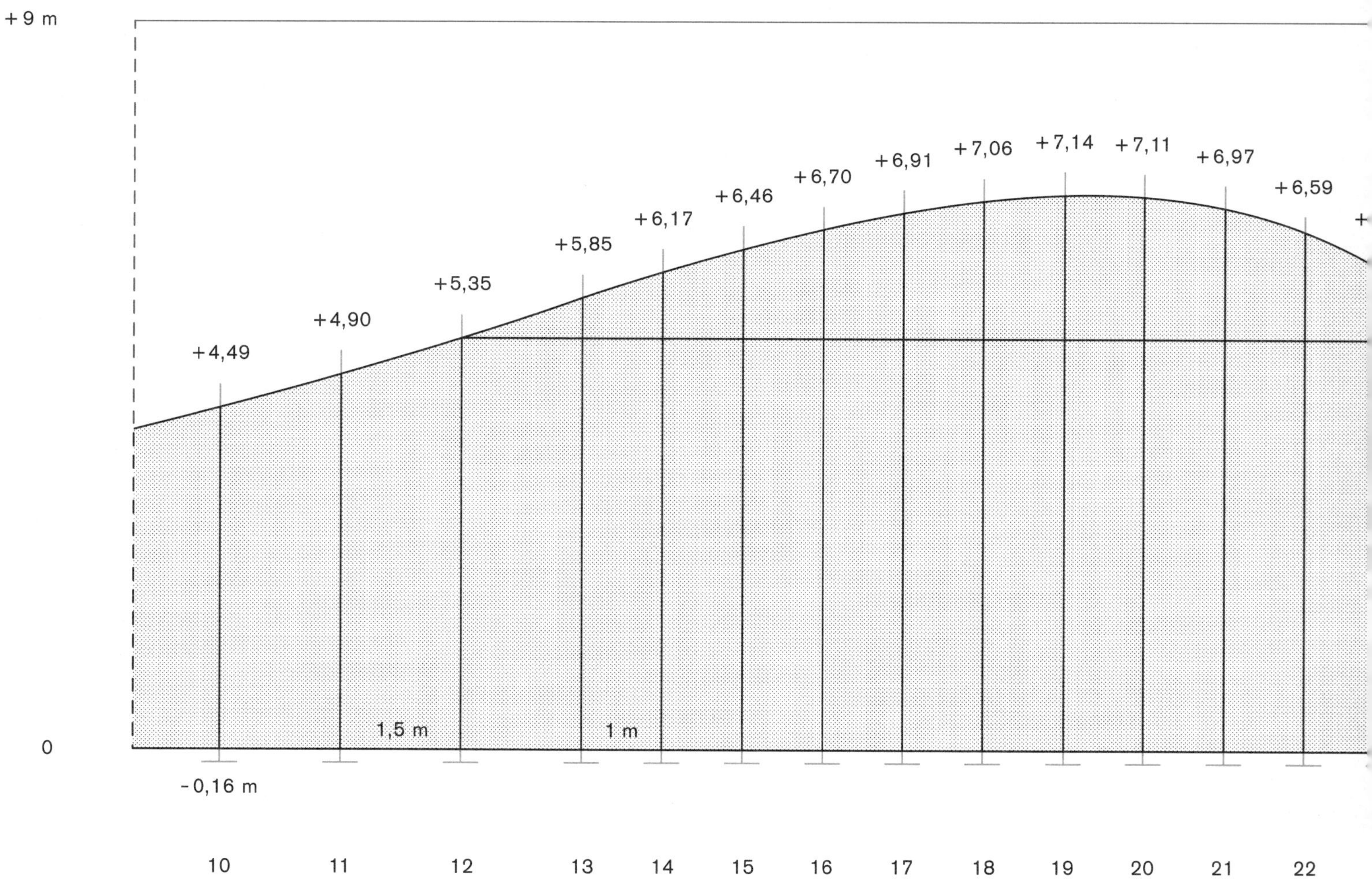
+9 m
0
+4,49
+4,90
+5,35
+5,85
+6,17
+6,46
+6,70
+6,91
+7,06
+7,14
+7,11
+6,97
+6,59
1,5 m
1 m
-0,16 m
10
11
12
13
14
15
16
17
18
19
20
21
22

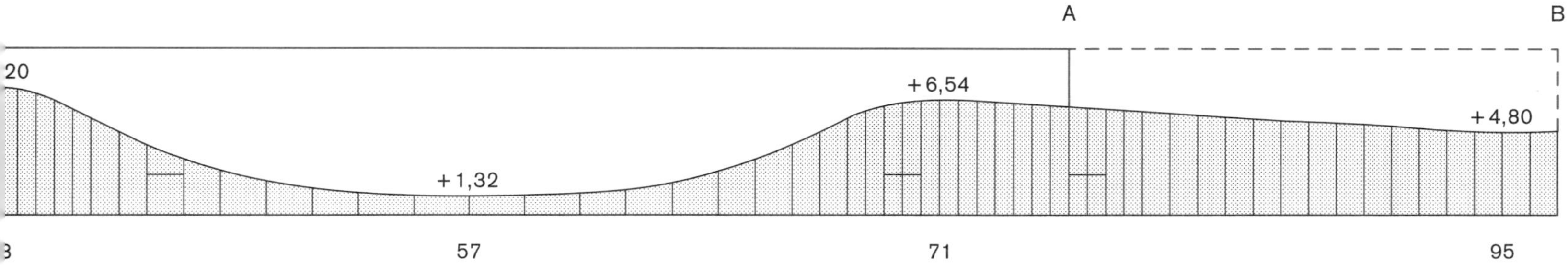

A
B
20
+6,54
+4,80
+1,32
3
57
71
95

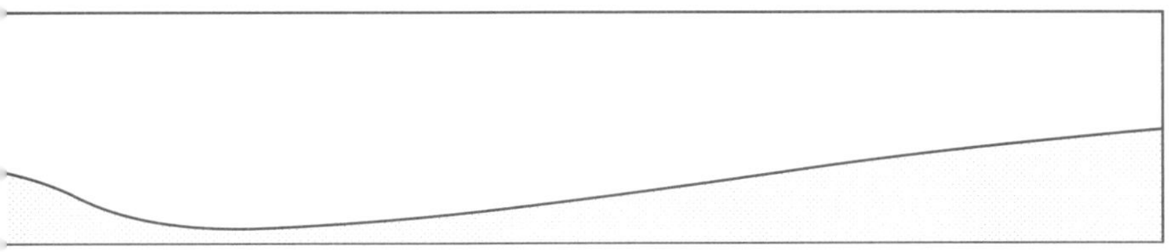

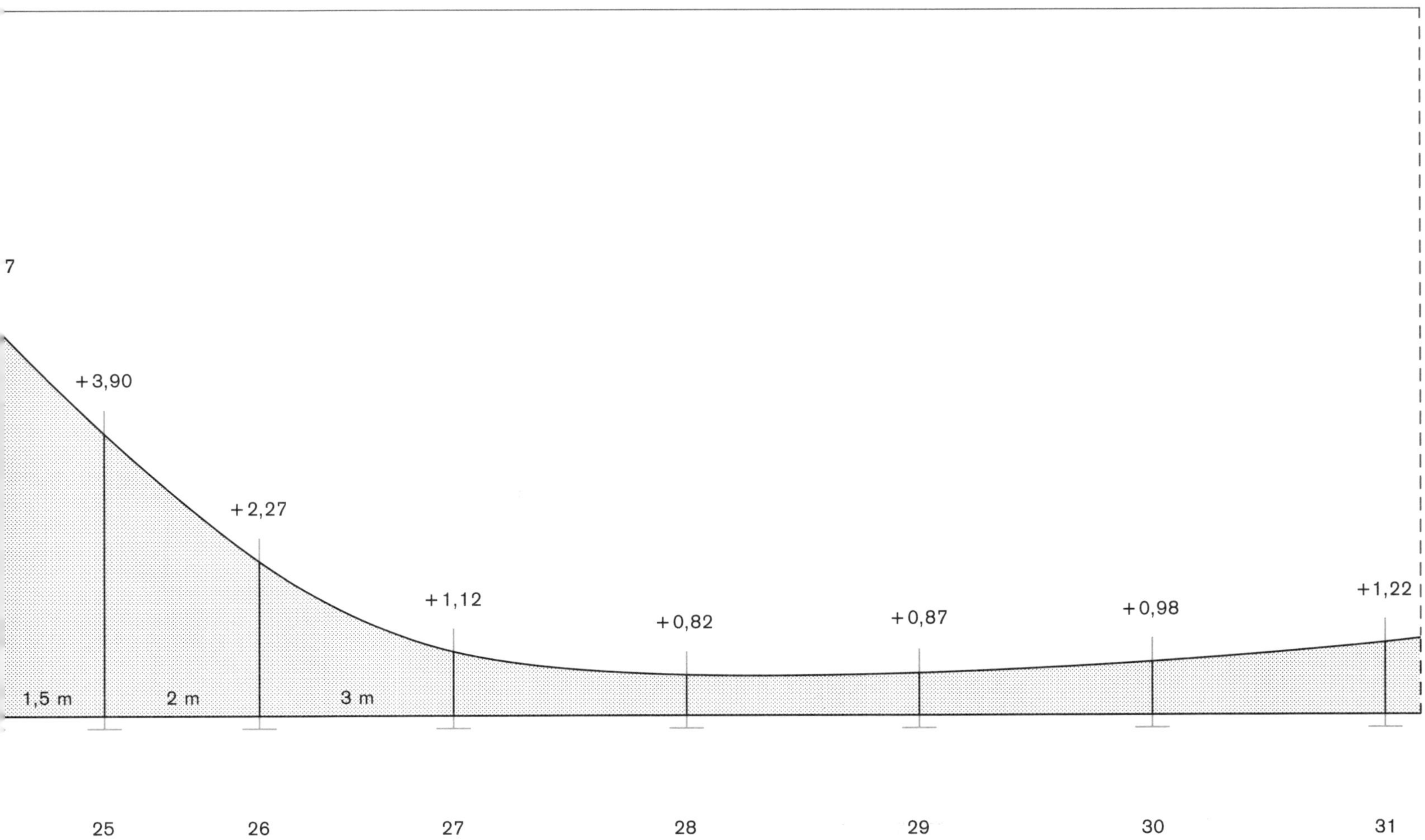

7
+3,90
+2,27
+1,12
+0,82
+0,87
+0,98
+1,22
1,5 m
2 m
3 m
25
26
27
28
29
30
31

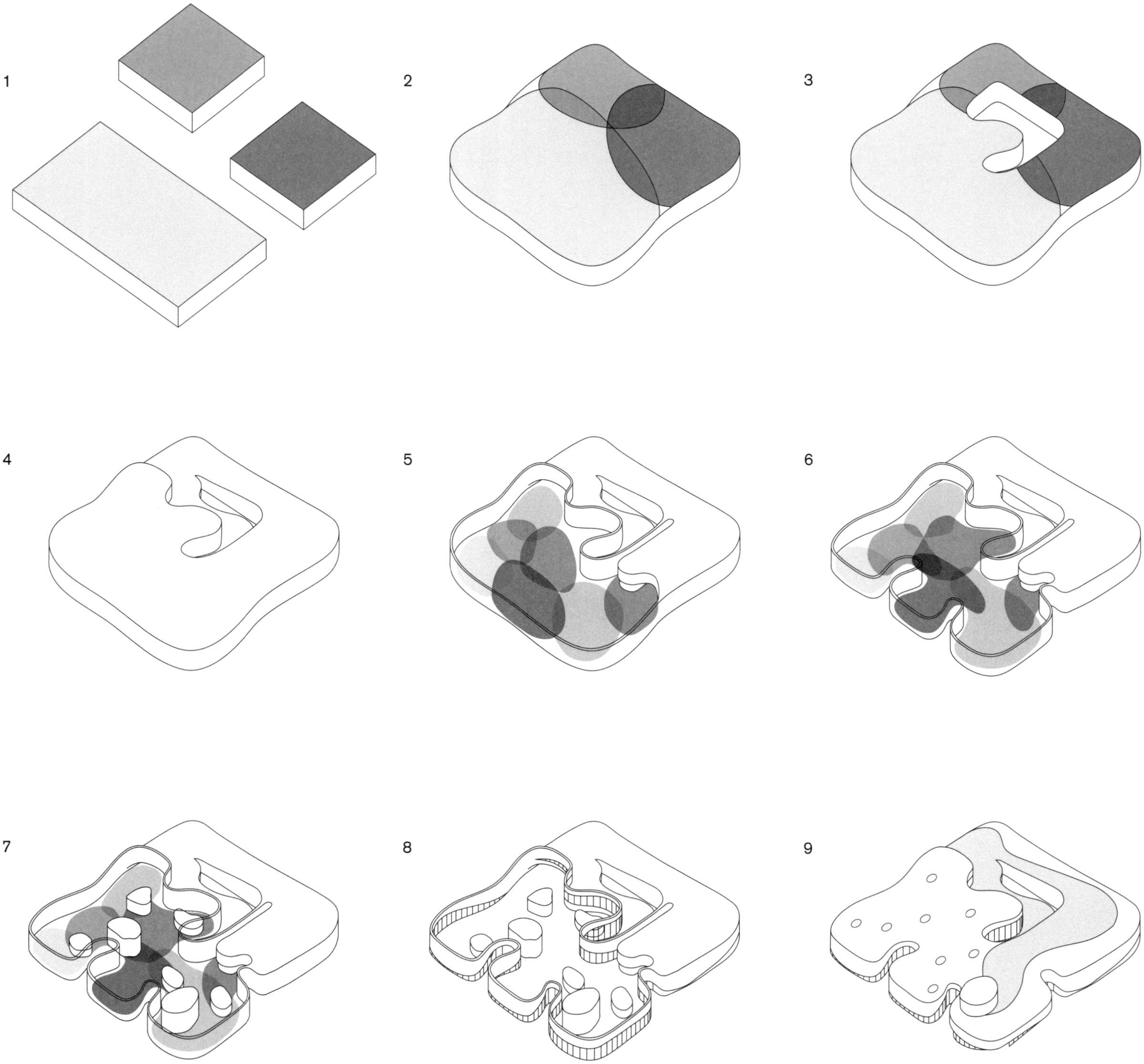

1 Media library, creation studio, administrative area and plant. 2 Interaction areas. 3 Patio.
4 Ramp and rooftop garden. 5 The media library's six universes and creation studio. 6 Hierarchy between the universes.
7 Position of the bubbles. 8 Transparency. 9 Overhead natural lighting and layout of the rooftop garden.

N

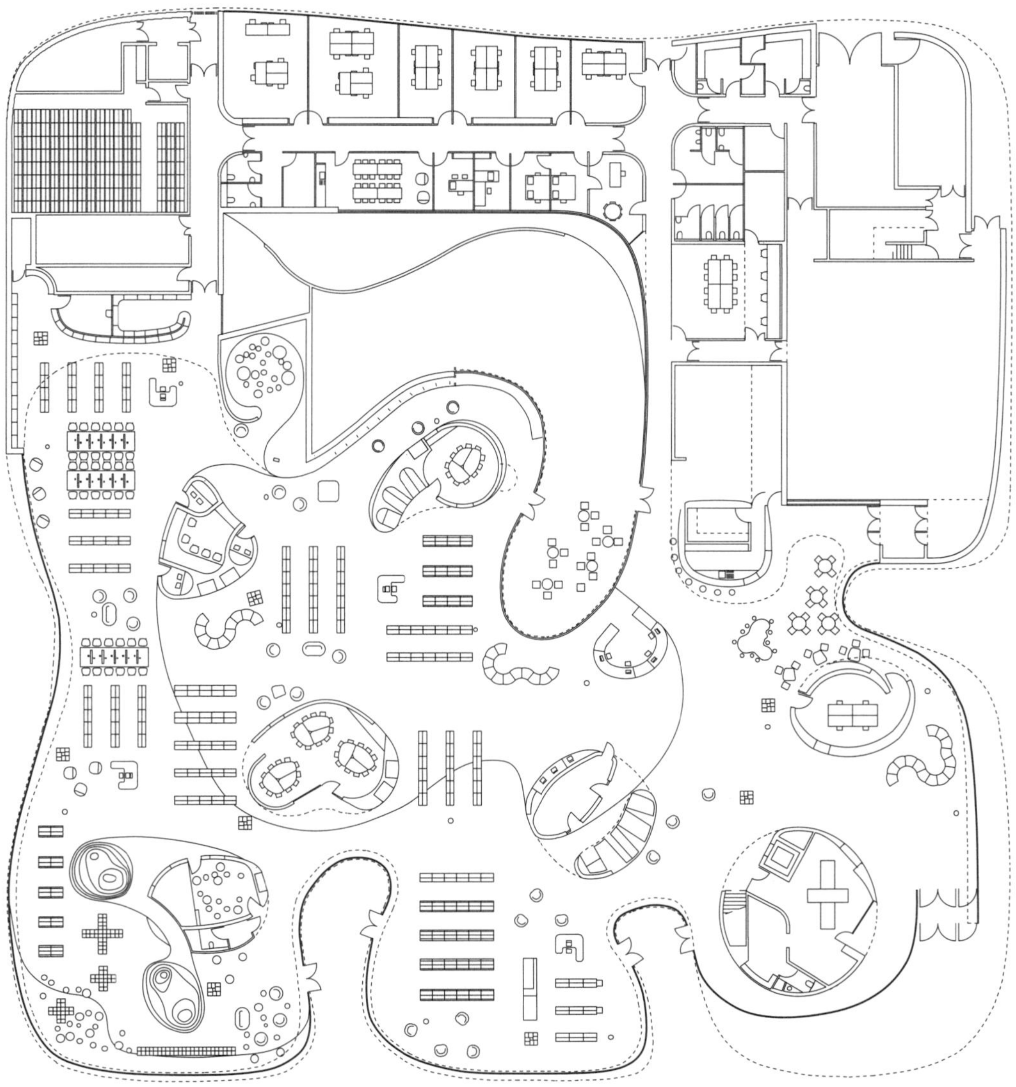

0

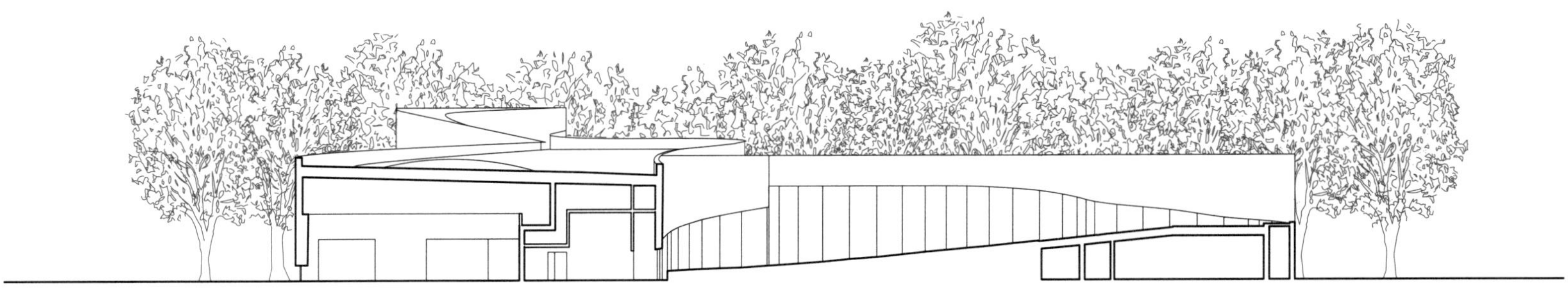

10 m

Third place —— Intended as a new type of media library, the project in Thionville sets out to question the classic functions of such an institution, proposing a programme christened ‘third place’ where the user is active as much as passive, and both receives and conceives. In addition to the usual activities, the building includes exhibition halls, creative spaces, music studios and a café-restaurant. In order to do justice to this ambitious programme, we felt it was necessary on our part to question the usual modes of fabrication of this type of institution; the various functions are mixed in a dynamic organisation of space that is based in a non-hierarchical superimposition of different systems. The multimedia library is set within a square that is suggested by the site’s geometry and which is marked at its perimeter by rows of plane trees. Built close up against the latter, and thus following the contours of an isotropic figure which has no hierarchy of direction, the façade wraps round the structure like a ribbon that plays off the colonnade of trees, its folds and hollows containing the different aspects of the programme while still bringing a feeling of spatial continuity. Intended as a membrane that protects and contains the interior while still allowing exchange with outside world, the external envelope narrows as it approaches the street and thickens elsewhere. In the hollows, the limit between outside and in diminishes, inviting passers-by to enter, at least visually. The solids and voids blur the relationship between inside and out, challenging the limits of public space. Deprived of clear contours, the interior becomes uncertain, calling into question habit and use. Light washes over the ribbon, and is redistributed via the hollows into the heart of the building. A green ramp climbs up towards a rooftop garden and bar, which prolong the interior circuit. On the roof, the town disappears behind the leafy crown of the trees, and new behaviours become possible: reading under the open sky, taking a sun-soaked nap, picnicking, or simply chilling out with friends.

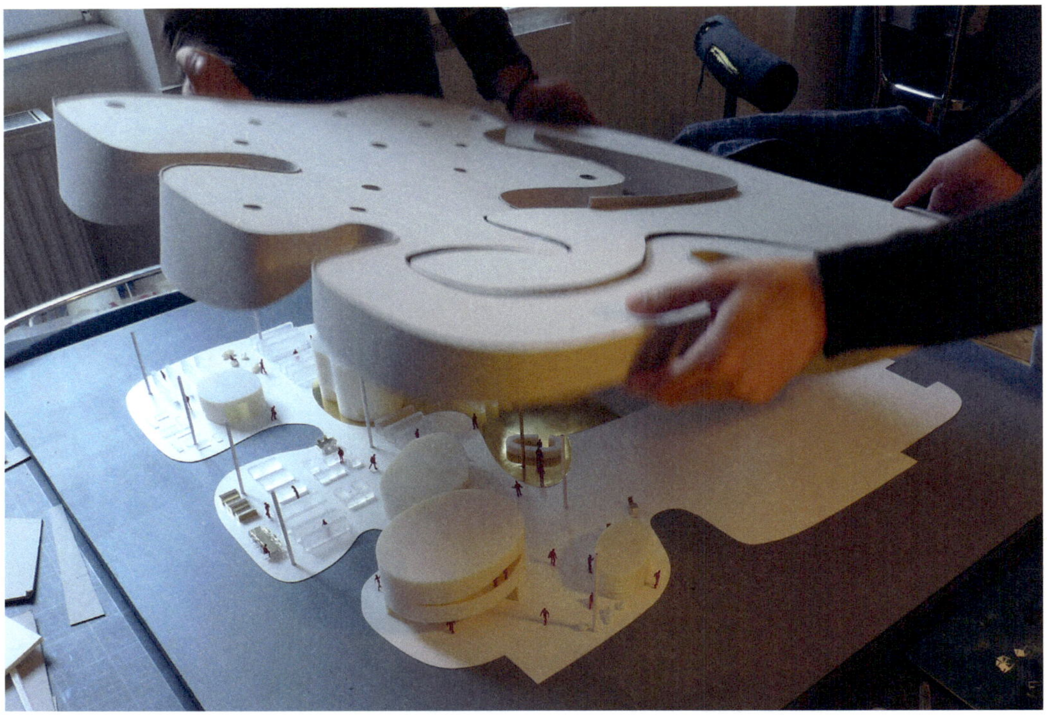

Fleeing the straight lines of Euclidean geometry, the building is based on the juxtaposition of simple, separate but irregular systems, their autonomous logic creating a tension in both the space and its comprehension. The columns seem to have been disposed randomly, following no obvious pattern, and yet their spacing is a precise response to structural requirements. An appearance of freedom and disorder replaces the shackles of ortho-normalised space. Scattered throughout the interior, bubble-shaped structures contain certain requirements of the brief: the storytelling space for toddlers, for example, but also language labs, video-gaming spaces, an art-making workshop, etc. Each bubble is adapted to the specific activities it houses in its form, dimensions and also materials: dark, rough-finished cork, pink carpet, immaculate white. Cut off from the comings and goings in the other areas of the building, these are the most intimate parts of the library, refuges that again refuse Cartesian logic. The distances separating them were calculated according to their sphere of influence and their size. In the main volume, floors and ceilings are treated discontinuously, following their own paths, while white or reflecting walls produce variations in light intensity that contrast with the materiality of the bubbles. The use of green flooring echoes the plane trees and brings the garden, so to speak, inside the building. Space is fluid, the many different routes through the library offering a variety of unusual viewpoints that are constantly renewed. The discovery of the building's different ambiences becomes a playful promenade, while the unwinding of the ribbon façade accentuates the impression of infinite, inexpressible space where the idea of gravity evaporates, walls and ceilings appearing to float. The ergonomics of the interior spaces suggest new ways of inhabiting them: snuggling up, lying down, leaning over the heights or swinging in a suspended chair—the body's centrality is reconsidered in a playful manner. Different strata of the programme are superimposed but preserve their own logic, the structural, spatial and functional elements of the project coming together without conflict and mutually enhancing each other. Out of this complexity comes forth, to borrow a phrase from Le Corbusier, a 'plastic acoustic': an atmosphere that transports and modifies the relationship to the body and whose many layers of meaning reveal a wealth of unsuspected interpretations. The 'third place' is a space of freedom.

PARIS
Animalium
CHEVAUX
Nina

PREMIERS DOCS
CINÉMA
CINÉMA
MUSIQUE

labo de langue

2015
Retirement home

Orbec

Open landscape —— Orbec is a village in the Normandy *bocage*, an hour from the Channel, which spreads out either side of its main street, the Rue Grande. Economically times are hard, business being on the wane and the population getting older. The local authority decided to replace a run-down retirement home, which backed onto a church, with a new building in a development zone in the south of the village, on the eastern flank of the Orbiquet Valley. The new retirement home, which rejects the usual look of health-sector buildings, is perfectly aligned with the slope of the valley and harmoniously moulds itself to the contours and topography of the site. At the time of writing, it stands alone in this lovely wooded landscape, the surrounding plots, earmarked for suburban housing, having failed to find buyers. In order to reduce its visual impact, the building has been fragmented into several volumes and dressed up in military green—set on stealth mode, it blends into the rural background. The white base and undersides of the cantilever lift up the volumes to give them a certain lightness. Organisation of the programme is simple: the volumes containing the living areas sit atop a base, partly buried in the slope, which houses the ancillary spaces—entrance desk, administration, kitchen, laundry and plant. To get around the programme's monotony—one hundred and fifteen rooms divided into nine living units—each unit is housed in a distinct volume, none of which lines up with the others but all of which give onto a double-height internal street. A north–south axis running along the hill, the latter offers views out to either side and provides a light-cadenced walkway in a plan echoing the layout of Orbec itself. To the east is the slope and nearby nature, protected from the wind, to the west the wide-open landscape. A place of promenade, like a long gallery, the internal street accesses living units that are also intended as social spaces. The red 'thread' running through the interior destructures and animates space, as well as defying the traditional colour palette of medical facilities. The bedrooms feature large windows whose thick carpentry frames become desks and cupboards inside. Each enjoys generous light and a view out onto the landscape, but none overlooks any of the others, guaranteeing privacy. Colours vary according to aspect, with warm tones to the north and cooler hues to the south and west, every bedroom therefore being unique.

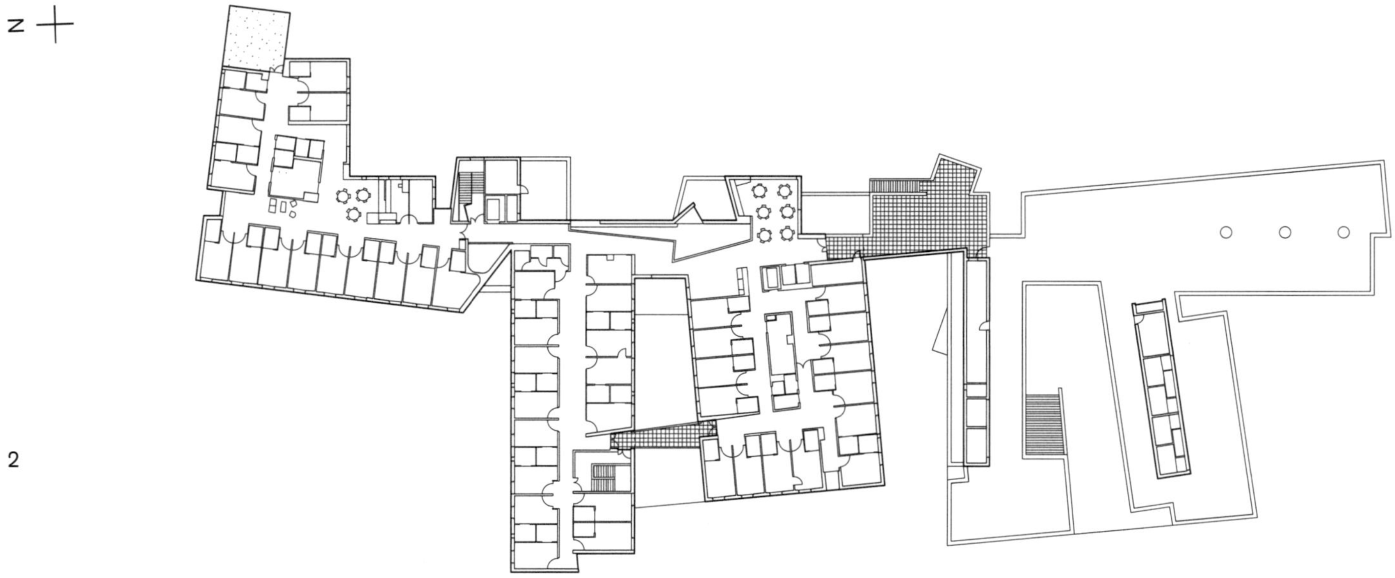

2

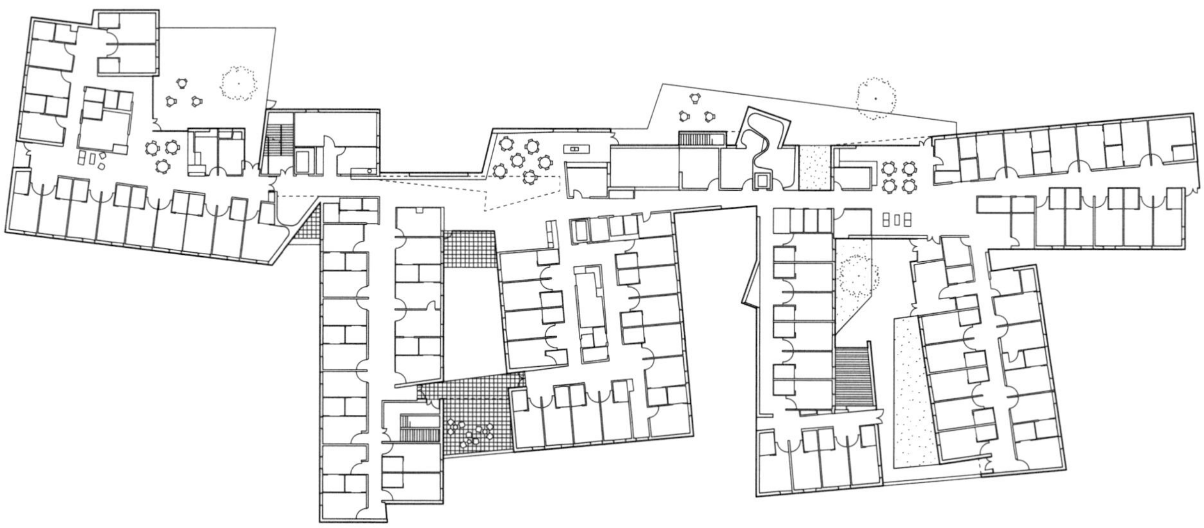

1

0

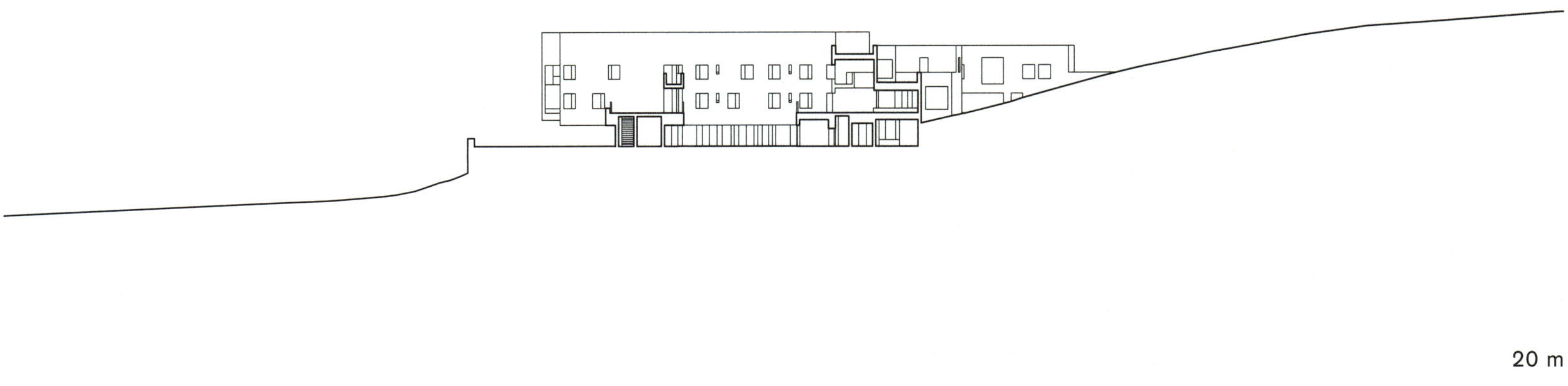

20 m

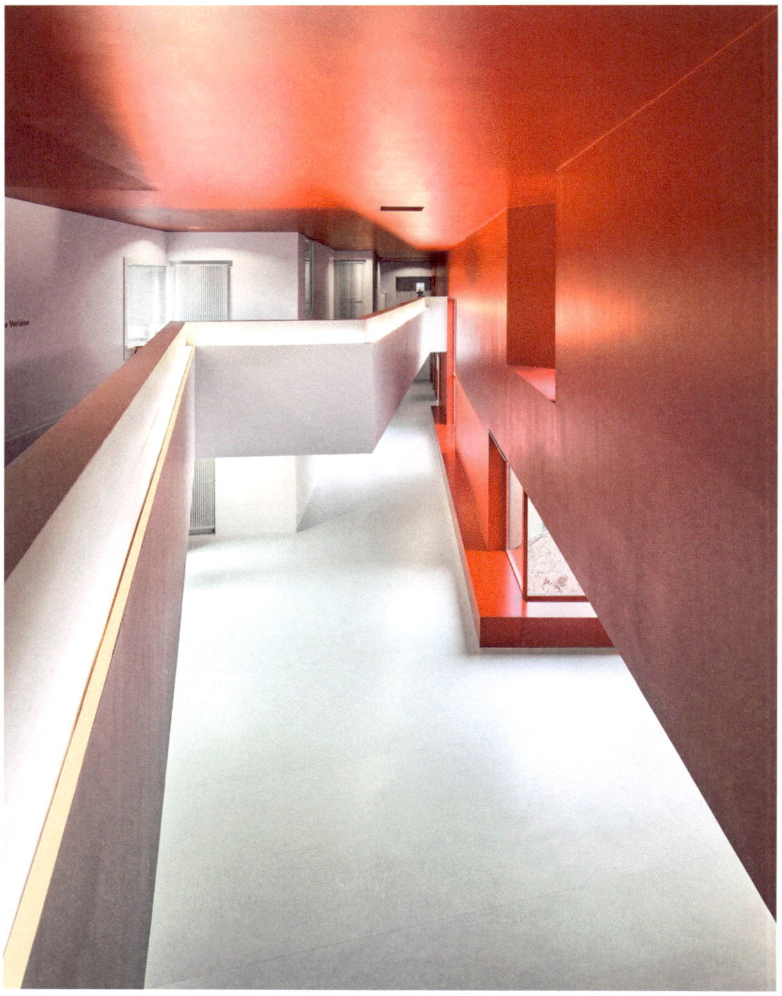

1

10 m

Maizières-lès-Metz

Carapace —— In a crumbling edge-of-town environment, surrounded by suburban housing and near to the motorway, the municipal music conservatoire in Maizières-lès-Metz is home to a diverse cultural programme: an auditorium, a music school, an events space, after-school facilities and a neighbourhood youth space. A concrete monolith forty meters wide and one hundred meters long, the building is set perpendicular to the main road and structures the disparate landscape with its brut mass. Dropped without fuss onto the slope of the terrain, it sits at the centre of a large public plaza which slips under the building's sixteen-meter cantilever, creating a fissure-like entrance via which the surrounding landscape comes right into the conservatoire's heart. A monumental outdoor stair leads up through a large internal courtyard whose walls are treated with phosphorescent paint, which captures light by day that it gives back at night, in a strange hue. The programme's complexity is processed within a single building, engendering a contrast between the different activities that brings unexpected richness. Deviating from the ortho-normalised geometry of the building envelope, the internal volumes are deformed by a play of obliques, fragmenting in a generous chaos. The result is an autonomous universe, isolated from a difficult environment by its thick concrete carapace.

SALLE FESTIVE

0

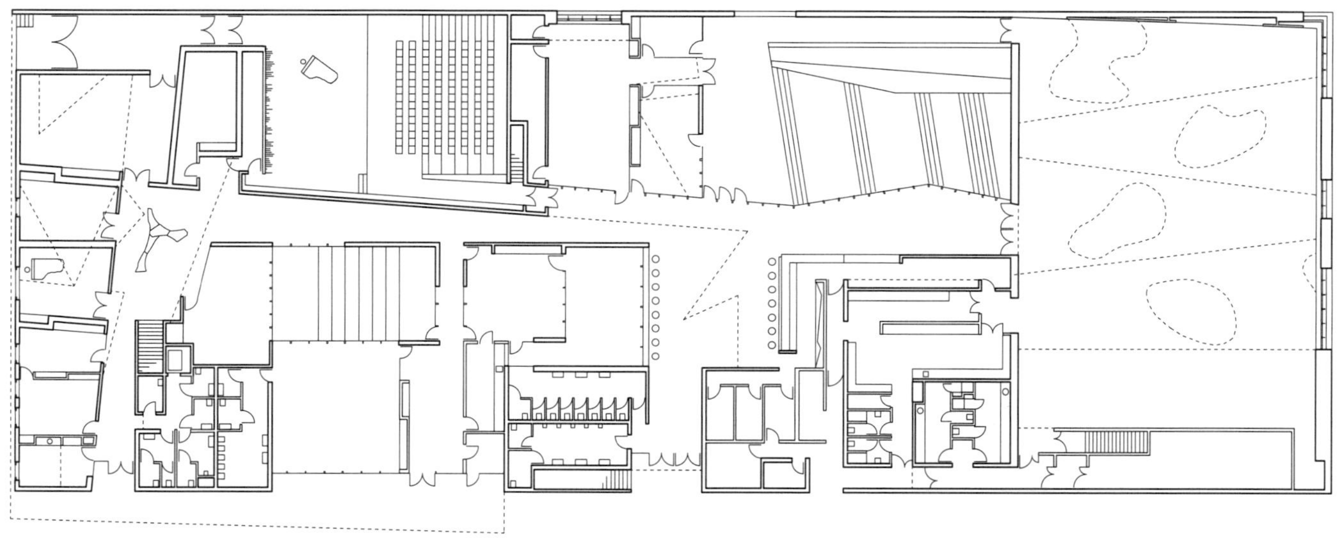

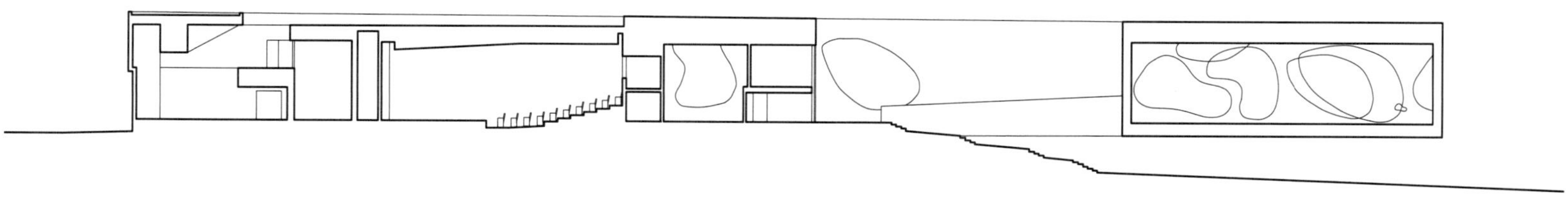

10 m

1

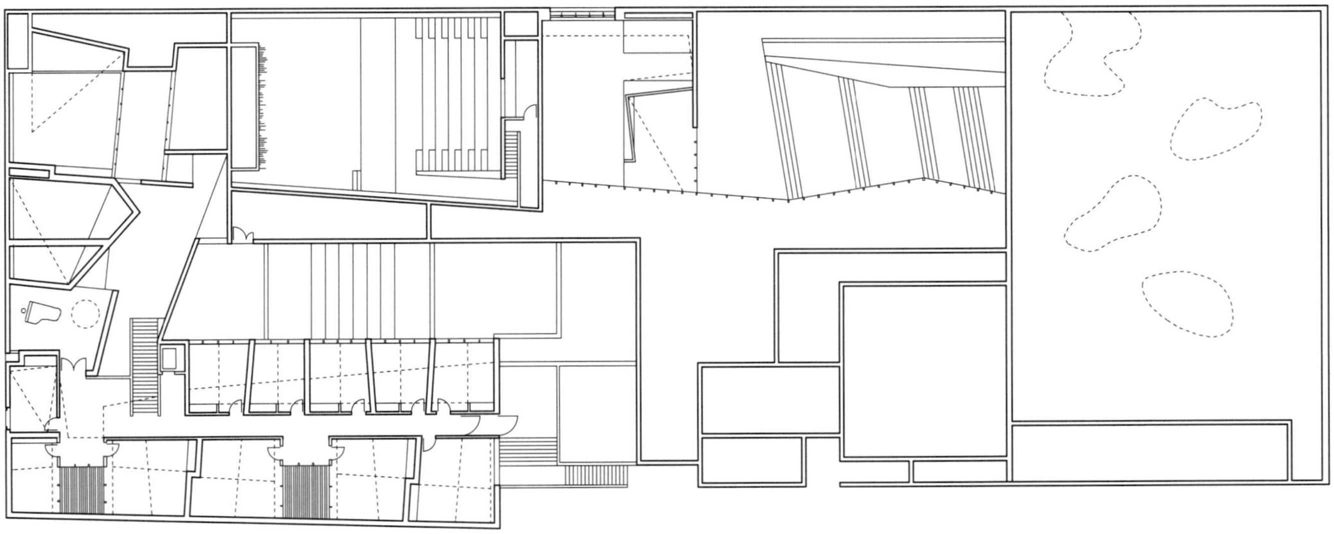

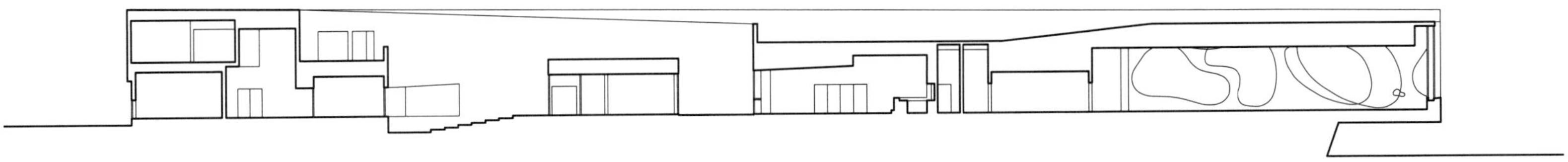

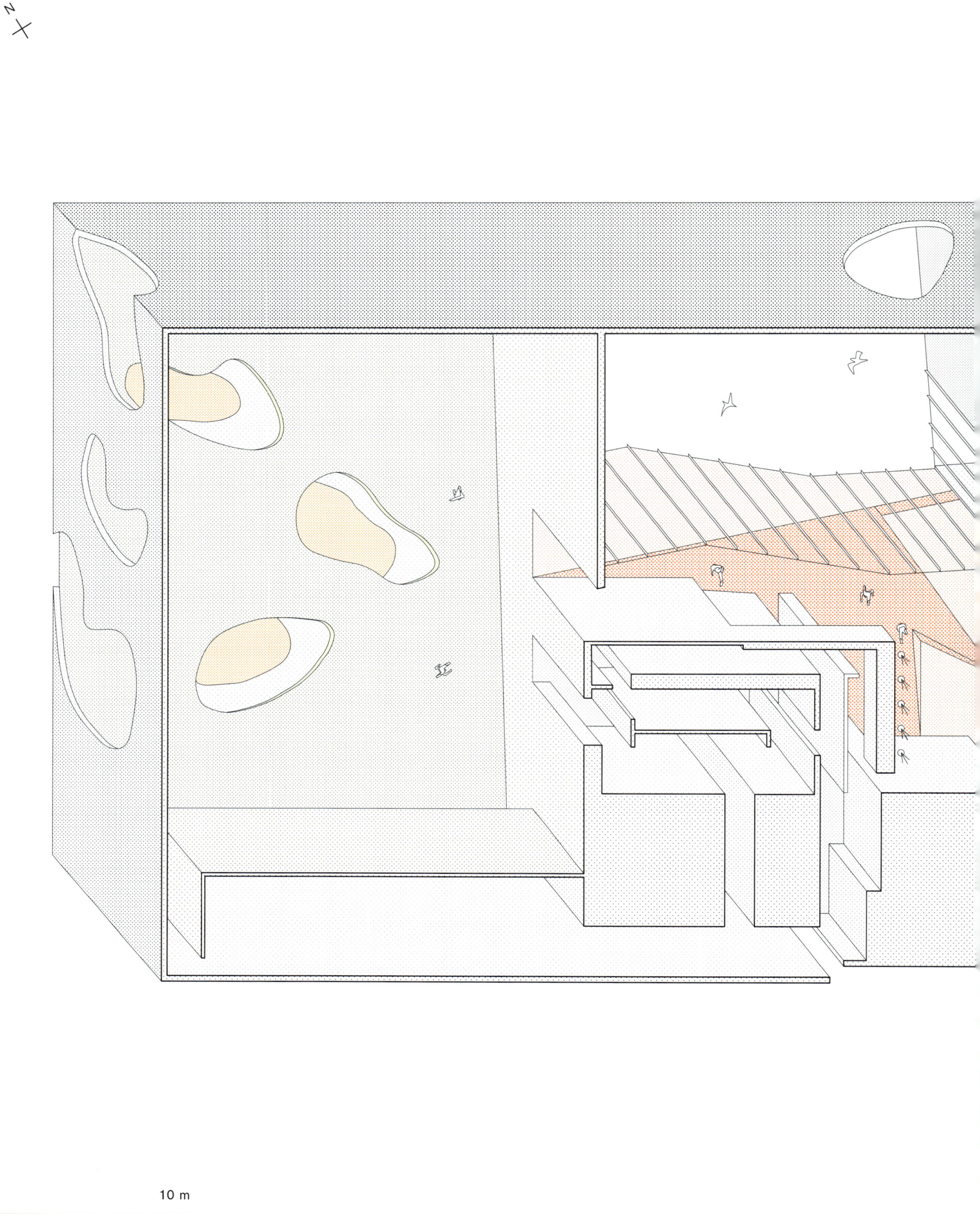
N
10 m

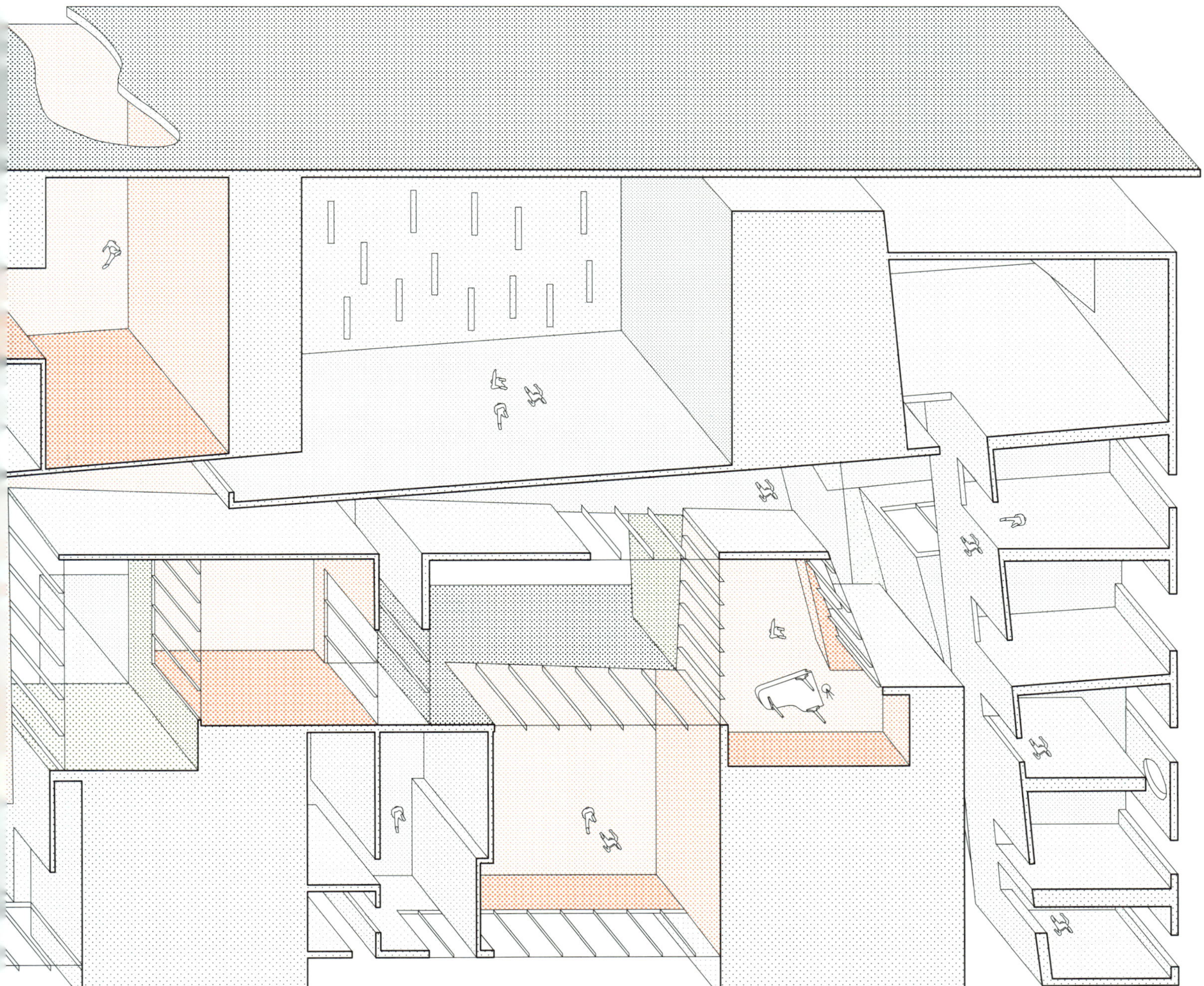

Anzin

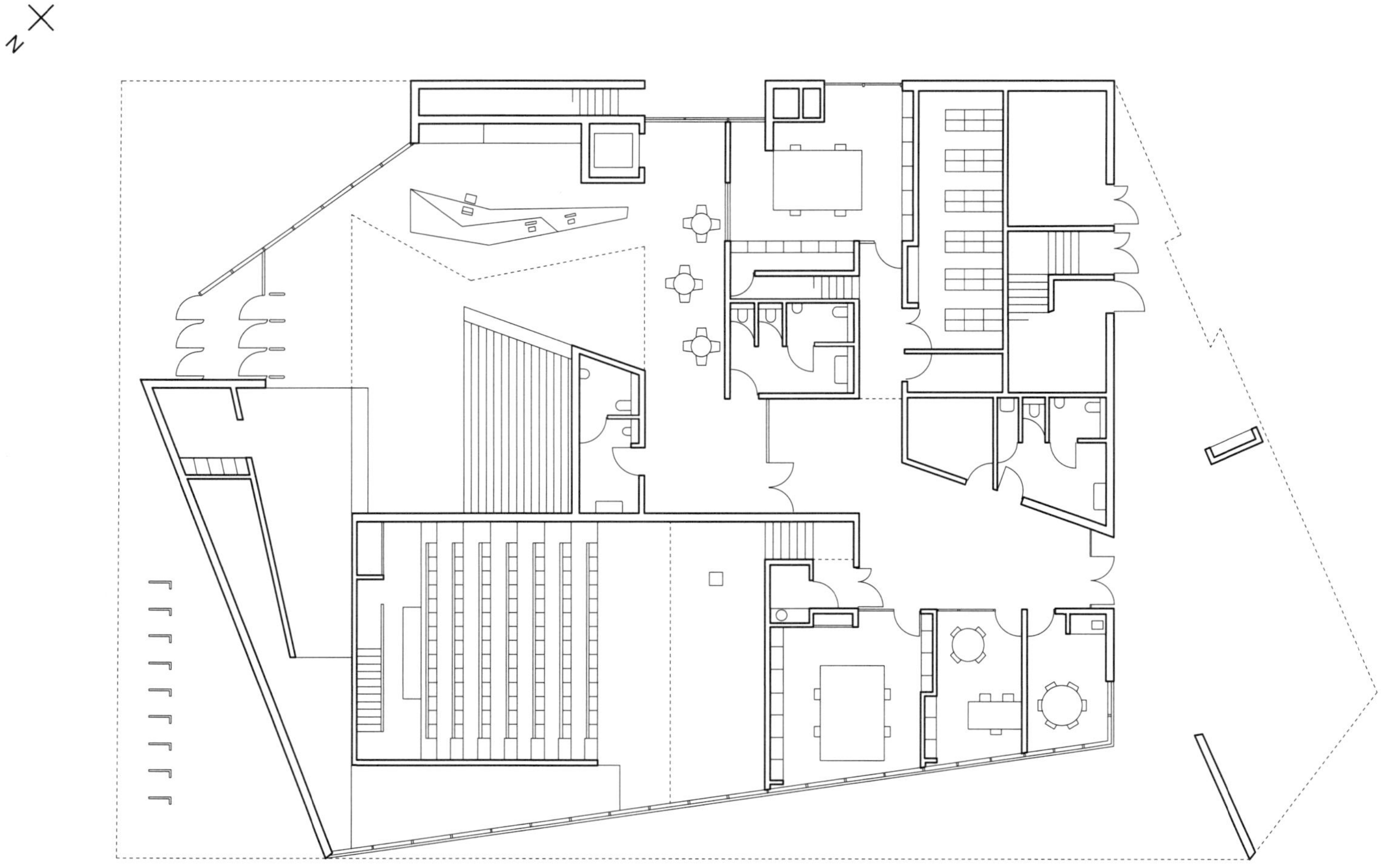

0

5 m

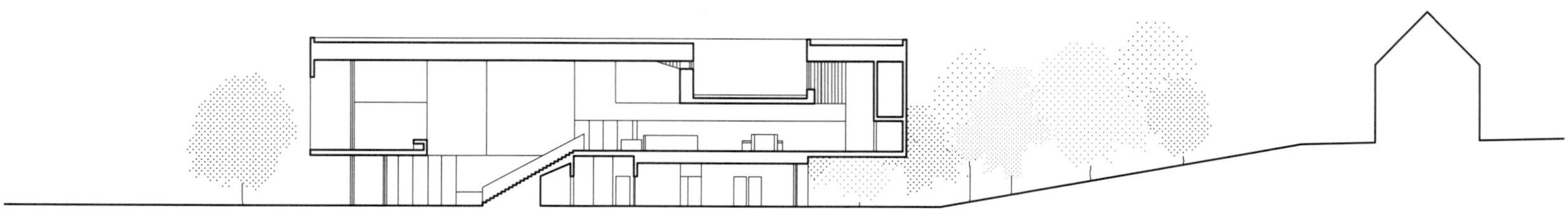

10 m

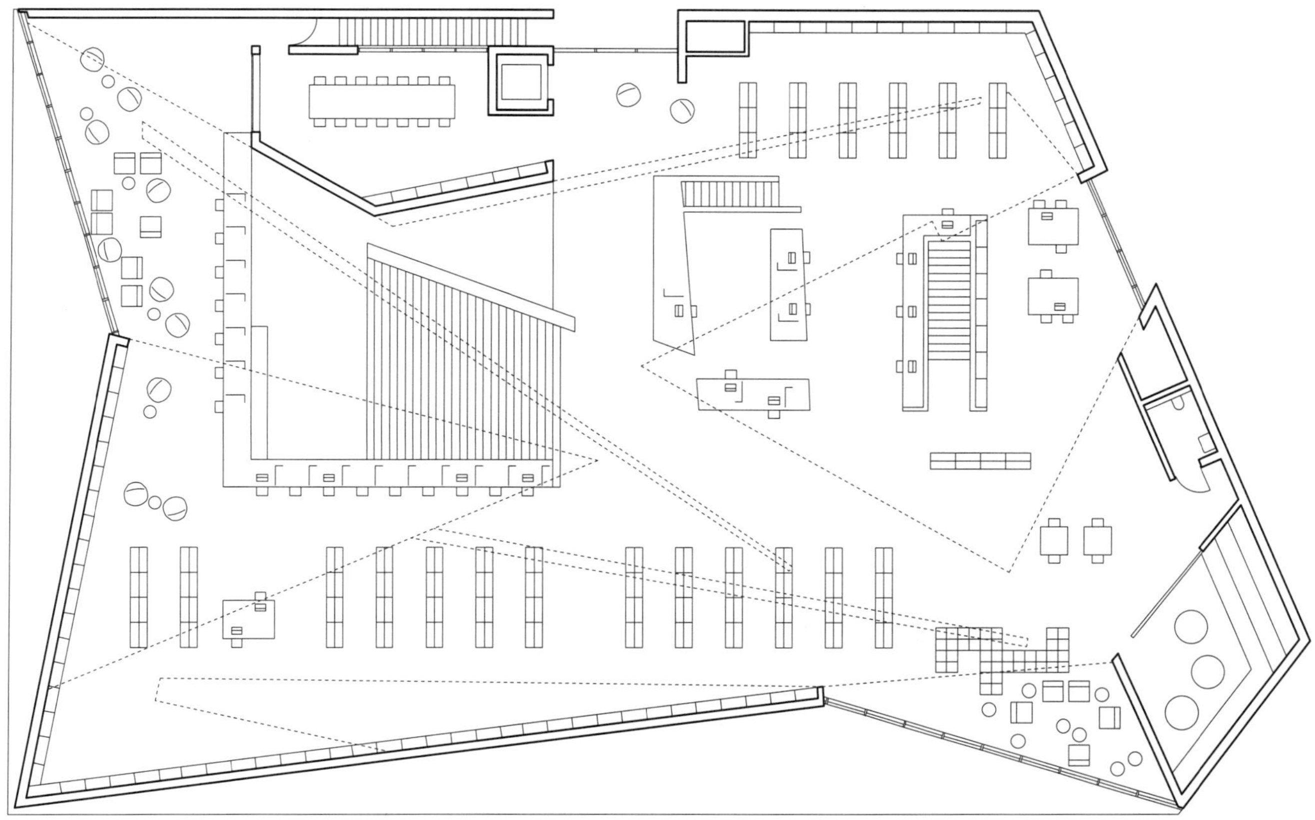

1

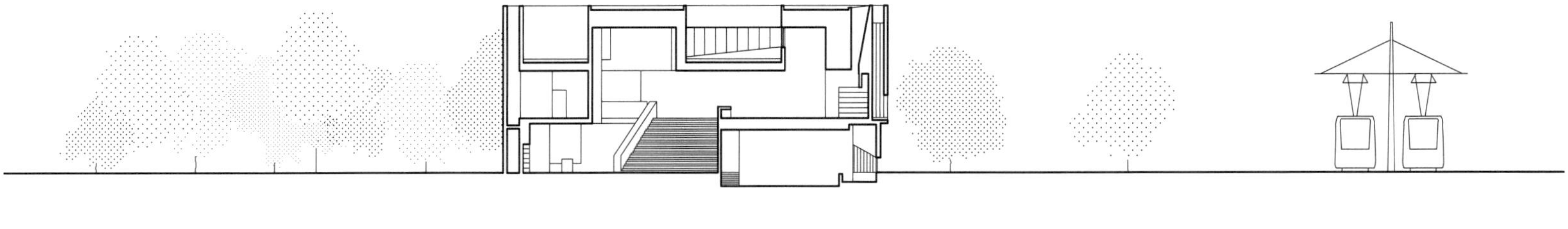

Contrast —— It was in Anzin that Émile Zola wrote his great novel *Germinal*—and yet the authorities didn't want their new multimedia library to bear his name. The painful history of the mining community was too recent and had been dwelt on enough; the mayor wished to break with the past, and brick had thus become a forbidden material. It was, moreover, the first time we tried our hand at a multimedia library, and, at this particular moment in the digital revolution, we were asked for flexible spaces that could adapt to technological evolution, the brief calling for a neutral, entirely modifiable space—a sort of supermarket of culture. But we were convinced that, on the contrary, a versatile building could easily accommodate spaces with a marked character, and this quest to produce strong and differentiated atmospheres, contrasting through effects of light and proportion, became the leitmotif running through the whole project. We chose to design a building that breaks with the red and brown of the surrounding urban fabric: its precious, reflecting whiteness is deployed in great walls of concrete whose folds and cutaways break up light. Areas of glazing giving onto the reading space invite passers-by to enter, and once across the threshold they discover an interior that is luminous, free, fluid and alive, with its soaring separate spaces that nonetheless harmonise under the skylights. Each user can, from among the many sub-areas, find one where he or she feels at ease.

RECHERCHE
RENSEIGNEMENTS
toilettes

"Haut J
Poutre Voila Béton Armé ép. 20cm ht=4.43m, As=+62.50
Voile Béton Armé 20cm
As = +62.50
PVBA ép.20cm ht
As=+62.50
VBA20 As=+62.50
Poutre BA 20x125T
Ai=+61,25, As=+62,50
+61.96
23
Dalle pleine
Béton Armé
Poutre BA 20x125T
Ai=+61,25, As=+62,50
Poutre BA 20x125T
Ai=+61,25, As=+62,50
Voile Béton Armé de façade ép. 20cm
Ai = variable de +54.00 à +62.00
As = +62.50
Voile Béton Armé ép. 20cm As=+62.50
Poutre Béton Armé 20x125T
Ai=+61.25, As=+62.50
Acrotère 20x42T As=+62,15
Acrotère 20x42T As=+62,15
VIDE SOUS VERRIERE
VBA20
As=+62.50
Voile Béton Armé ép. 20
Voile Béton Armé de fa
Ai = variable de +54
As = +62.

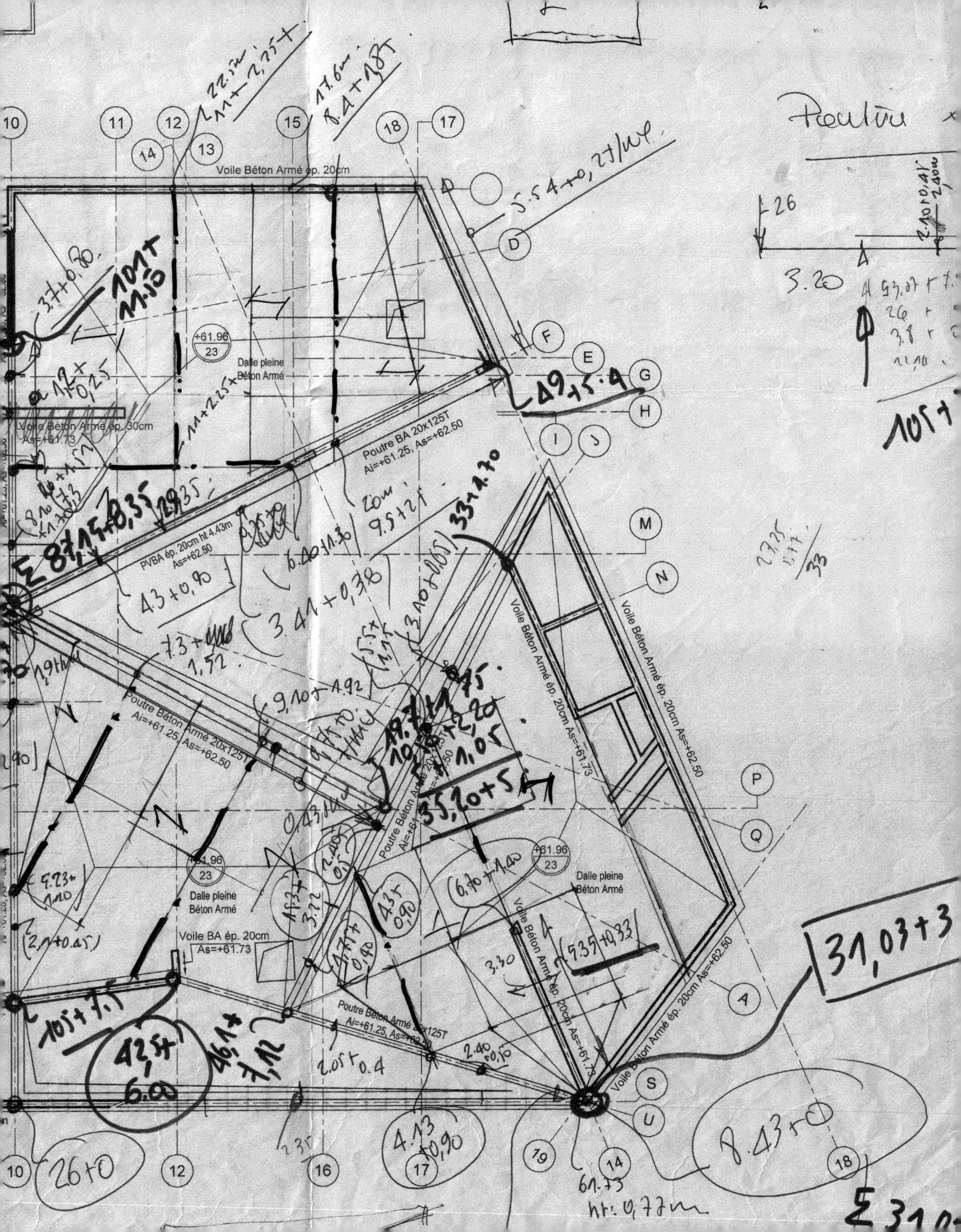

Voile Béton Armé ép. 20cm
Dalle pleine Béton Armé
+61.96
23
Voile Béton Armé ép. 30cm As=+61.73
Poutre BA 20x125T Ai=+61.25, As=+62.50
PVBA ép. 20cm ht 4.43m As=+62.50
Poutre Béton Armé 20x125T Ai=+61.25, As=+62.50
Voile Béton Armé ép. 20cm As=+61.73
Voile Béton Armé ép. 20cm As=+62.50
Voile BA ép. 20cm As=+61.73

2015
Sports hall

Clamart

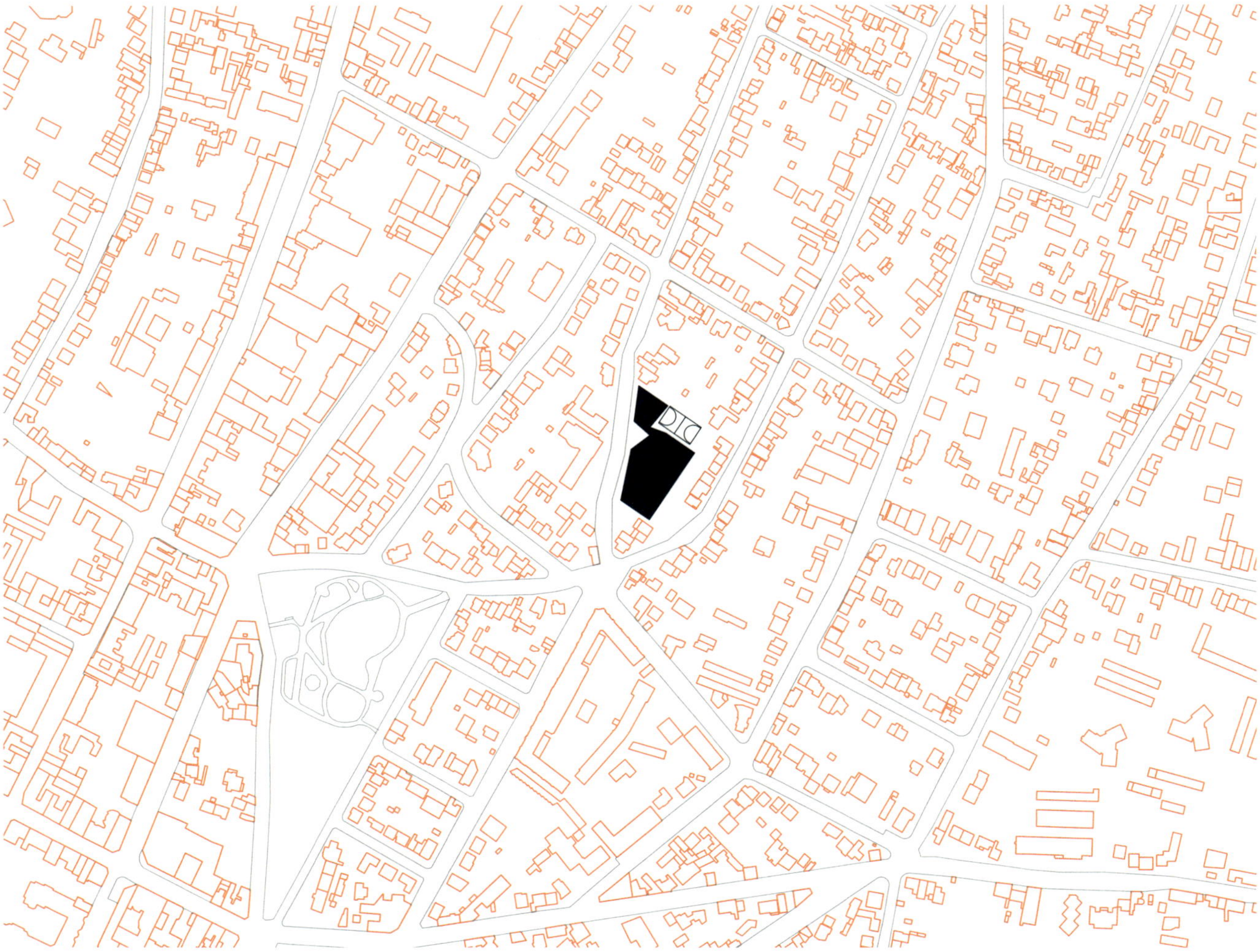

20 m

Transparency —— The programme for this sports hall, which is located among 1950s suburban housing south of Paris, includes three staff dwellings and an information and orientation centre. Pivoting at the rear of the plot, the sports hall frees up the width of the street, thereby providing the building with the external public space befitting its status as a municipal facility. Contained in a separate volume that is lined up with the neighbouring houses, the staff dwellings are nonetheless joined to the rest of the ensemble by a continuous canopy—a canopy which disrupts the perspective, whose lines are deformed by a series of obliques that obey the logic of invisible vanishing points. The fragmentation of the different aspects of the programme frees up a view into the gardens at the heart of the site, deconstructing the classic relationship between the street and the centre of the city block. Renouncing its role as a frontier between public and private space, the architecture offers up spaces that are traditionally hidden to the general gaze. A transparent gallery gives onto the street. The centrepiece of the project, the sports hall required the best possible natural light: tall clerestories on all four sides ensure abundant quantities, while the building's steel structure is hidden within their double glazing. The band of glass, insulating and translucent, diffuses a soft pearlescent brightness above which the ceiling appears to float. The lower part of the walls is clad in lightly spaced vertical strips which serve to hide technical equipment, their grey outer face contrasting with the black acoustic covering. The reliefs and hollows bring depth to this graphic display, while the contrast between matte, glossy and glassy surfaces accentuates the abstraction of the space. In this minimalist, pared-down hall, where prosaic features keep a low profile, grey concrete and vitreous glass model an atmosphere that is disconnected from time.

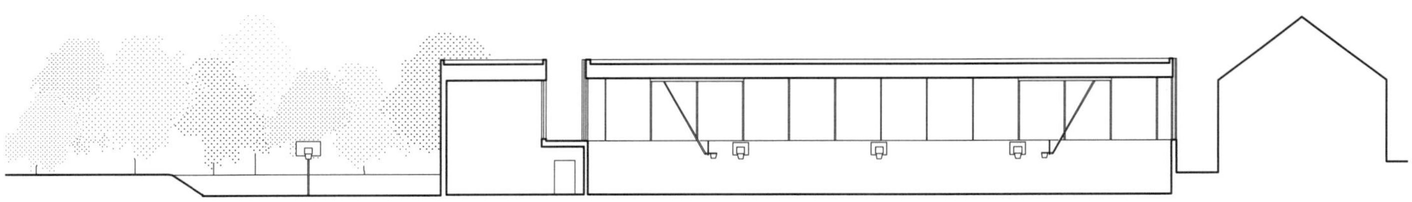

2

1

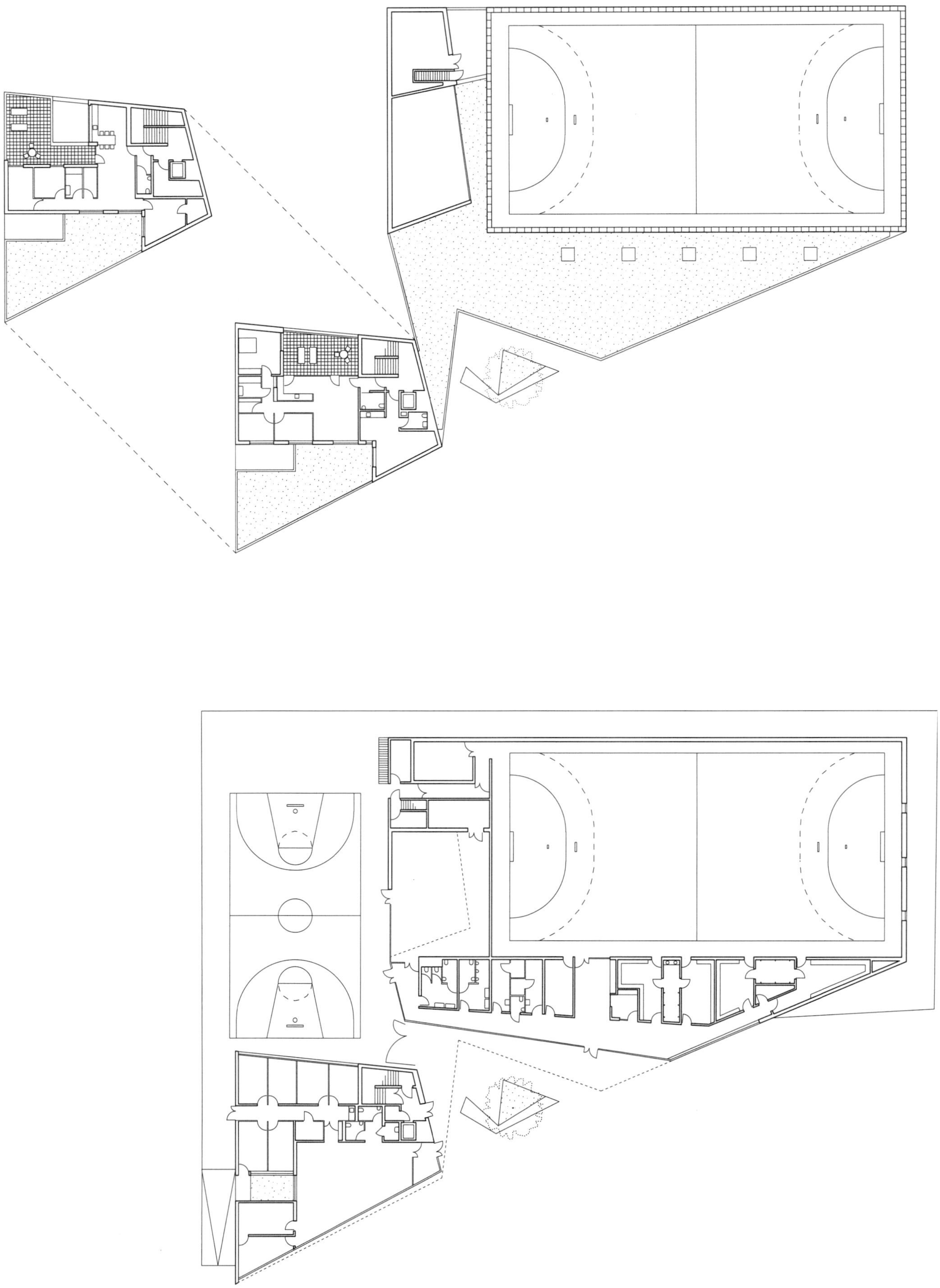

0

20 m

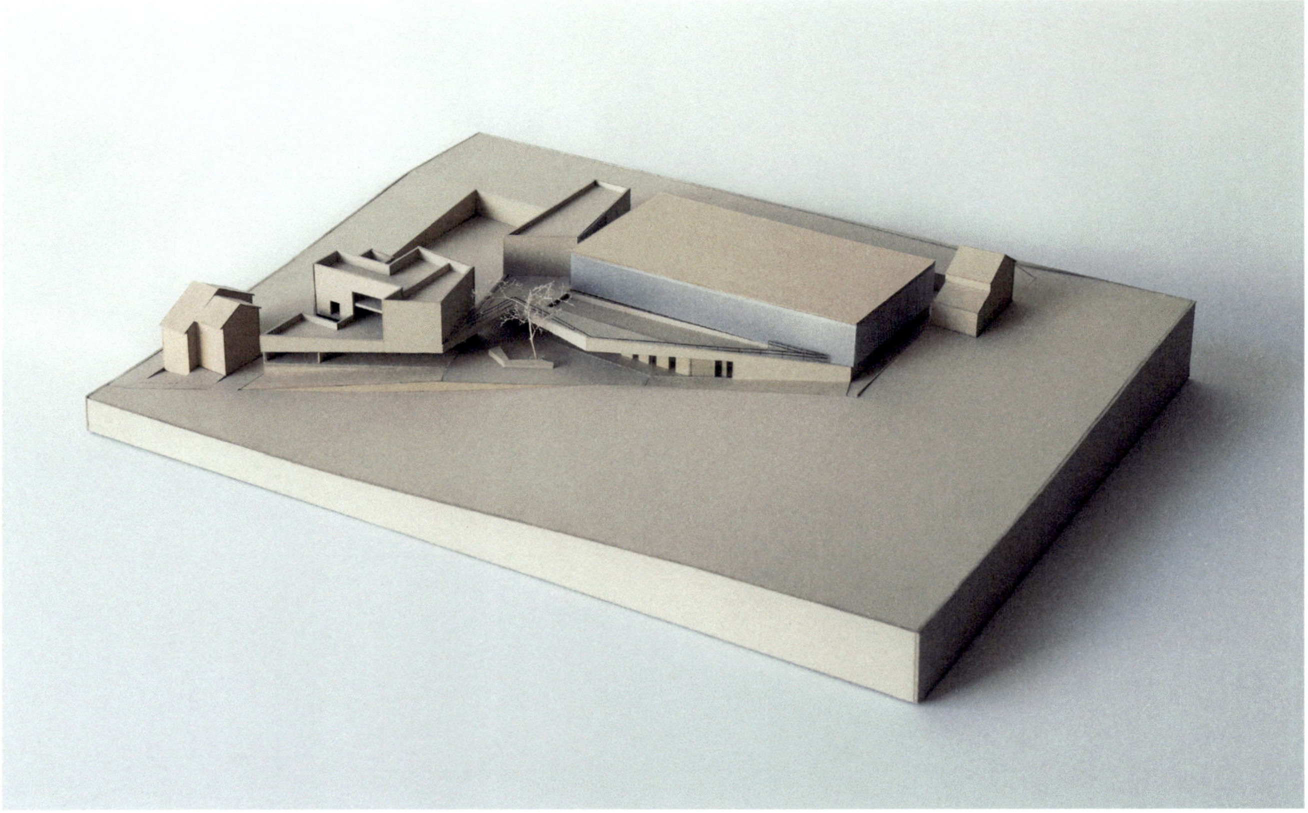

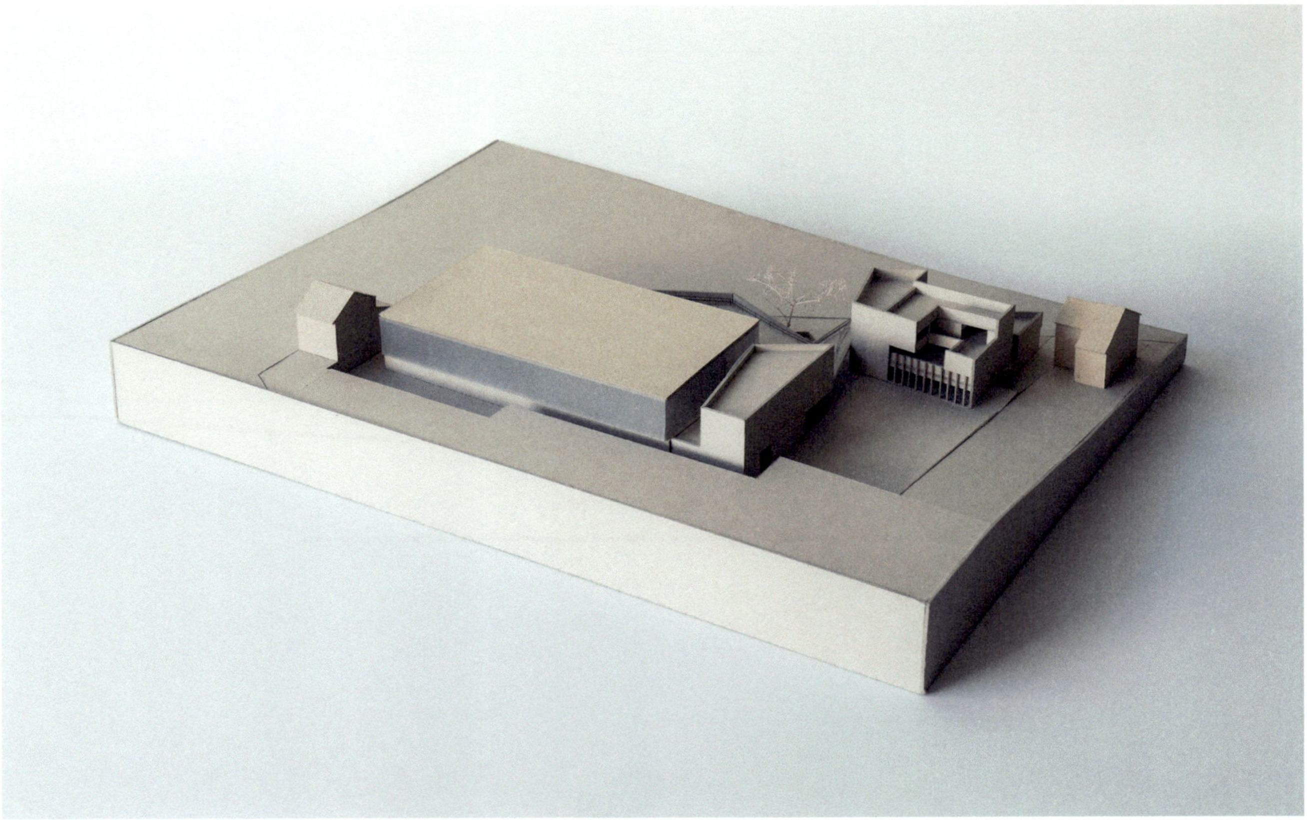

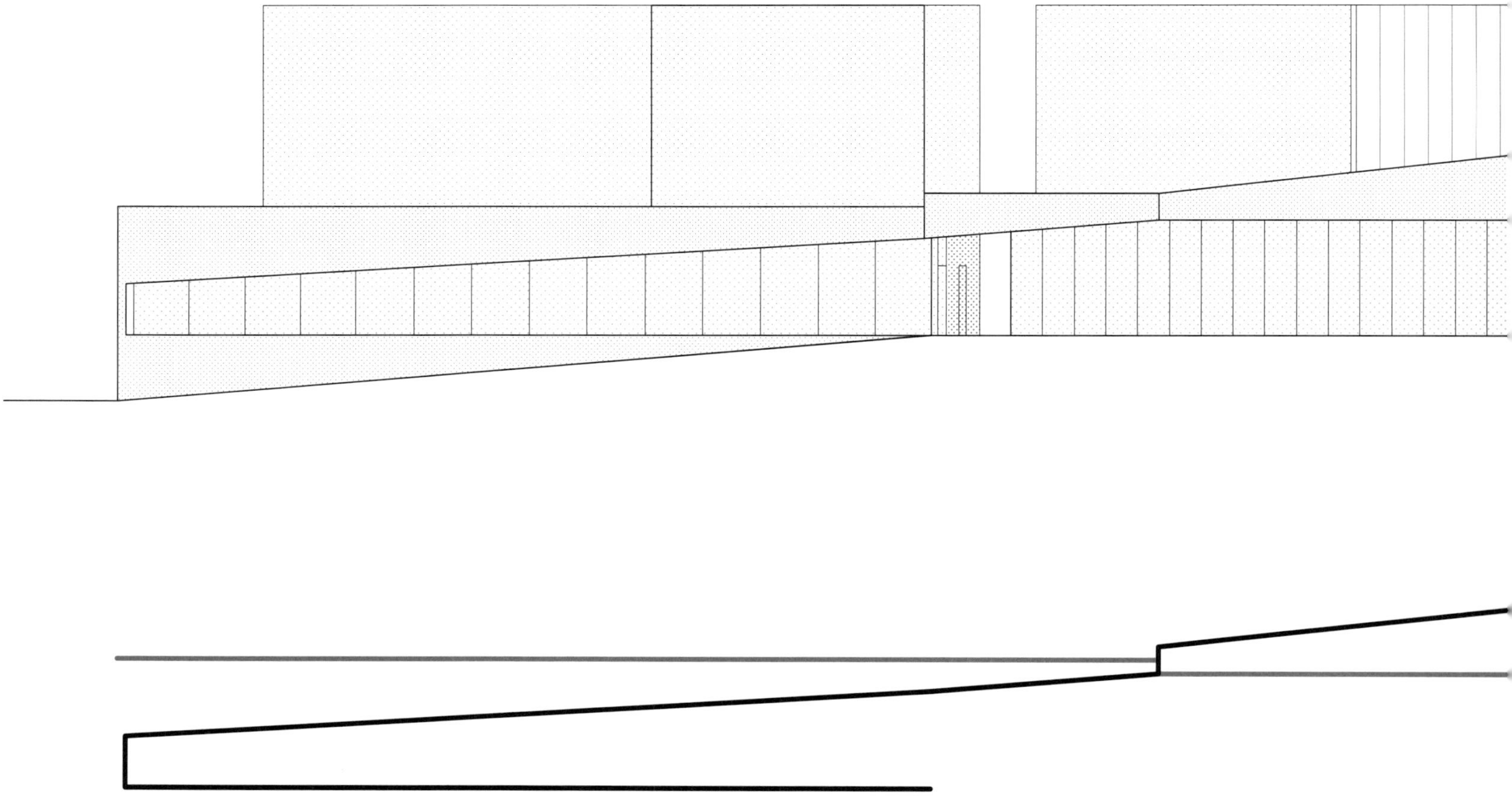

5 m

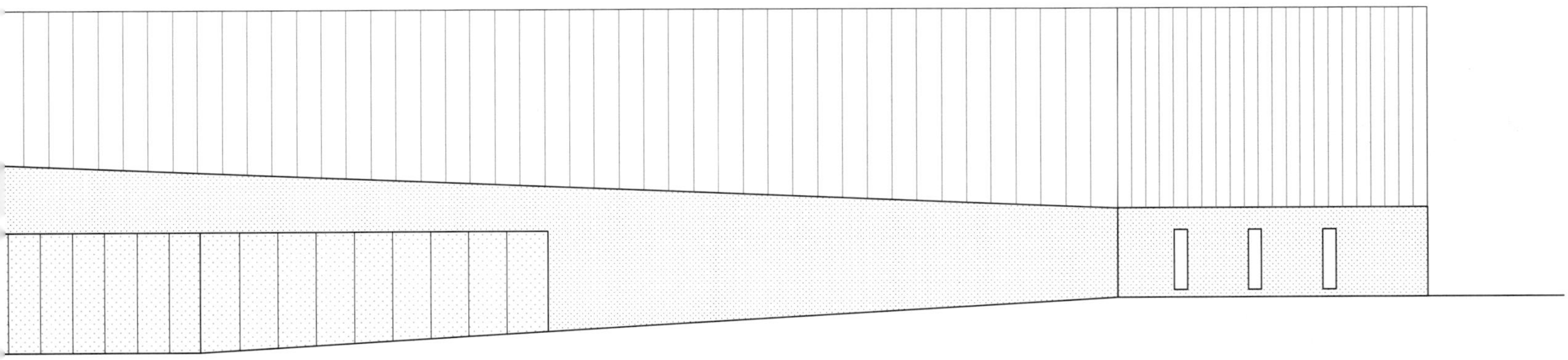

2013
Cultural centre

Isbergues

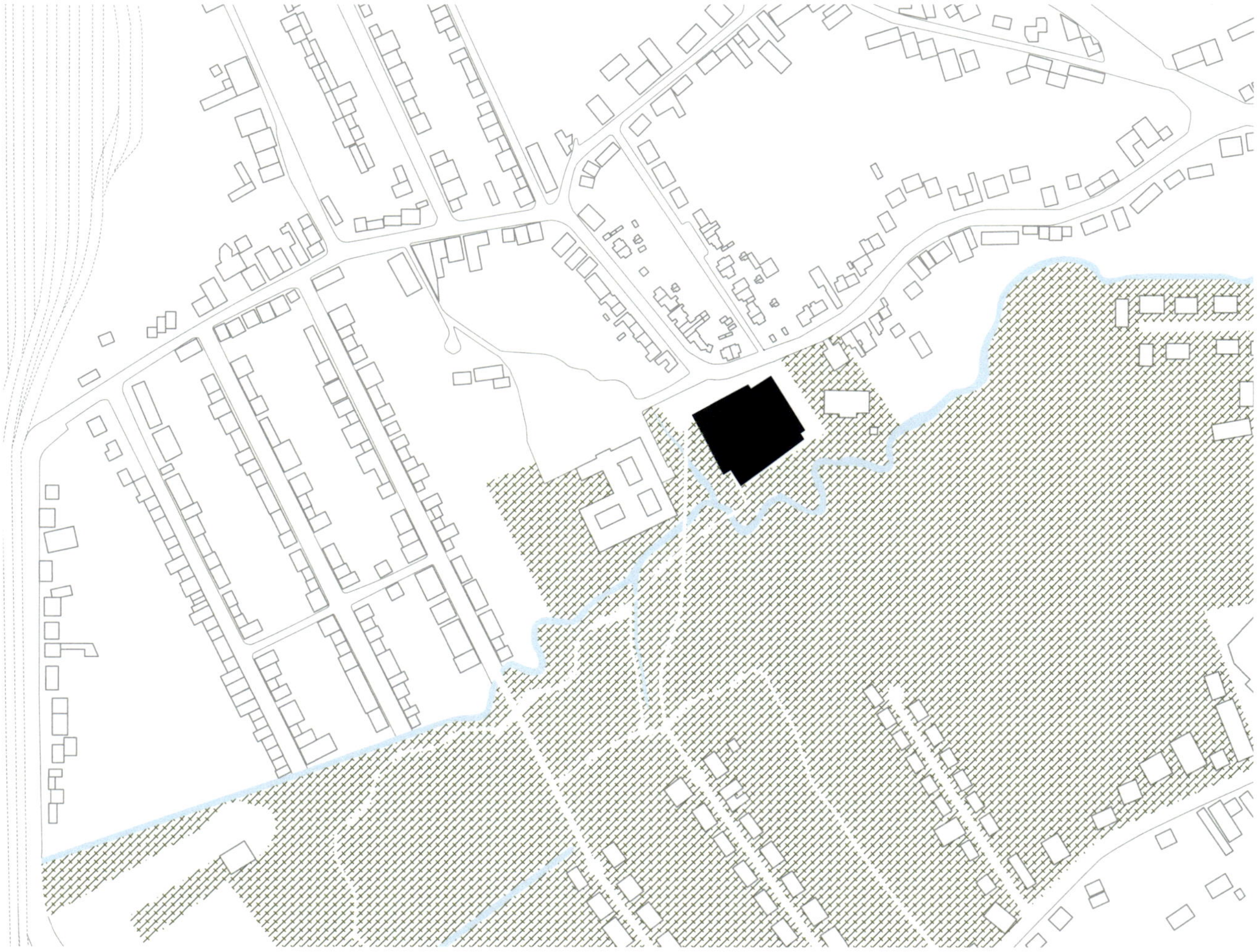

Interface —— The Isbergues cultural centre, in the northernmost part of France, hinges on the relationship between two programmes and two landscapes. On one side of the building there is a park and a river, and on the other the rendered brick houses of the town, whose silhouette is dominated by the local steelworks—today booming after a difficult period in the 1990s and 2000s. Among them is the Aperam plant, a leader in stainless steel in Europe and Latin America, which is the area's biggest employer. The cultural centre's programme combines a multimedia library and a theatre, gathering together different audiences in a public facility that the town has long been waiting for, a symbol of Isbergues' attachment to culture and community cooperation. The multimedia library and the theatre stand next to each other on either side of an axis that crosses the site from northwest to southeast. With its two entrances, one on either side, the building acts as an interface between the park and the town, while its central axis acts as an interface between the programmes. Since direct access is provided to the upper tiers of seats, the theatre deploys itself vertically; the multimedia library, on the other hand, unfurls horizontally, all its public spaces being located on the ground floor. From outside, the theatre is an opaque mass while the library is a model of transparent fluidity. The interface between the two is the pivotal space in the project, a limit we sought to make as unbrutal, hazy and ambiguous as possible, the expression of a fortunate encounter between two opposites. Large, emphatically defined masses slip past each other, blurring the differences in volume between the two programmes and hiding the building's functional duality from the external gaze. Vertically jointed Isbergues stainless steel clads the entire structure, its three finishes—satin, mirror-polished and matte—radiating an ever-changing image of the building under the effects of cloud and sun. The gaze is drawn towards it as the façade alternately blends with the grey of the sky or blazes with the brilliance of reverberating light. At the entrances, large glazed bays invite visitors to step inside: on the town elevation, the street line is carefully respected; by the river, the building opens onto a large plaza. As visitors move round the building, the sliding volumes frame different facets of the surrounding landscape. Inside, the central circulation area is a destination in itself, bringing together all the programme's collective spaces: the bar, the exhibition gallery, the theatre entrances and the periodicals reading room. Within the circulation space, the auditorium's hollow volume forms a series of solids that populate the void. A yellow ribbon runs along the walls and the floors, following a route made entirely of obliques that superimpose themselves on the masses, folding and unfolding according to the obstacles in their way. Colour traverses the space and warms up the light that emanates from it, its reflections, escaping via a series of interstices, serving to guide visitors.

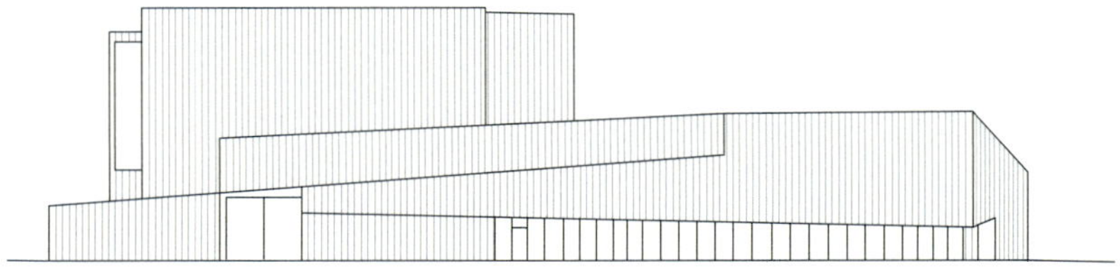

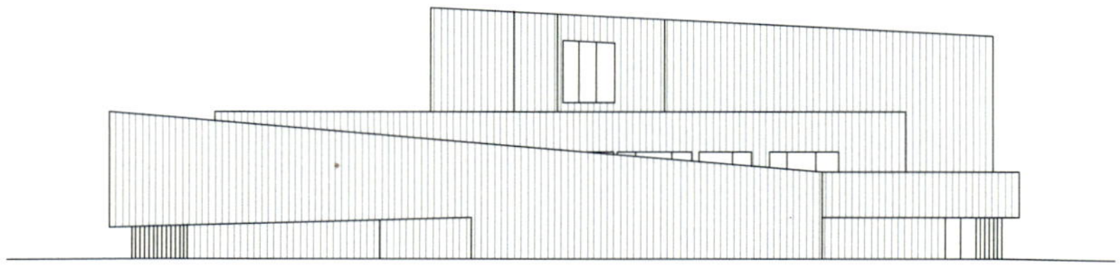
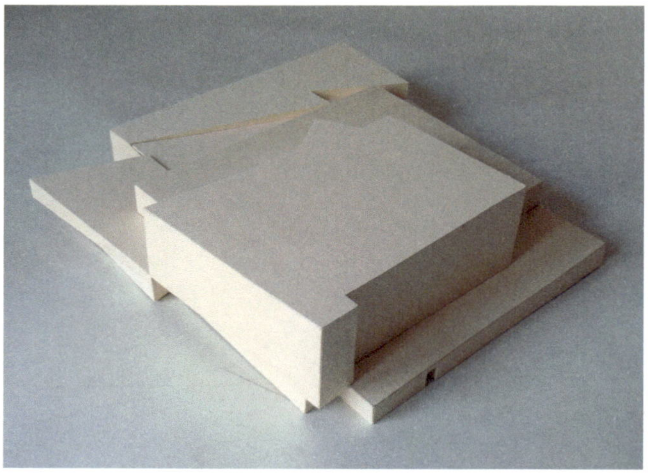
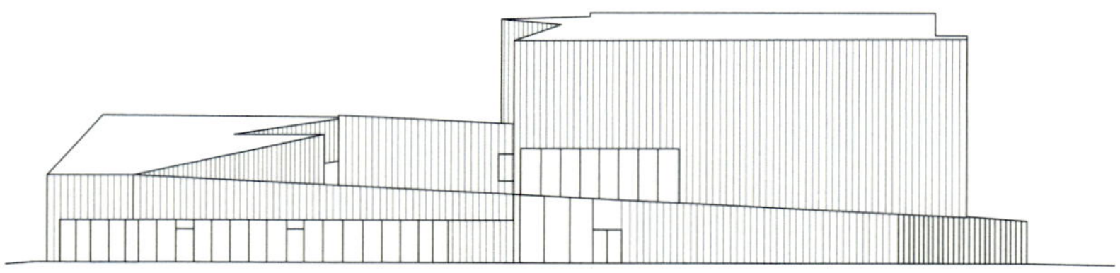

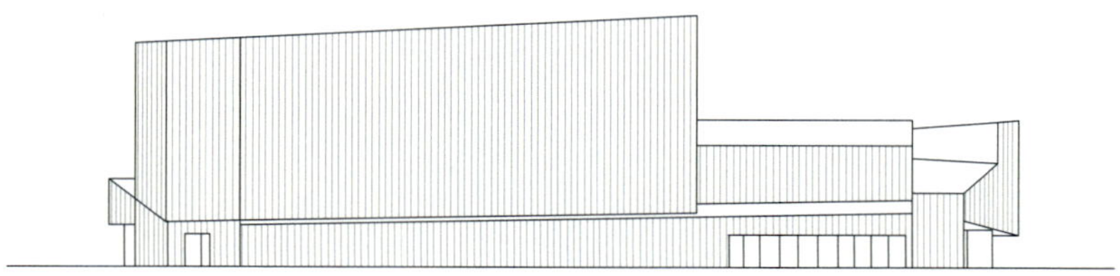

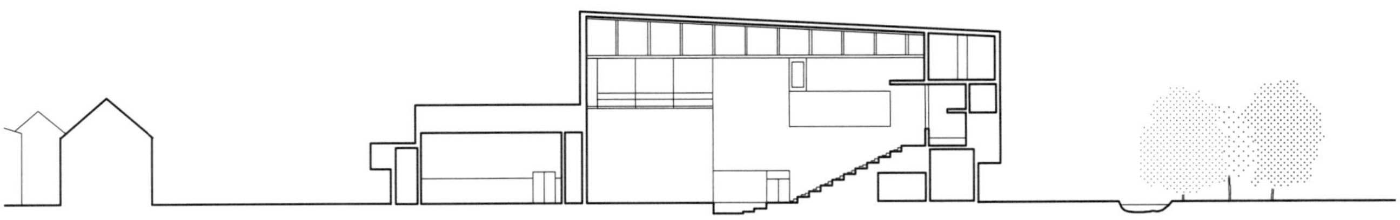

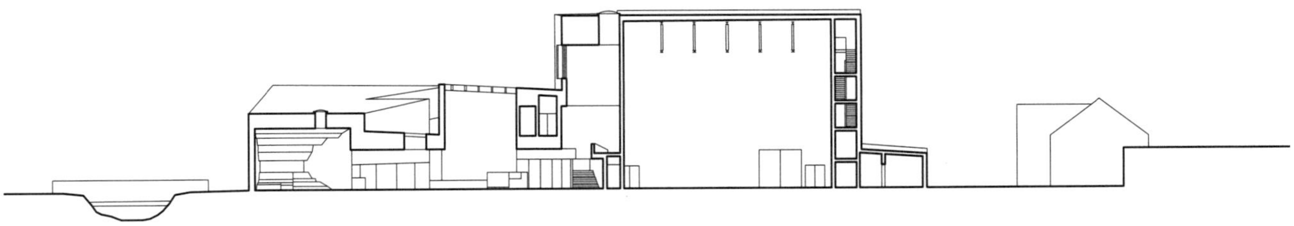

20 m

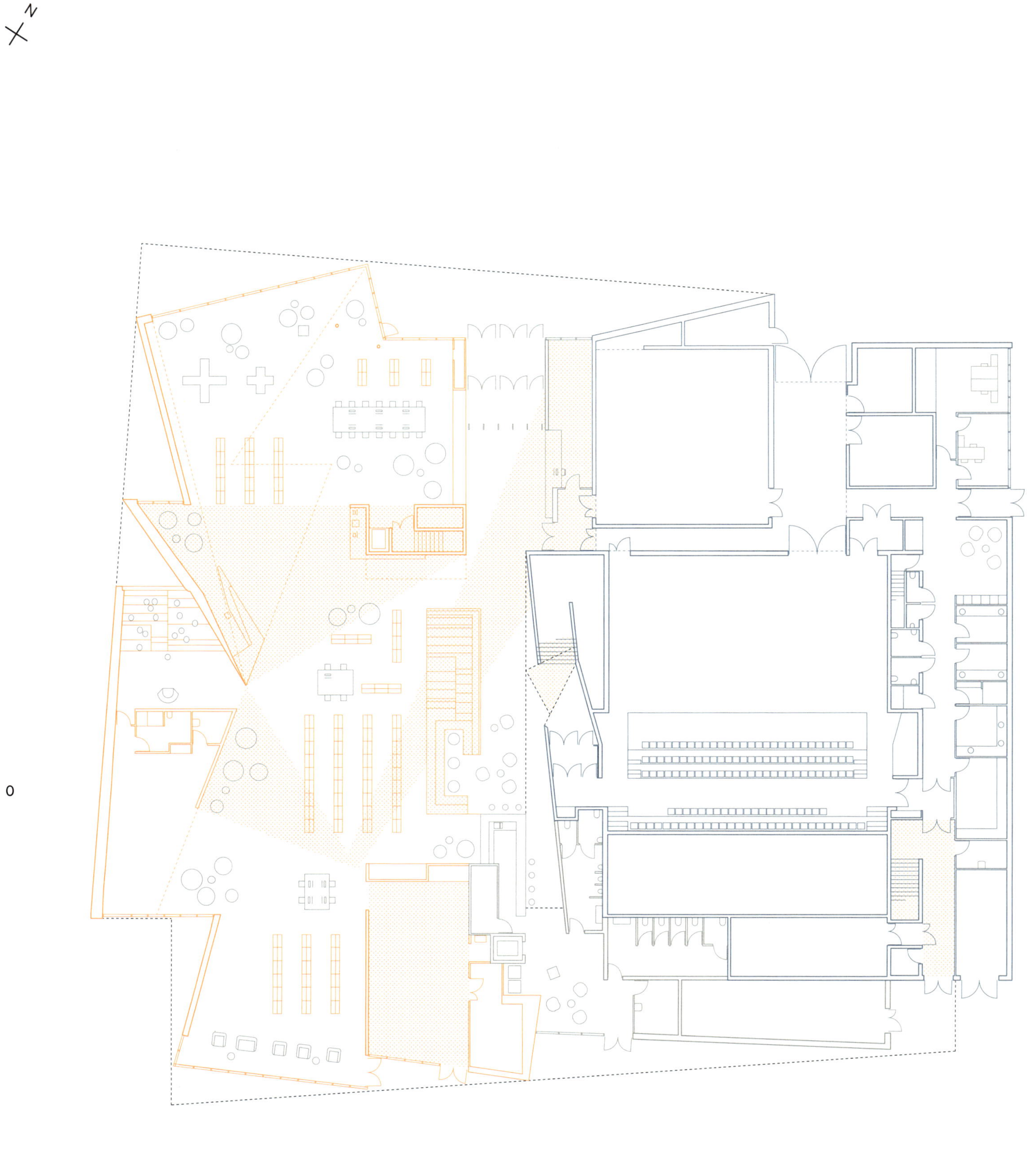
N
0
10 m

1

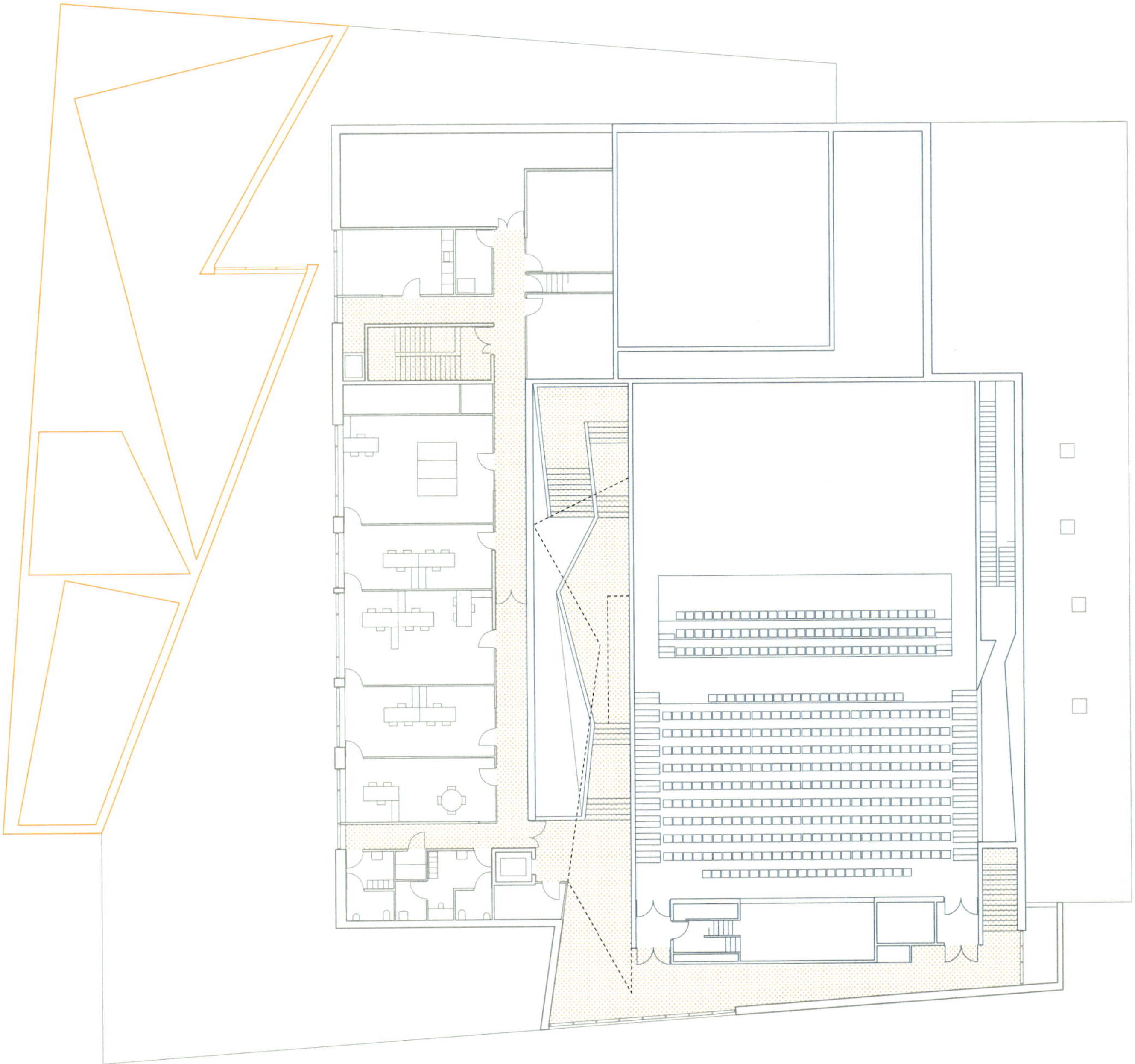

INFORMATION INSCRIPTION

2010
School complex

La Courneuve

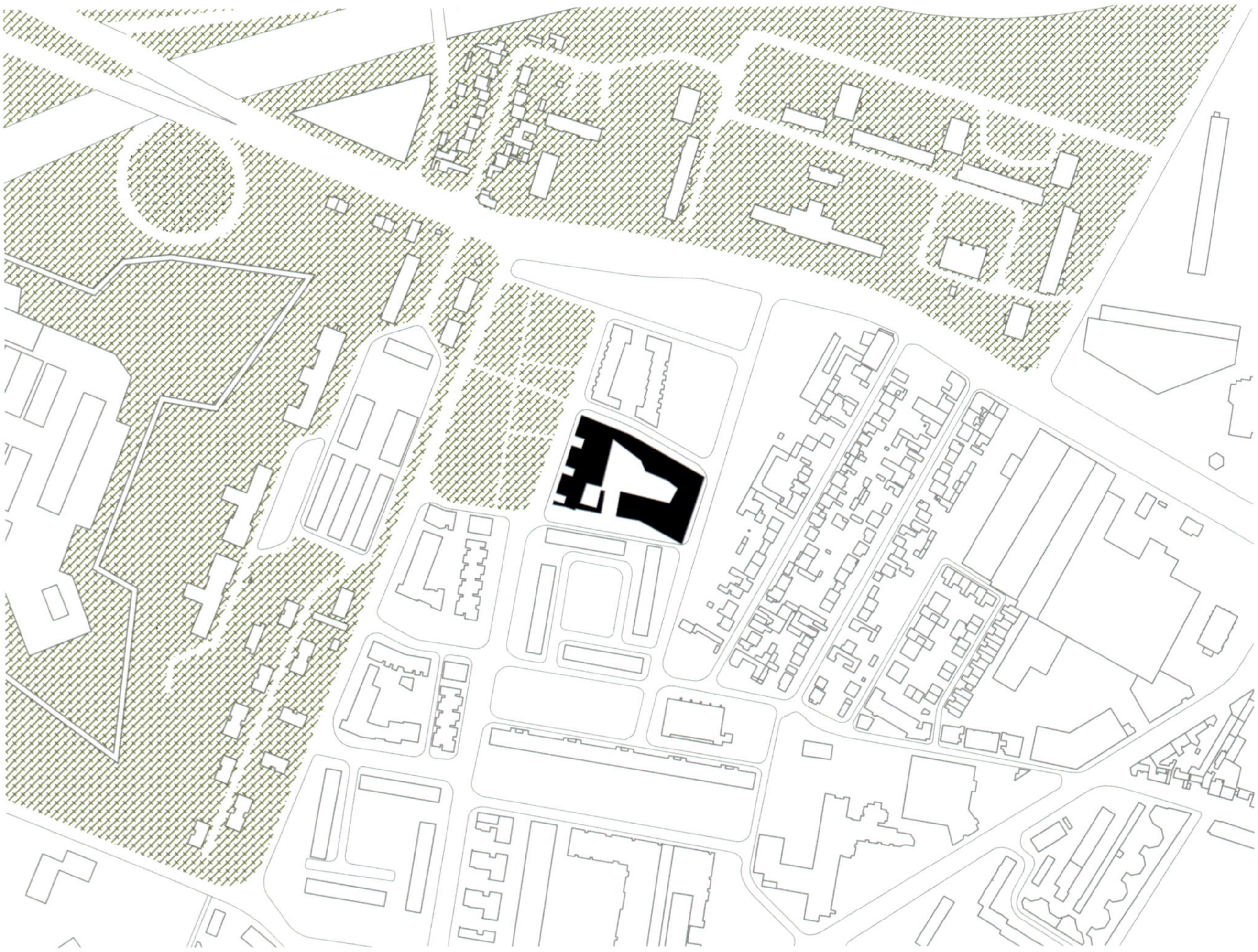

Memory —— Located within the limits of the Cité des 4000 housing estate, this school complex is one of several urban-renewal schemes realised in the wake of the widely reported demolitions at La Courneuve. The urban planners had decreed a non-built void on the site of the demolished Ravel block, but in return gave us carte blanche with respect to our interpretation of the programme. Inspired by the rather 'free' geometry of the plot, we undertook a dislocation of the volumes, multiplying obliques to bring a sculptural quality to the building. Its cantilevers, along with the thick slabs over the covered play areas, add an airy quality, as does the primary school's playground which is up on the roof, reached by a ramp. The bright-orange undersides and floors reflect onto the white walls with varying intensity according to light conditions.

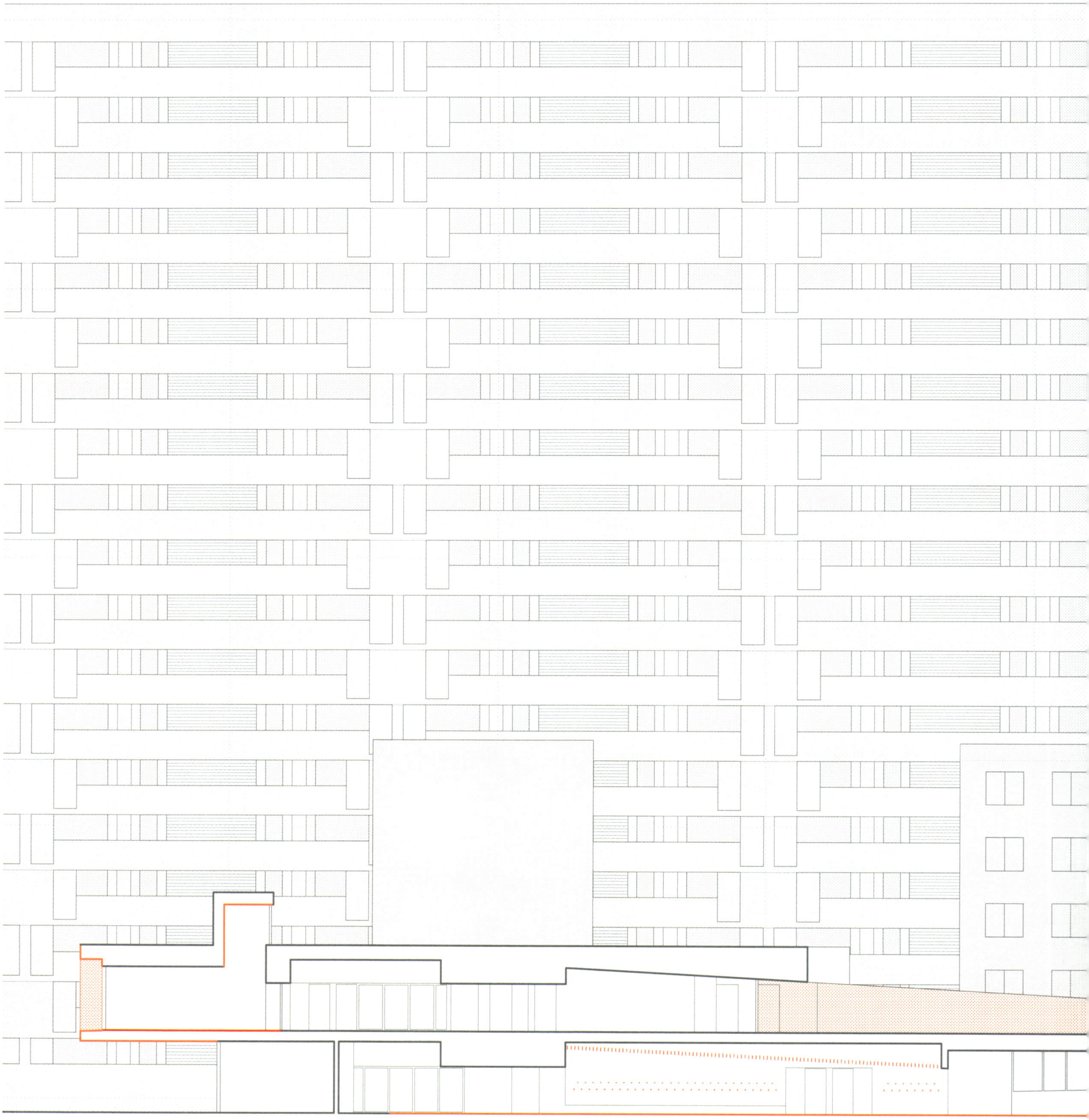

10 m

RESILIENCE

While the school complex manages to take root in the difficult context of the Cité des 4000 housing estate in La Courneuve—a site marked by the painful memory of the demolished Ravel and Presov blocks—it also manages to open internally onto another landscape—an elsewhere, a utopia.

The project takes its place in Bernard Paurd's very subtle urban plan, which seeks to reference the different signs and traces that are superimposed on the site like the different layers of writing that make up a palimpsest. The plan reorganises the neighbourhood according to the meeting at right angles of two historic axes, one going from the Fontaine Saint-Michel in Paris to the former Abbey of Saint-Denis, the other from the abbey church (now cathedral) to the Church of Saint-Lucien. This crossing of abscissa and ordinate makes visible the emergence of diverse traces—the ruins of a Gallo-Roman necropolis or the scars that bear witness to the Ravel and Presov blocks, which were brought down with explosives on 23 June 2004—as though a series of old maps had been tattooed onto the terrain.

The school complex occupies an irregular plot that is cut in two by the unbuilt zone which follows the contours of one of the demolished blocks. While respecting Bernard Paurd's plan, as well as his intentions, Dominique Coulon seems to view this scar as the medium for an act of resilience—the psychological process analysed by Boris Cyrulnik which allows the human psyche to overcome traumatic situations—rather than the stigmata of an irreversible situation. And so he spontaneously revisits the research into forms in torsion which he has been pursuing from project to project. The fact that the building regulations forbade any closed volumes being built on the rectangle which cuts through the plot, as well as imposing constraints of height and density, allowed him to call into question the brief's separation of the primary and infant schools, which he replaced with a combined scheme. Handled with virtuosity in three dimensions between two poles joined by a system of ramps, his design places the infant-school classrooms to the east, in a cantilevered floor above the entrance, while the primary-school classes occupy little plots to the west that open onto interstitial gardens. The big kids' playground intrudes into the block reserved for the little ones, which also contains the common dining hall, while the sports courts are displaced onto the roof of the other block, which houses a joint library for both schools.

Despite its sliding volumes, its folds and its twists and turns, the building asserts itself right away as a closed and little-fenestrated form. The primary-school classrooms, stacked in their plots, only open generously onto the lateral gardens. Though outside, verticality dominates through the multiple indents that cadence the façades, paradoxically it's the horizon that takes precedence once inside, as though an infinite universe were opening up within a rigorously delimited space enclosing a children's heterotopia—an initiatory place where pupils are cut off from the world of adults so as to have the necessary distance and momentum to plunge back into it once they are ready and of age.

But by far the greatest attention seems to have been paid to crossings and thresholds: entering the school; taking off one's coat and hanging it on the wall before going through the classroom door to sit down in front of the teacher; going out laughing into the covered play area at break time. From the entrance onwards, the building puts into play a subtle double movement of advance and retreat, a mechanism that recalls the curves and counter-curves of Borromini's church of San Carlo alle Quattro Fontane in Rome. As though in a gesture of protection, the upper floor comes forward to welcome the children, while the glazed ground floor beats a retreat, hollowing out so as to de-dramatise the separation of children from their parents. The corridors thicken and dilate at the doors to the classrooms and are flooded with abundant light from above, as though seeking to define themselves better as decompression zones before the holding-of-breath that is going into class. Finally, the covered play area's canopy soars well beyond the ramp that climbs up to the sports grounds, which spread out at their ease across the roof.

This game of compression and dilation, which brings a sort of organic quality to this building in concrete, is further accentuated by the orange colour used for the floors, which sometimes spreads onto the walls and ceilings, and is set alight by the slightest ray of sun—the accessible roof space, in particular, burns incandescent, offering itself up like an open hand beneath the complementary blue of the sky, which in turn is revealed in all its power.

Too often, as was the case in the nineteenth century, schools seem to be designed for adults reduced to the size of children. But here the way spaces link up together and the design of the classrooms demonstrate a different relationship between the child's body and space, a relationship that's all the more cohesive for not yet being entirely mediated by language. Classrooms, corridors and playgrounds at the 'Josephine Baker' School stretch and dislocate around an as-yet-indeterminate body, a body in perpetual transformation, a body of sensations ready to emote at the slightest ray of sunshine and to perceive in the slightest change in the weather a thousand playful opportunities.

The use of natural products, like the linoleum on the floor or the wood of the window frames, and the attention paid to the slightest detail help make this building almost luxurious. It was warmly welcomed, at its inauguration, by local families who wish to turn the page with respect to past demolitions and instead look resolutely towards the future.

Richard Scoffier, Paris, on 3 February 2011

The scar left by the Ravel block crosses through the building.

N

1

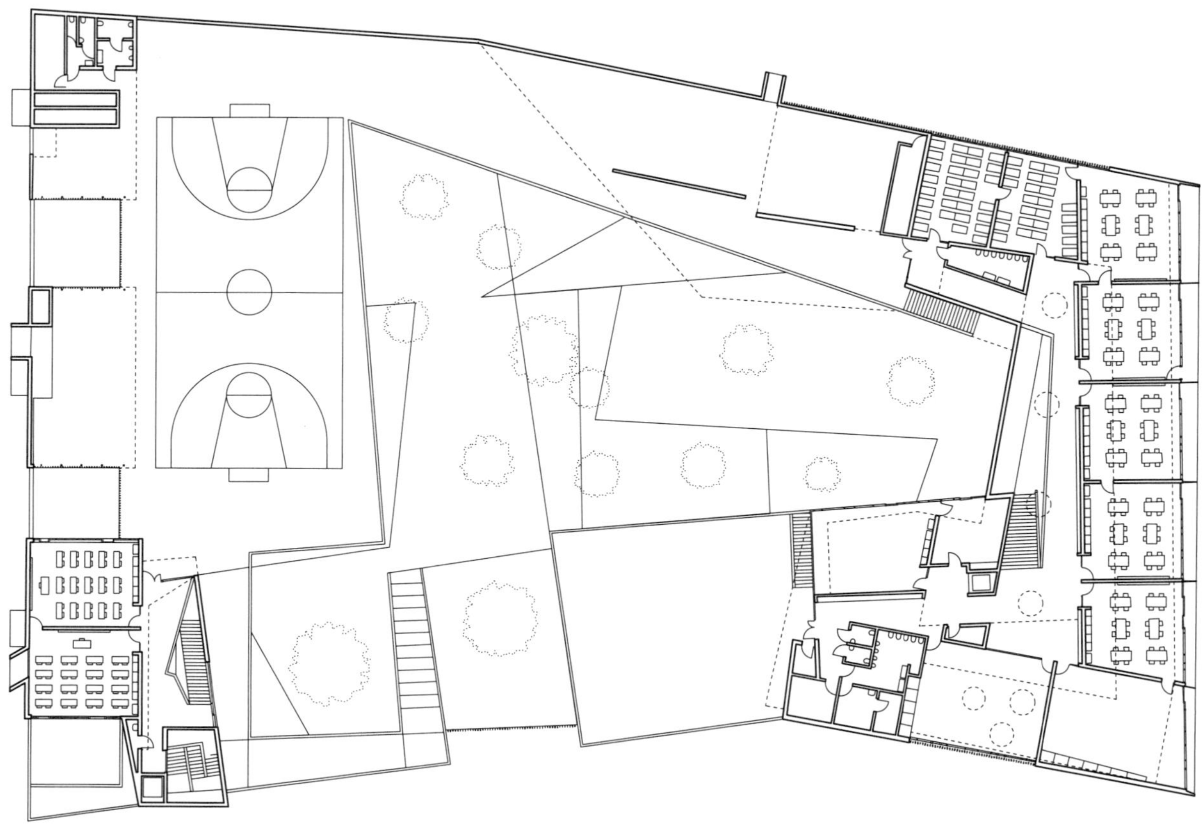

0

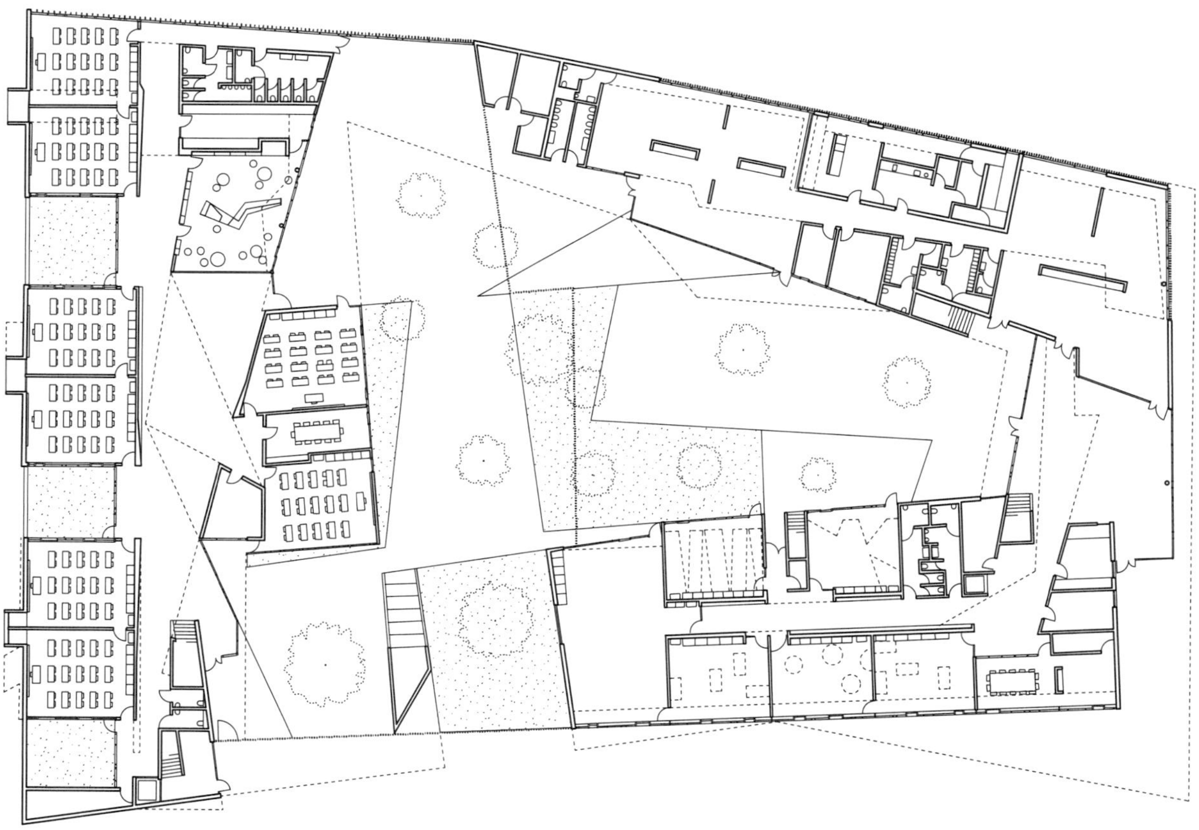

20 m

2

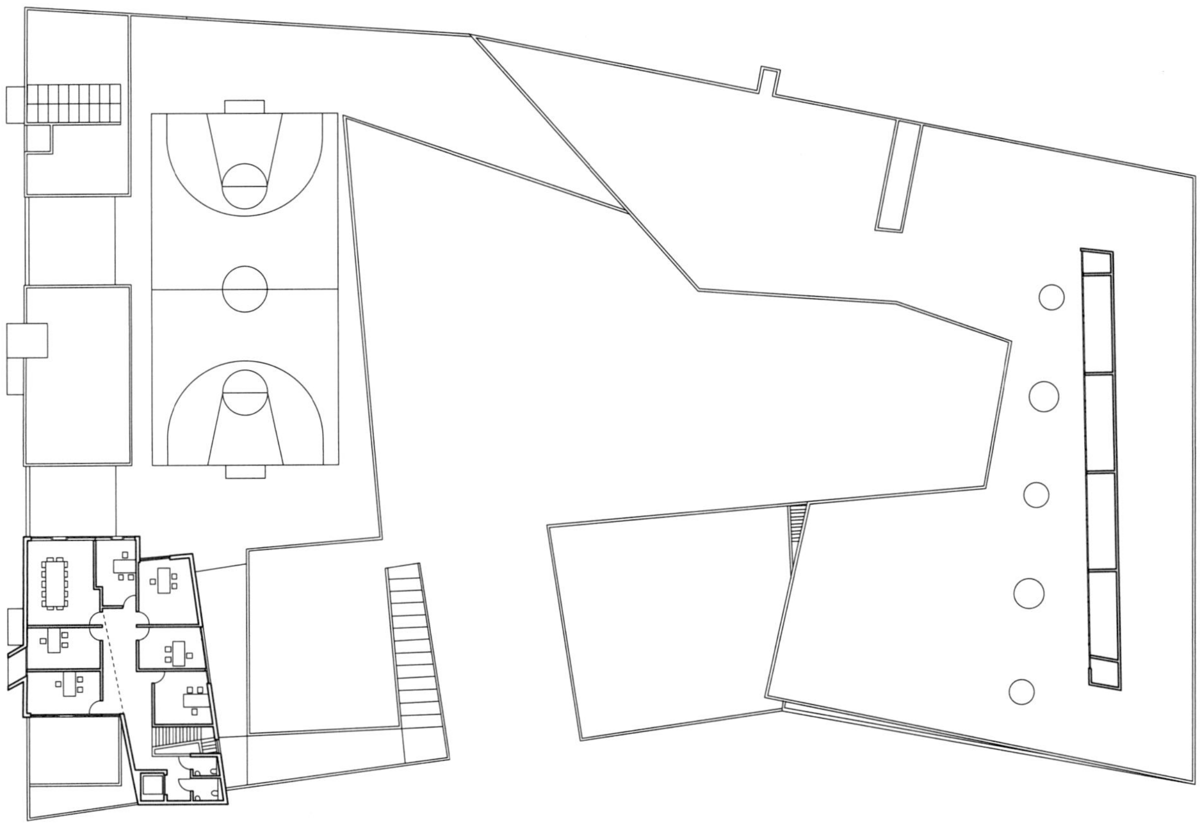

LA TERRE EST BLEUE COMME UNE

COMME UNE

LA TERRE EST BLEUE COMME UNE ORANGE

2015
School complex

Colombes

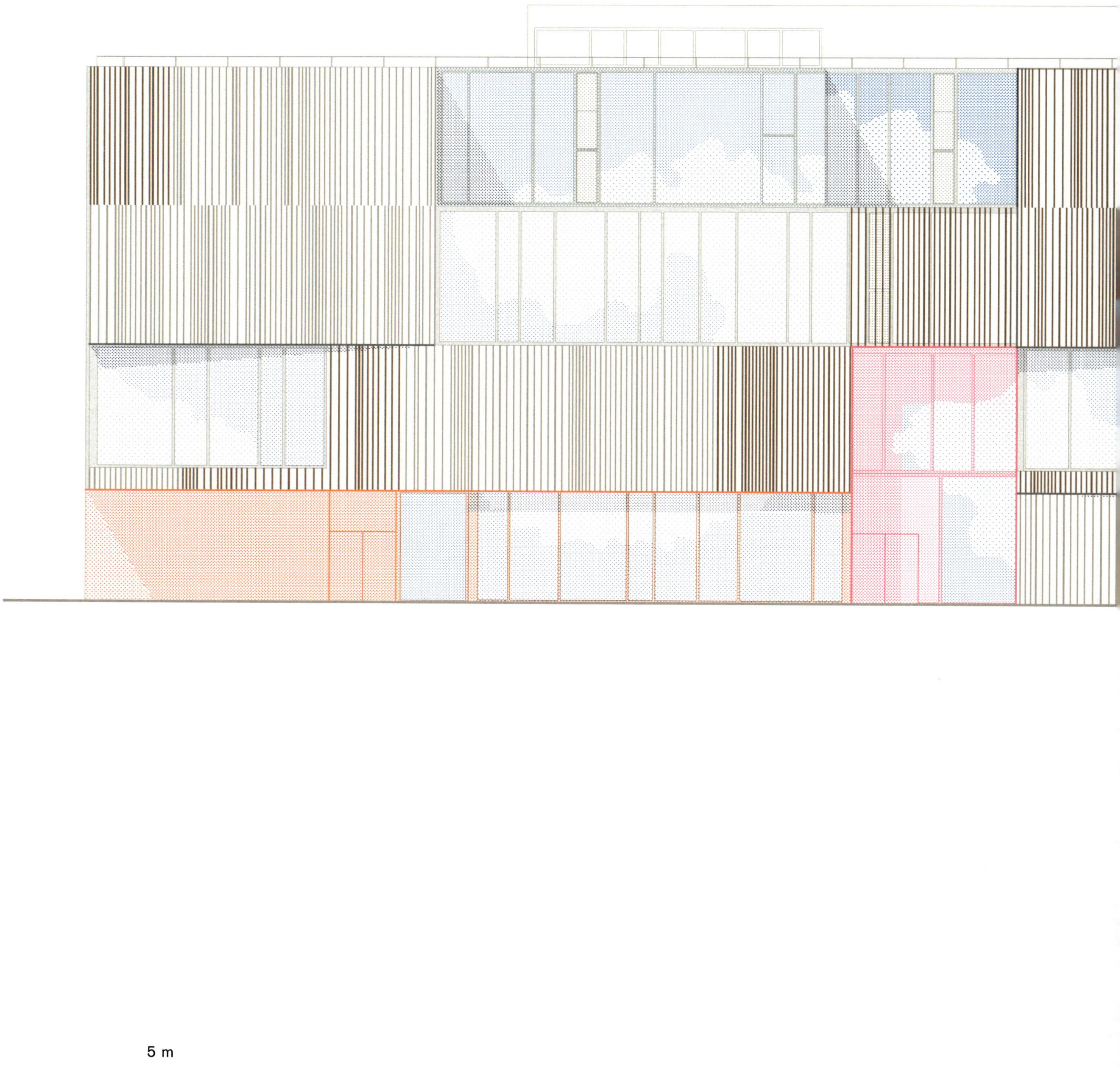
5 m

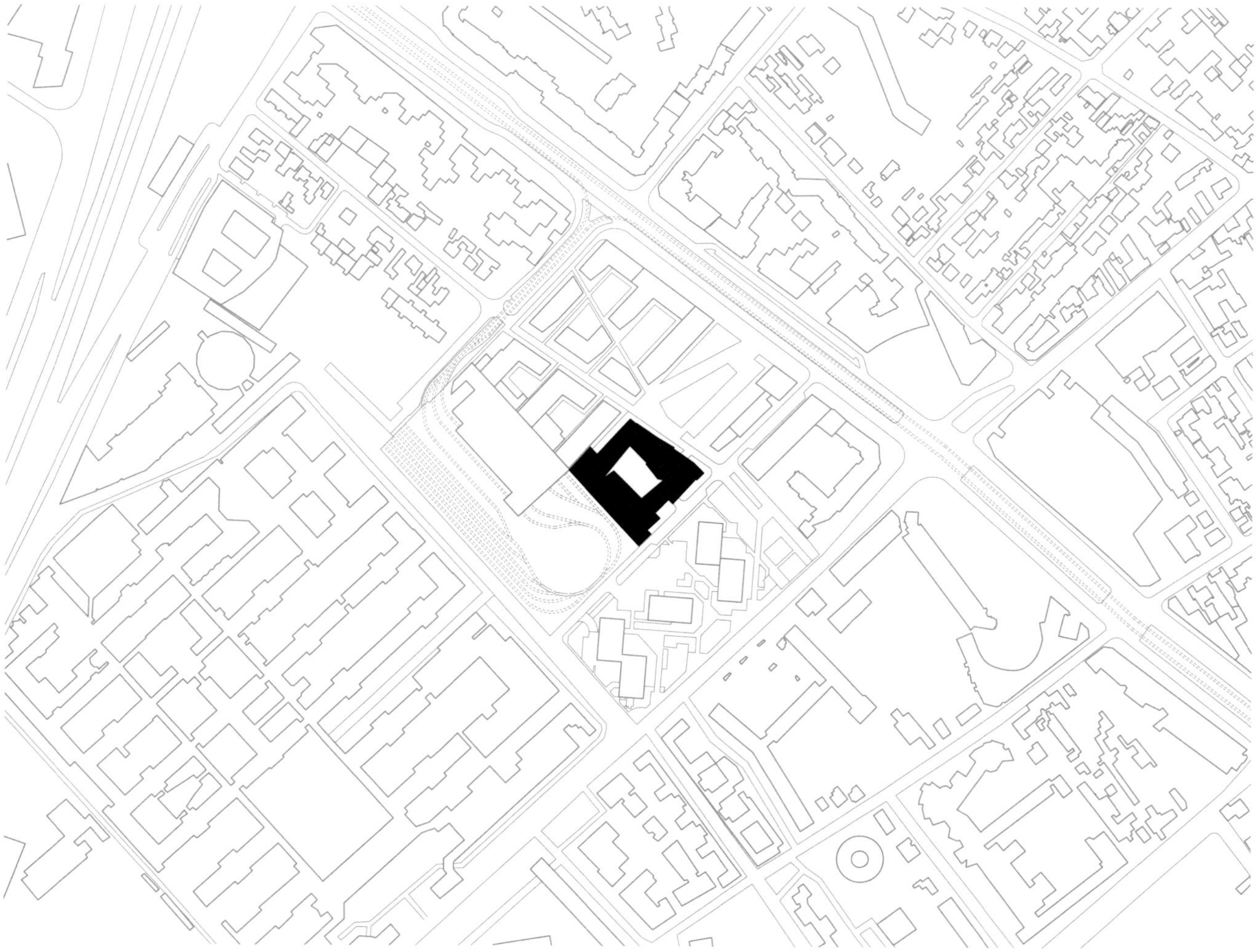

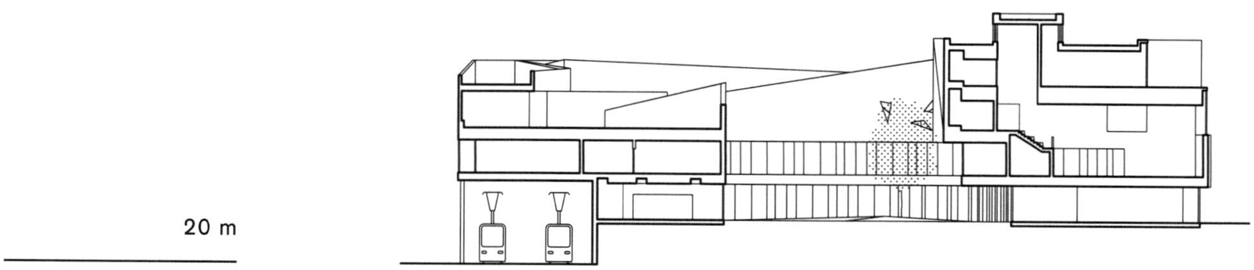
20 m

Interlinking —— This school complex plays an important role in the urban composition of a new eco-neighbourhood in Colombes. Set in a dense urban fabric, it faces a park on one side and adjoins the maintenance workshops of a new tram line on the other. Rising four storeys on a restricted plot, the building incorporates the primary school's playgrounds on its roof, alongside pedagogical gardens. The programme also includes a sports hall, a restaurant, a library and spaces for after-school activities. Glazed hollows in the façade fragment and reflect the light. Given the building's depth, the circulation spaces take refuge at the perimeter, providing light-filled, varied trajectories. Courtyards bring daylight into the heart of the school, while glimpses through into other spaces bring supplementary variety to the routes through the complex. Clothed in rough-hewn wood strips that still have their bark, the building offers a coarse visage to the street. From the ground floor, which is open to the surrounding urbanity, one glimpses through the covered playground the highly coloured courtyard, which was designed as a unique autonomous universe. Colour, which accentuates the expansion of the building's volumes, makes this aerial space a place of awakening and liberty. Colour is also present in the infant school, while the classrooms of the primary school are more soberly dressed in wood and concrete. The design eschews repetition: the treatment of light and the variety of materials and trajectories create a succession of micro-events and fragments of architecture that come together in a joyous and eclectic ensemble.

1

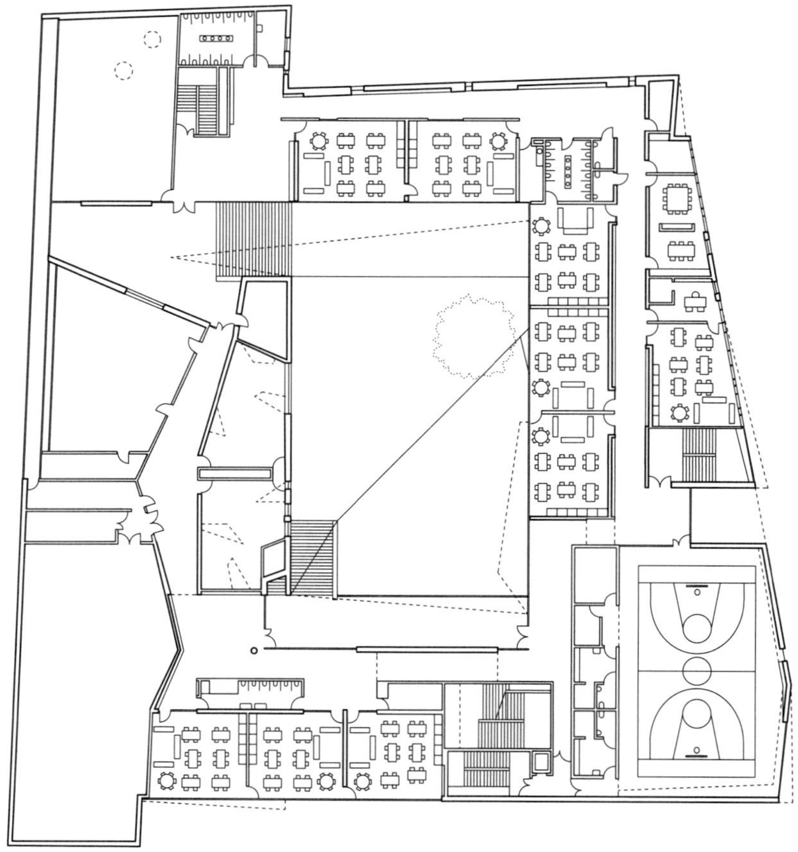

0

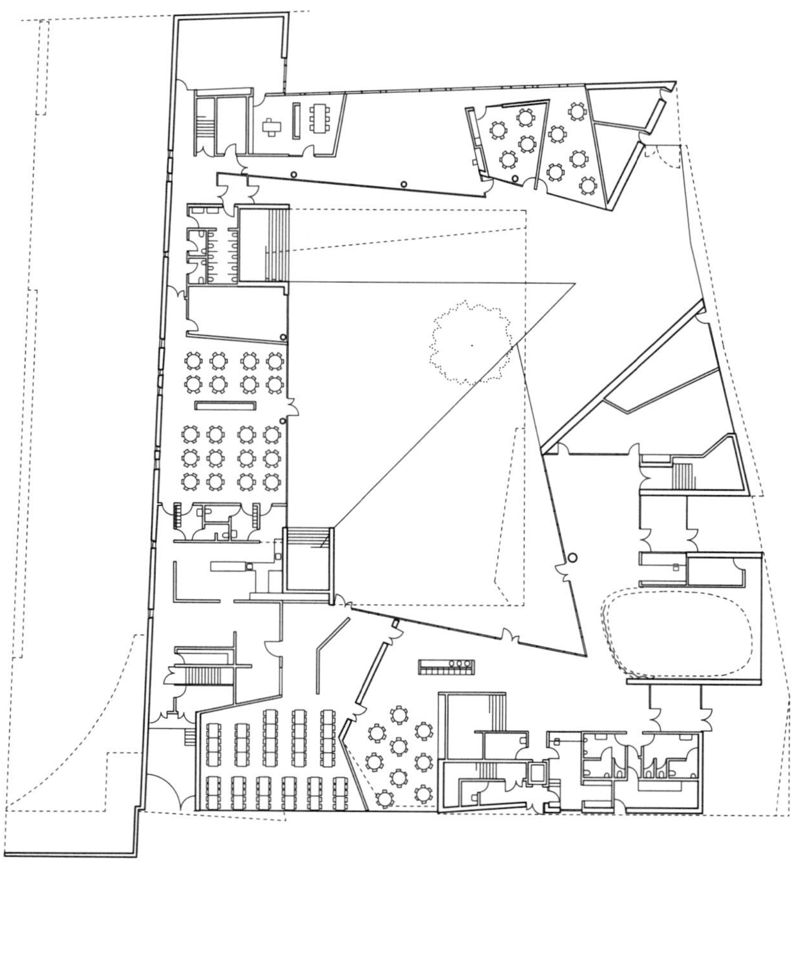

3

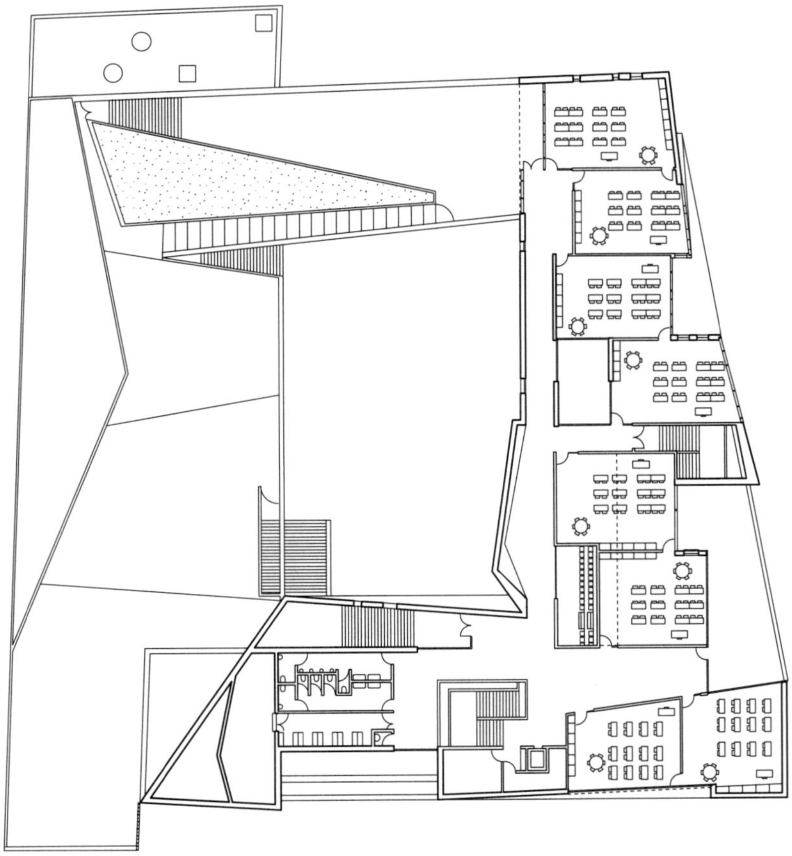

2

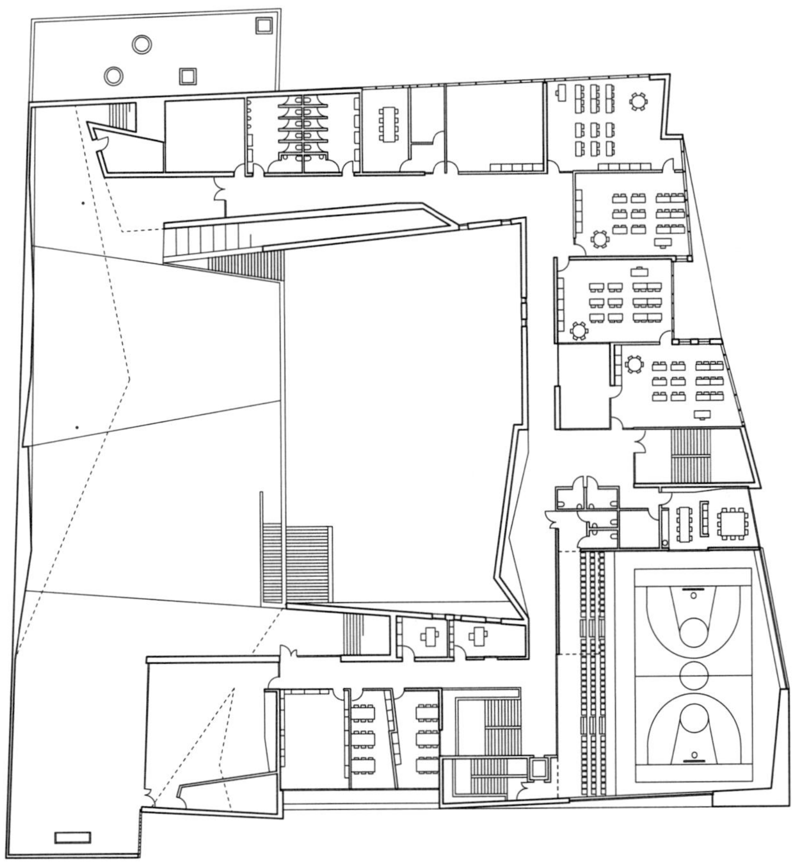

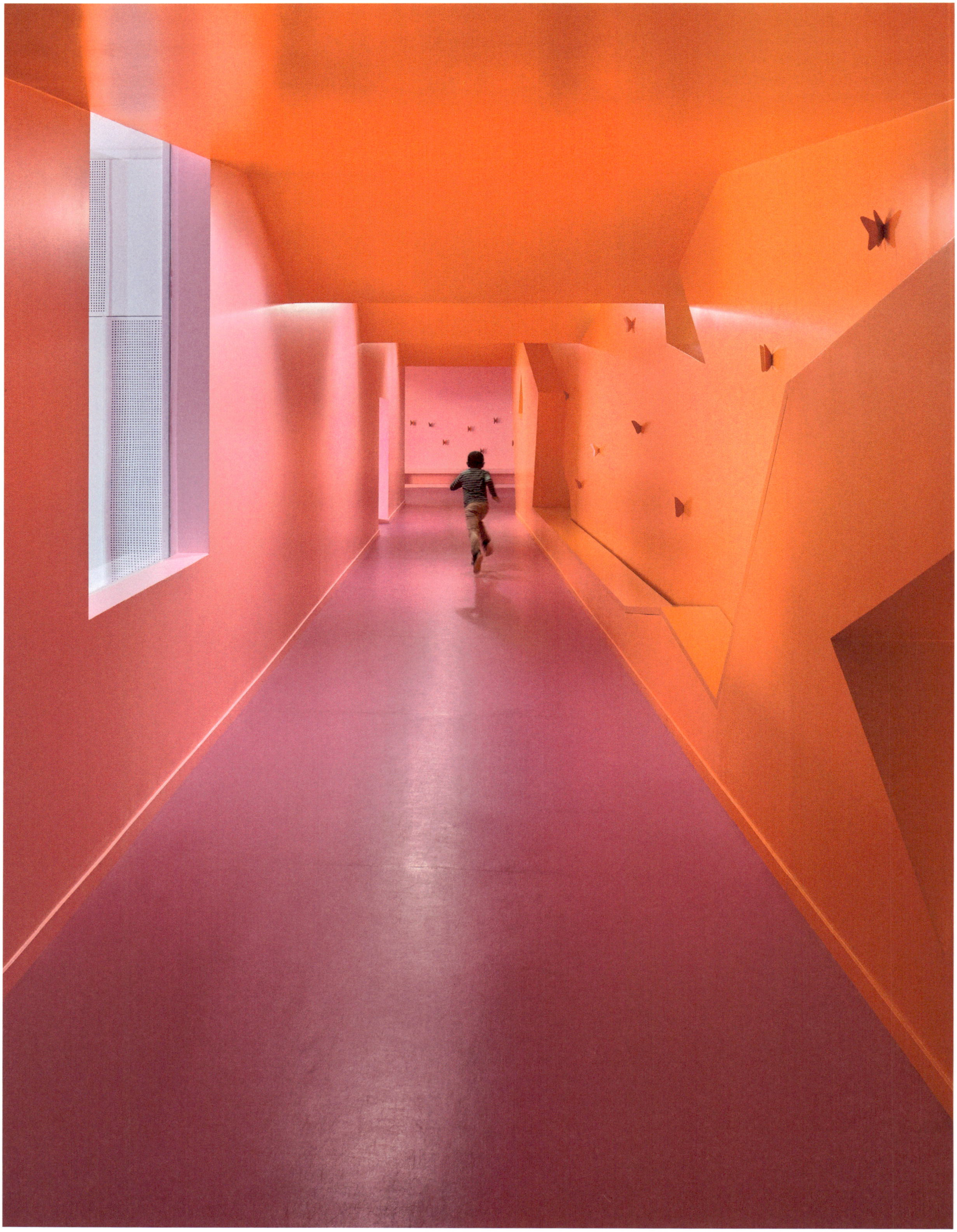

Freyming-Merlebach

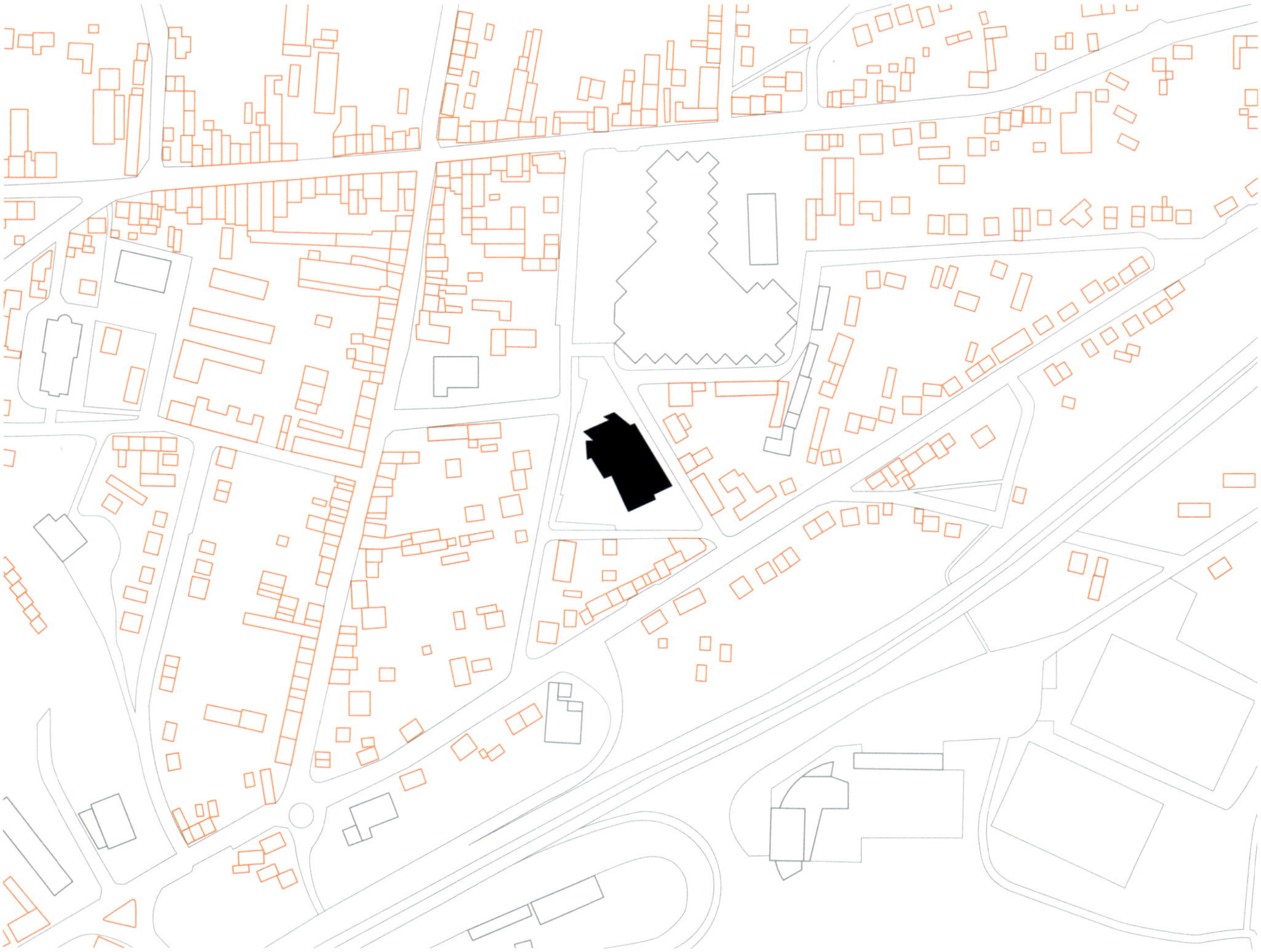

Renaissance —— Like many towns in north-eastern France, Freyming-Merlebach grew significantly in the first half of the twentieth century with the development of coal-mining. But its history, bound to that of the pits, has been one of high unemployment and decline since their closure in the 1980s. The abandoned coal tunnels are, moreover, unstable, resulting in frequent collapses, one of which put paid to the town's old theatre when the site on which it stood caved in. Convinced that culture has an important part to play in the fight against the socio-economic hardships of post-industrial transition, the municipal authorities resolved to build a new, seven-hundred-seat theatre with dressing rooms and technical spaces that would allow the staging of everything from musicals to experimental dramas. Located not far from the new town hall, opposite a little-frequented shopping centre, the theatre creates a new public space in a changing urban centre and sets up a strong dialogue with the disparate surroundings. Its distinctive volumes give it a streamlined silhouette whose height variations were calculated to ensure visual transition between the different elements of the programme while respecting the local urban scale. A symbol of renewal, the building stands out in the townscape thanks to its plastic effects, which include a 'stepping down' from the large mass of the fly tower to the surrounding piazza. The theatre's white exterior sparkles at the heart of this mining town, its animated play of volumes attracting attention. On the upper level, the foyer juts out in a cantilever to mark the main entrance, while from the street discreet views into the building give a tantalising idea of its complex interior layout. The modest entrance is located to one side, allowing the foyer to make full use of the building's width. Inside, the first flight of steps is still fairly discreet, but the extent of the interior void becomes apparent as one climbs and walls begin to dissolve. In a play of diagonals that emphasises the building's complex geometry, the progressive dilatation of space creates a dizzying sensation, the staircases intertwining on their way to the auditorium in a spectacular *promenade architecturale* which, thanks to a homogeneous treatment of raw plaster and soft carpet, envelops the theatregoer in a fragmented cocoon. Along the way, natural light picks out volumes and facets, modelling the space in a constantly changing, theatrical progression. Little by little the building reveals itself: from the immaculate whiteness of the façades to the off-white tones of the foyer and the walkways all the way to the auditorium, where a total and deliberate break occurs. Here, in the heart of the building, the containing volume is shallow and compact—the furthest spectator is only twenty meters from the stage—and colour bursts forth in red, orange and pink, bringing a unique density to the space and sanctifying the act of performance.

1

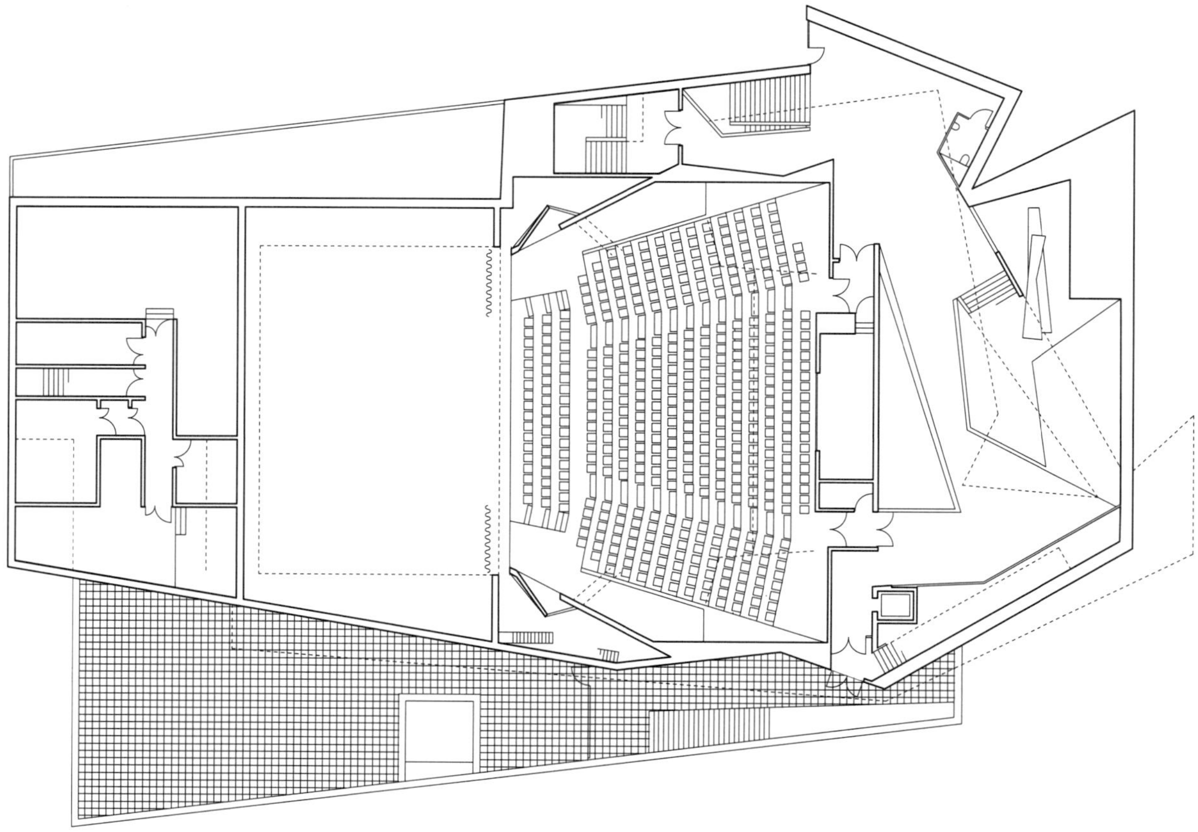

0

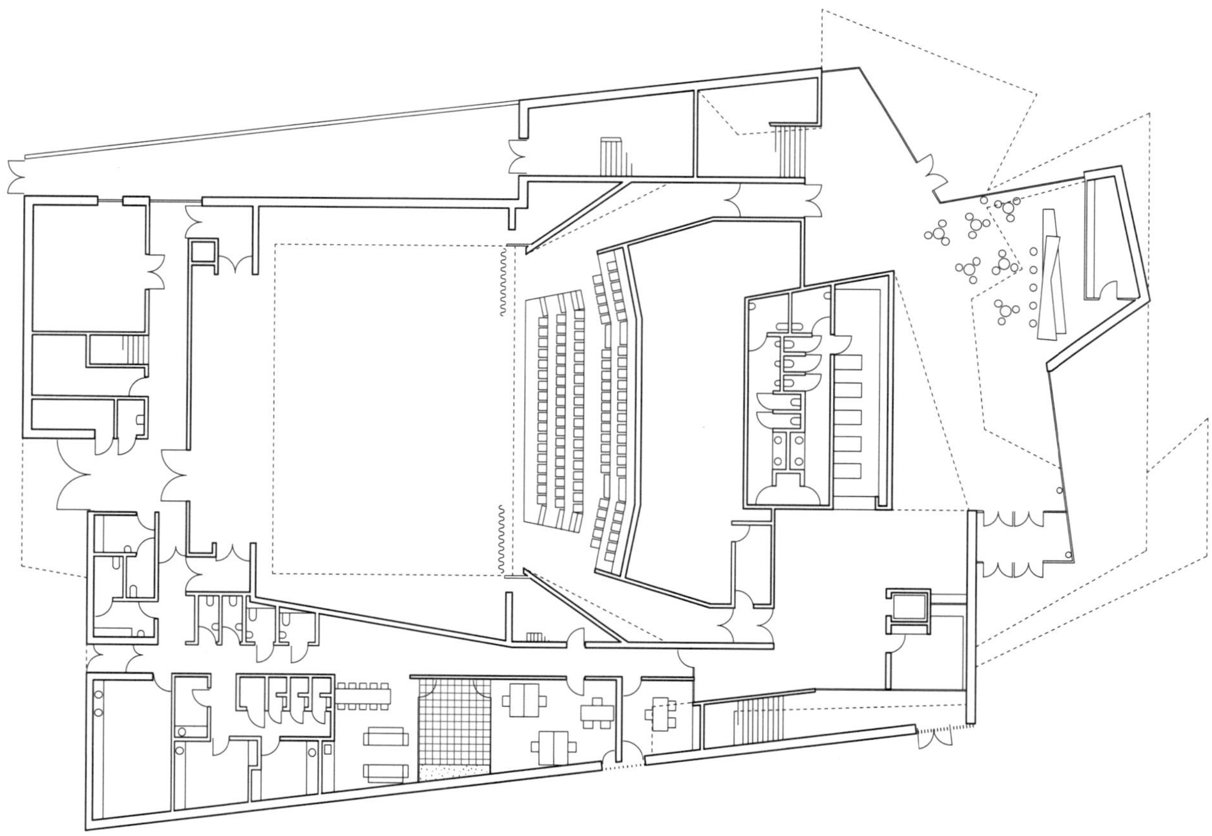

10 m

2

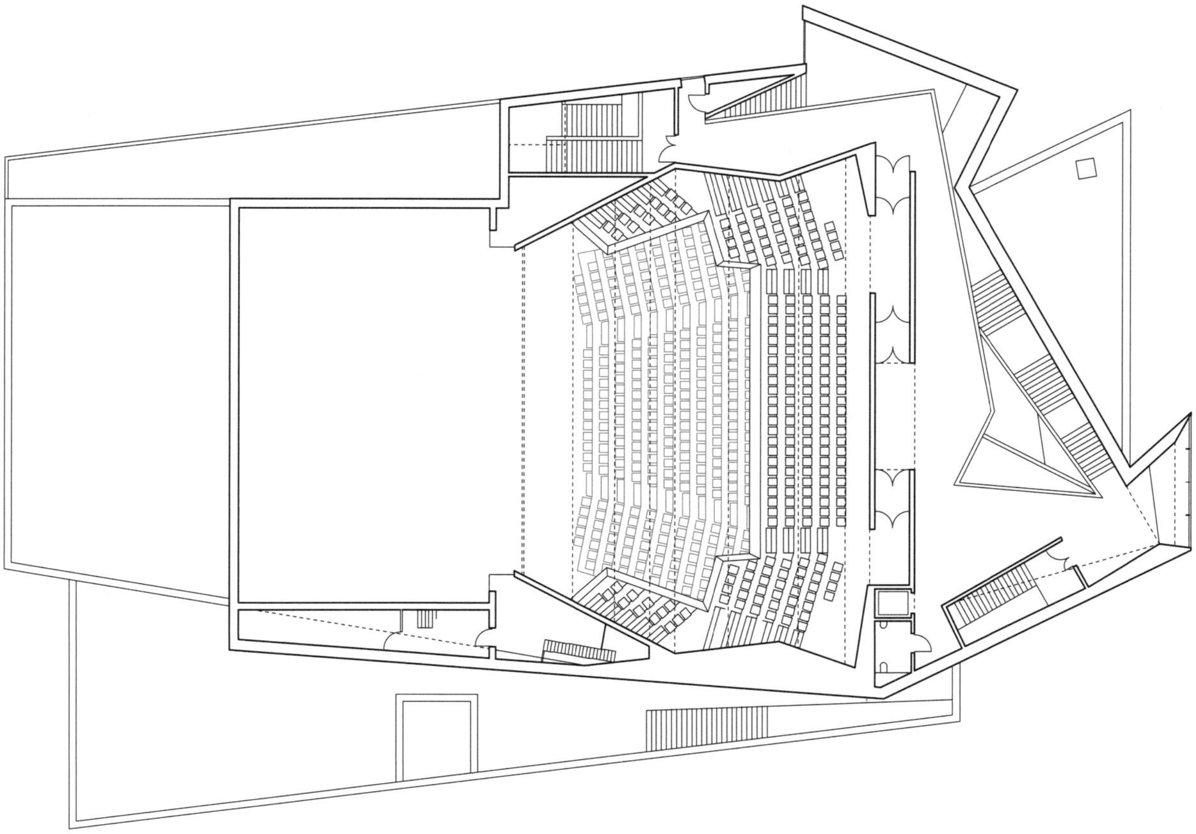

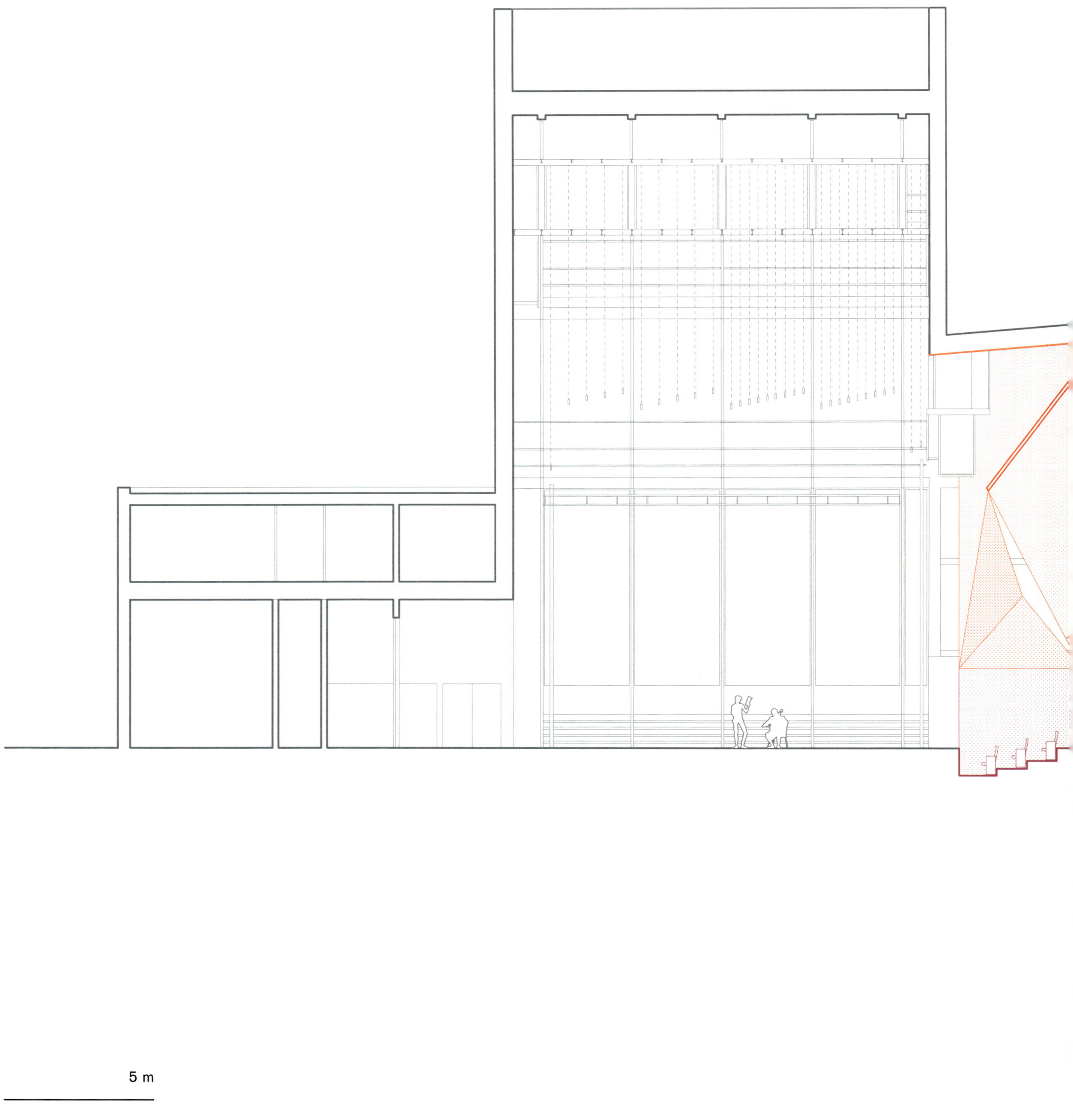
5 m

M
L
K
J

Strasbourg
Secondary school
1994–1996
Client: Conseil Général du Bas-Rhin
Programme: Secondary school for 700 pupils
Cost: 30 000 000 F incl. tax
Area: 5 800 m²
Stage: Built
Address: Allée Colette Besson, 67100 Strasbourg

Saverne
Sixth-form college
2000–2003
Client: Région Alsace
Programme (construction and extension): Mass catering for 700 meals, multi-purpose projection room, classrooms, computer room, laboratories, staff accomodations
Cost: 4 560 000 euros incl. tax
Area: 3 389 m²
Stage: Built
Address: 1 rue de Haegen, 67700 Saverne

Ingwiller
Nursing home
1995–1999
Client: Asile du Neuenberg
Programme (construction and extension): Nursing home, retirement home and link to the existing hospital
Cost: 39 000 000 F incl. tax
Area: 4 700 m²
Stage: Built
Address: 38 rue du Pasteur Herrmann, 67340 Ingwiller

Strasbourg
University canteen
2003–2004
Client: Direction départementale de l'Équipement du Bas-Rhin
Programme (extension): Canteen
Cost: 219 277 euros excl. tax
Area: 100 m²
Stage: Built
Address: 4 Allée du Sommerhof, 67200 Strasbourg

Reims
Infant school
1998–2001
Client: Ville de Reims
Programme: Infant school for 112 pupils
Cost: 13 400 000 F incl. tax
Area: 1 660 m²
Stage: Built
Address: 15 rue des Sculpteurs Jacques, 51100 Reims

Reims
School complex
2000–2005
Client: Ville de Reims
Programme: Infant school, primary school, catering, computer room, multi-purpose hall, projection room, staff accomodation
Cost: 6 009 000 euros excl. tax
Area: 3 880 m²
Stage: Built
Address: 12 ter rue Passe Demoiselles, 51100 Reims

Marmoutier
Infant school
2004–2006
Client: Ville de Marmoutier
Programme: 5 classrooms, activity room, library, rest area
Cost: 1 400 000 euros excl. tax
Area: 1 160 m²
Stage: Built
Address: 1 chemin du Schlossgarten, 67440 Marmoutier

Corbara
Individual house
2006–2008
Client: Private
Programme: House
Cost: 300 000 euros incl. tax
Area: 139 m²
Stage: Built
Address: 20256 Corbara

Montreuil
Theatre
2003–2007
Client: Ville de Montreuil
Programme: 400-seat theatre, rehearsing halls
Cost: 9 030 000 euros excl. tax
Area: 2 600 m²
Stage: Built
Address: 10 place Jean Jaurès, 93100 Montreuil

Paris
Nursery
2003–2008
Client: Ville de Paris
Programme (restructuring): Nursery of 60 cradles, separate areas for each age, daycare
Cost: 1 800 000 euros excl. tax
Area: 990 m²
Stage: Built
Address: 11 bis rue Édouard Robert, 75012 PARIS

Strasbourg
Administrative Centre
2004–2007
Client: Direction départementale de l'Équipement du Bas-Rhin
Programme (restructuring of six buildings): Two separate regional management offices with common meeting room
Cost: 4 682 919 euros incl. tax
Area: 6 683 m²
Stage: Built
Address: 14 rue du Maréchal Juin, 67000 Strasbourg

Maizières-lès-Metz
Music conservatoire
2005–2009
Client: Ville de Maizières-lès-Metz
Programme: Music conservatoire, 130-seat auditorium, reception hall, extra-curricular activities centre, area for the young
Cost: 6 200 000 euros excl. tax
Area: 3 400 m²
Stage: Built
Address: 1 avenue Marguerite Duras, 57280 Maizières-lès-Metz

Mattaincourt
Specialised care home
2004–2010
Client: Centre hospitalier Ravenel
Programme: 40-bedroom specialised care home, restaurant, outdoor and indoor common areas
Cost: 4 700 000 euros excl. tax
Area: 2 300 m²
Stage: Built
Address: 39 rue du Général de Gaulle, 88500 Mattaincourt

Strasbourg
School complex
2009–2013
Client: Ville de Strasbourg
Programme (restructuring): 10-classroom infant school, 18-classroom primary school, music school, school canteen, extra-curricular activities centre, sports hall
Cost: 10 700 000 euros excl. tax
Area: 8 731 m²
Stage: Built
Address: 13 rue des Bonnes Gens, 67000 Strasbourg

Anzin
Media library
2006–2010
Client: Ville d'Anzin
Programme: Reading and document-consulting areas, 100-seat multi-purpose hall, administration
Cost: 3 750 000 euros excl. tax
Area: 1 750 m²
Stage: Built
Address: Place de Boussu, 59410 Anzin

Isbergues
Cultural centre
2010–2013
Client: Ville d'Isbergues
Programme: Media library, 400-seat performance hall, rehearsing halls
Cost: 6 200 000 euros excl. tax
Area: 3 928 m²
Stage: Built
Address: Rue Léon Blum, 62330 Isbergues

La Courneuve
School complex
2007–2010
Client: Ville de La Courneuve
Programme: 6-classroom infant school, 10-classroom primary school, 6-room leisure centre, school canteen, 5 offices for educational inspectorates, meeting room
Cost: 8 000 000 euros excl. tax
Area: 4 500 m²
Stage: Built
Address: 2 rue des Clos, 93120 La Courneuve

Montmorency
Regional court and industrial tribunal
2011–2013
Client: Ministère de la Justice
Programme: Courtrooms, 1 floor regional court offices, 1 floor industrial tribunal, archives, library, coffee room, main hall, technical facilities
Cost: 4 367 100 euros excl. tax
Area: 2 110 m²
Stage: Built
Address: 137-143 avenue Charles de Gaulle, 95 160 Montmorency

Bagneux
Swimming pool
2009–2014
Client: Communauté d'agglomération Sud de Seine
Programme (restructuring and extension): 25-metre swimming pool, teaching pool, paddling pool, sauna, hammam, relaxation aeras, dressing rooms, showers, outdoor solarium
Cost: 8 038 000 euros excl. tax
Area: 3 431 m²
Stage: Built
Address: 1 avenue de Stalingrad, 92220 Bagneux

Strasbourg
Combined workshop and home
2009–2015
Client: Private
Programme: Private appartment, architecture office
Cost: 1 320 000 euros excl. tax
Area: 500 m²
Stage: Built
Address: 13 rue de la Tour des pêcheurs, 67000 Strasbourg

Pont-sur-Yonne
Retirement home
2010–2014
Client: Maison de retraite Lamy-Delletrez
Programme: 92-bedroom retirement home with 14-bedroom Alzheimer unit, guest rooms, reception and animation centre, care and medical consultation facilities, administrative area, staff facilities, logistic and technical facilities
Cost: 9 304 560 euros excl. tax
Area: 5 395 m²
Stage: Built
Address: Le Ravillon, 89140 Pont-sur-Yonne

Colombes
School complex
2010–2015
Client: Ville de Colombes
Programme: 9-classroom infant school, 12-classroom primary school, infant school leisure centre, primary school leisure centre, canteen, sports hall
Cost: 16 300 000 euros excl. tax
Area: 7 600 m²
Stage: Built
Address: 3 rue Marguerite Yourcenar, 92700 Colombes

Orbec
Retirement home
2008–2015
Client: E.P.M.S. Marie du Merle
Programme: 85-bed care home for dependent ederly people, 30-bed nursing home, day-centre providing adapted activities and treatment, kitchen, canteen, administrative areas, treatment department
Cost: 12 279 536 euros excl. tax
Area: 5 833 m²
Stage: Built
Address: 8 rue de la Source, 14290 Orbec

Belfort
Conservatoire
2011–2015
Client: Communauté d'agglomération Belfortaine
Programme: 32 classrooms, 6 collective classrooms, 4 collective rehearsing rooms, 4 studios, 140-seat auditorium, 70-seat amphitheatre, dance hall, drama room, percussions room, library
Cost: 6 326 000 euros excl. tax
Area: 3 895 m²
Stage: Built
Address: 1 rue Paul Koepfler, 90000 Belfort

Venarey-Les Laumes
Art and conference centre
2012–2015
Client: Ville de Venarey-Les Laumes
Programme: Performance hall, tourist office, intergenerational centre, day-nursery
Cost: 3 600 000 euros excl. tax
Area: 1 646 m^2
Stage: Built
Address: Avenue de la gare, 21150 Venarey-Les Laumes

Clamart
Sports hall
2010– 2015
Client: Conseil départemental des Hauts-de-Seine
Programme: Sports hall, outdoor sports area, staff accomodations, secondary school's courtyard
Cost: 7 400 000 euros excl. tax
Area: 2 596 m^2
Stage: Built
Address: 28 rue des Closiaux, 92140 Clamart

Montpellier
School complex
2012–2015
Client: Ville de Montpellier
Programme: Primary school, infant school, canteen, extra-curricular activities centre
Cost: 7 300 000 euros excl. tax
Area: 3 444 m^2
Stage: Built
Address: 89 avenue Joan Miró, 34 000 Montpellier

Thionville
Media library
2010–2016
Client: Ville de Thionville
Programme: Media library/third place, creation studios, auditorium/broadcasting room
Cost: 11 000 000 euros excl. tax
Area: 4 590 m^2
Stage: Built
Address: 1 place Malraux, 57100 Thionville

Buhl
Nursery
2013–2015
Client: Communauté de communes Région de Guebwiller
Programme: 40 children nursery, daycare and childminders' relay
Cost: 1 700 000 euros excl. tax
Area: 763 m^2
Stage: Built
Address: 14 rue de la Fabrique, 68530, Buhl

Freyming-Merlebach
Theatre
2011–2017
Client: Communauté de communes Freyming-Merlebach
Programme: 700-seat performance hall (223-seat balcony, 477-seat parterre)
Cost: 7 700 000 euros excl. tax
Area: 3 068 m^2
Stage: Built
Address: 1 place des Alliés, 57800 Freyming-Merlebach

Strasbourg
Sports hall
2012–2017
Client: Ville de Strasbourg
Programme: Sports hall, multi-purpose hall, changing rooms, infirmary, staff accomodation
Cost: 4 300 000 euros excl. tax
Area: 2 660 m²
Stage: Built
Address: 9 rue Peter Schwarber, 67000 Strasbourg

Huningue
Housing for the elderly
2013–2018
Client: Ville de Huningue
Programme: 22 assisted housing units, lounge rooms, winter garden, catering, multimedia room, hall, activity room, craft workshop, parking
Cost: 4 000 000 euros excl. tax
Area: 2 121 m²
Stage: Built
Address: 41 rue du Maréchal Joffre, 68330 Huningue

Mons-en-Barœul
Cultural centre
2012–2017
Client: Ville de Mons-en-Barœul
Programme: Performance hall (500 seats, 1000 standing places), rehearsing hall, recording studio, musical creation studios
Cost: 6 000 000 euros excl. tax
Area: 2 336 m²
Stage: Built
Address: 2 Avenue René Coty, 59370 Mons-en-Barœul

Schiltigheim
Covered market and exhibition area
2014–2018
Client: Ville de Schiltigheim
Programme: Rehabilitation of the former butchers' cooperative: covered market, exhibition area, café, convivial place, ticket office, administrative area
Cost: 3 600 000 euros excl. tax
Area: 2 100 m²
Stage: Built
Address: 17 rue Principale, 67300 Schiltigheim

Strasbourg
Café
2017
Client: Privé
Programme (restructuring): Transformation of a room into a café
Cost: 120 000 euros excl. tax
Area: 36,5 m²
Stage: Built
Address: 2 place des Meuniers, 67000 Strasbourg

Pélissanne
Media library and garden
2013–2018
Client: Ville de Pélissanne
Programme: Areas for children of different ages, news area, cultural area, storytelling space for toddlers, documentary area, sound and multimedia area, staff facilities, outdoor garden
Cost: 3 054 111 euros excl. tax
Area: 991 m²
Stage: Built
Address: Rue de la République, 13330 Pélissanne

Gidy
School complex
2015–2019
Client: Commune de Gidy
Programme: 6-classroom infant school, 8-classroom primary school, administrative and extra-curricular areas, canteen, schoolyards
Cost: 6 387 360 euros excl. tax
Area: 3 364 m²
Stage: Built
Address: Rue du Stade, 45520 Gidy

Gif-sur-Yvette
School complex
2015–2019
Client: Établissement public d'aménagement Paris-Saclay
Programme: 8-classroom infant school, 12-classroom primary school, 11-room leisure centre, sports hall, canteen, library, activity room, art room and physical mobility room
Cost: 12 300 000 euros excl. tax
Area: 6 828 m²
Stage: Built
Address: Rue Francis Perrin et rue André Blanc-Lapierre, 91190 Gif-sur-Yvette

Vaulx-en-Velin
School complex
2015–2019
Client: Ville de Vaulx-en-Velin
Programme: Childminders' relay, nursery, infant school, primary school, leisure centre, sports hall, library, school canteen, neighbourhood multi-purpose hall, staff accomodation
Cost: 11 378 000 euros excl. tax
Area: 6 720 m²
Stage: Built
Address: 69120 Vaulx-en-Velin

Moscow
Infant school
2016–2019
Client: PIK
Programme: Infant school for 225 children
Area: 3 510 m²
Stage: Built
Address: Selskokhoziaystvennaya Street, Moscow

Villejuif
School complex
2015–2019
Client: Ville de Villejuif
Programme: 6-classroom infant school, 11-classroom primary school, extra-curricular activities centre, activity rooms, canteen, staff accomodation, parking
Cost: 13 100 000 euros excl. tax
Area: 4 561 m²
Stage: Built
Address: 5 passage de la Pyramide, 94800 Villejuif

Rennes
Neighbourhood facility
2013–
Client: Ville de Rennes
Programme: Municipal library, contemporary music stage, youth cultural centre, administrative areas
Cost: 11 500 000 euros excl. tax
Area: 5 824 m²
Stage: Construction
Address: Avenue Jules Maniez, 35000 Rennes

Sarlat
Cultural centre
2014–
Client: Communauté de communes de Sarlat-Périgord noir
Programme: Cultural centre, media library, music school, youth centre
Cost: 3 454 539 euros excl. tax
Area: 2 059 m²
Stage: Construction
Address: 7 rue Jean-Baptiste Delpeyrat, 24200 Sarlat-la-Canéda

Porto-Vecchio
Media library
2016–
Client: Ville de Porto-Vecchio
Programme: Reading areas for children and adults, educational workshop, exhibition area, multi-purpose hall, open-air media library and garden, administrative area
Cost: 4 200 000 euros excl. tax
Area: 1 200 m²
Stage: Construction
Address: Lieu-dit Vignola, 20137 Porto-Vecchio

Poissons
Retirement home
2015–
Client: EHPAD Legay Colin
Programme: 63-bed care home for dependent ederly people, kitchen, catering, administrative areas, medical centre, community life centre, social facilities
Cost: 5 427 338 euros excl. tax
Area: 3 622 m²
Stage: Construction
Address: 37 rue de Saint-Amand, 52230 Poissons

Bourg-la-Reine
Cultural centre
2016–
Client: Ville de Bourg-la-Reine
Programme: Multi-purpose hall with grandstand, arts rooms, craft rooms, language labs, dance halls, science and technology room, multimedia room, music studios, violin-making workshop, exhibition area, educational kitchen, main hall, administrative areas
Cost: 5 870 000 euros excl. tax
Area: 2 550 m²
Stage: Construction
Address: 11 rue des Rosiers, 92340 Bourg-la-Reine

Fondettes
Swimming pool
2015–
Client: Communauté d'agglomération Tour(s)plus
Programme: 25-metre sports swimming pool, leisure pool, wellness area: 2 saunas, hammam and hot tub, 3-lane multi-slide, lawned solarium, beach-volley court
Cost: 6 610 700 euros excl. tax
Area: 2 340 m²
Stage: Construction
Address: Rue Alfred de Musset, 37230 Fondettes

Saint-Dié-des-Vosges
Cultural centre
2017–
Client: Communauté de communes de Saint-Dié-des-Vosges
Programme (restructuring): Third place: media library, tourist office, exhibition area, lecture hall, workshops
Cost: 8 770 000 euros excl. tax
Area: 4 200 m²
Stage: Construction
Address: Place Jules Ferry, 88100 Saint-Dié-des-Vosges

Still
Specialised care home
2017–
Client: Associations Adèle de Glaubitz & Les Maisons de la Croix
Programme: 30 bedrooms, catering, activity rooms
Cost: 2 600 000 euros excl. tax
Area: 2 500 m²
Stage: Construction
Address: 25 Grand Rue, 67190 Still

Ghisonaccia
Performance hall
2017–
Client: Communauté de communes Fium'orbu Castellu
Programme: 300-seat performance hall, dressing rooms, wings, public square and outdoor stage, administrative area
Cost: 4 900 000 euros excl. tax
Area: 1 355 m² (indoor) + 1 450 m² (outdoor)
Stage: Studies
Address: 20240 Ghisonaccia

Montigny-le-Bretonneux
Conservatoire
2018–
Client: Ville de Montigny-le-Bretonneux
Programme: Stage-rehearsing hall, 34-classroom theatre and music school, 3-hall dance school
Cost: 7 100 000 euros excl. tax
Area: 5 270 m²
Stage: Construction
Address: Avenue Kessel, 78180 Montigny-le-Bretonneux

Strasbourg
Housing
2017–
Client: Stradim, Kaufman & Broad
Programme: Housing, offices, swimming pool, daycare and restaurant
Cost: 50 000 000 euros excl. tax
Area: 39 400 m²
Stage: Studies
Address: Route du Petit Rhin, 67000 Strasbourg

Talence
Dance and music school
2016–
Client: Ville de Talence
Programme: Orchestra hall, amplified-music hall, percussions room, individual and collective rehearsing studios, rooms for musical training, dance studios, 500-seat performance hall with retractable tiers, bar
Cost: 6 437 000 euros excl. tax
Area: 2 912 m²
Stage: Studies
Address: Allée du 7ᵉ Art, 33400 Talence

Strasbourg
Housing
2017–
Client: Stradim
Programme: 41 housing units with shared facilities: collective laundry room, party hall, guest rooms, roof terrace, vegetable garden, bicycle repair workshop
Cost: 4 500 000 euros excl. tax
Area: 3 270 m²
Stage: Studies
Address: Rue de Nantes, 67100 Strasbourg

Moulins
Retirement home
2017–
Client: EHD (Entreprendre pour humaniser la dépendance)
Programme: 90-bed care home for dependent ederly people
Cost: 7 204 000 euros excl. tax
Area: 4 648 m²
Stage: Studies
Address: Rue du commandant Jacques Morin, 03000 Moulins

Saint-Jean-de-Luz
Cultural centre
2018–
Client: Commune de Saint-Jean-de-Luz
Programme: 500-seat performance hall, music, dance and theatre school
Cost: 6 200 000 euros excl. tax
Area: 3 085 m²
Stage: Studies
Address: Rue Duconte, 64500 Saint-Jean-de-Luz

Illzach
Nursery
2018–
Client: Mulhouse Alsace Agglomération
Programme: Nursery for 50 children
Cost: 1 600 000 euros excl. tax
Area: 790 m²
Stage: Studies
Address: Rue des Carrières, 68110 Illzach

Saint-Vaast-la-Hougue
Retirement home
2018–
Client: EHPAD du Val de Saire
Programme: 63-bed care home for dependent ederly people with Alzheimer unit, shared catering areas on the groundfloor and upper floors, shared activities areas, kitchen, linen room
Cost: 6 720 000 euros excl. tax
Area: 4 150 m²
Stage: Studies
Address: Lieu-dit Le Marais, 50550 Saint-Vaast-la-Hougue

Nantes
School complex
2018–
Client: Ville de Nantes
Programme (extension): Infant school (6 classrooms, library, physical mobility room, 2 rest areas), primary school (10 classrooms, multi-purpose hall, library), school canteen, extra-curricular activities centre
Cost: 4 320 000 euros excl. tax
Area: 3 400 m²
Stage: Studies
Address: Boulevard Professeur René Auvigné, 44100 Nantes

Thionville
Sports centre
2018–
Client: Ville de Thionville
Programme: Multi-purpose hall, sports hall, dance hall, rhythmic gymnastics hall, climbing wall
Cost: 8 700 000 euros excl. tax
Area: 5 441 m²
Stage: Studies
Address: 57100 Thionville

2018
Media library and garden

Pélissanne

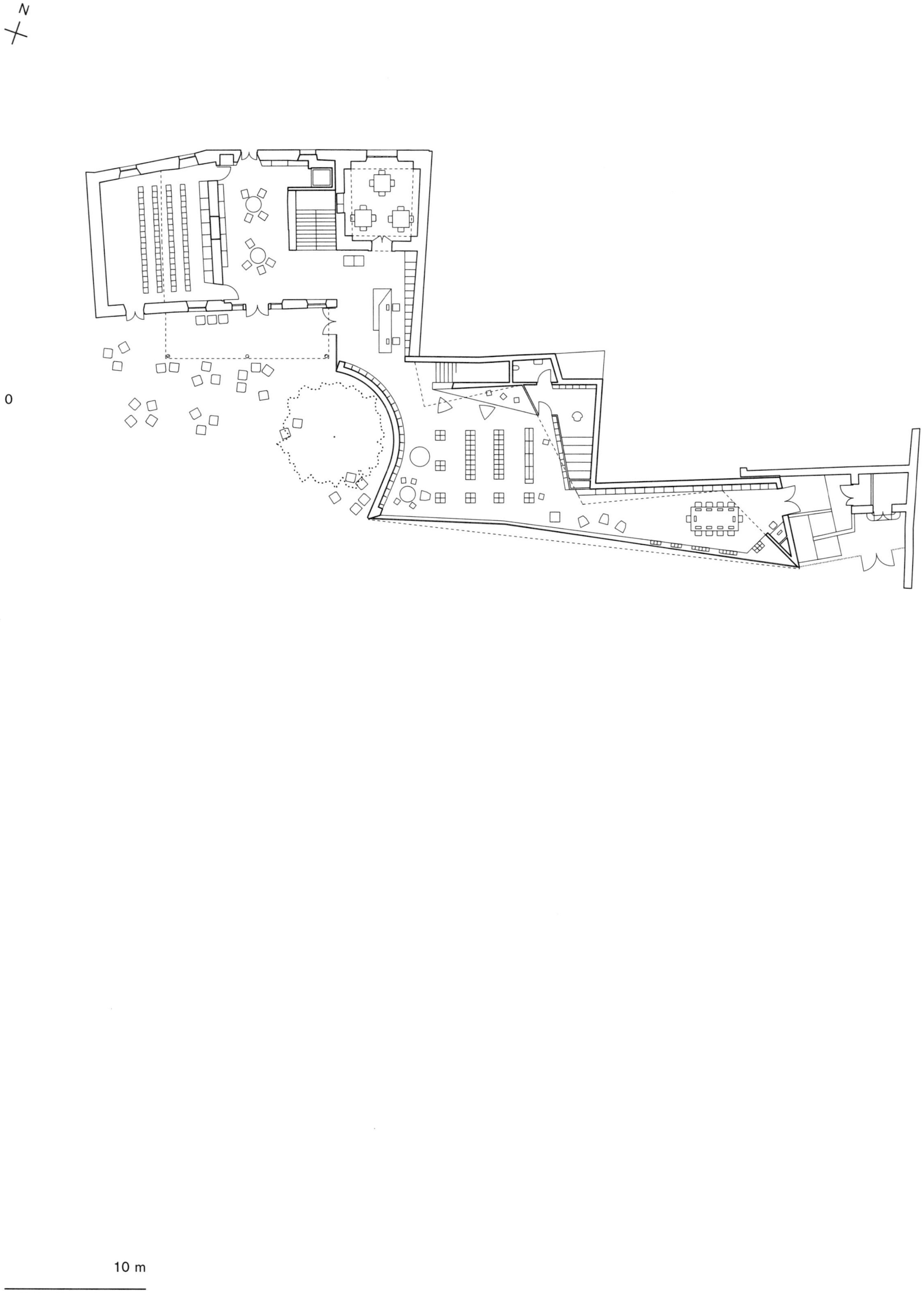
N
0
10 m

1

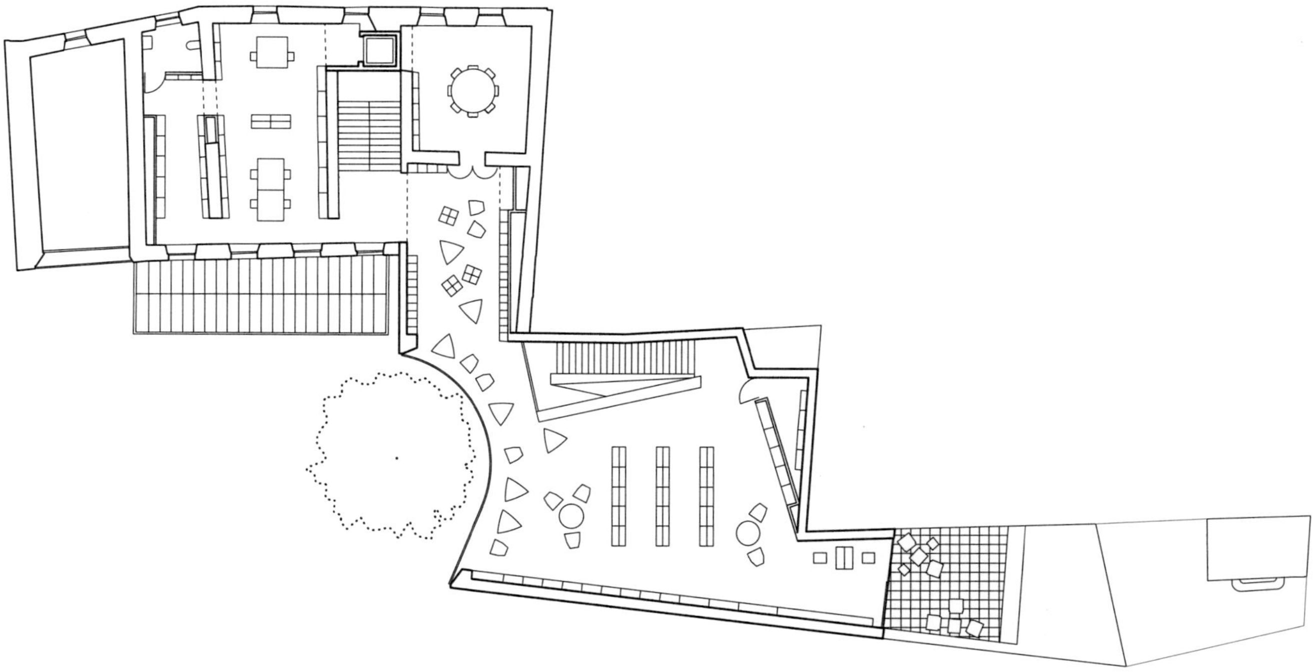

MEDIATHEQUE PIERRE

Buildings

Strasbourg, secondary school, 1996
Lead architect: Dominique Coulon; Architects: Michel Bayer, Jan Richter; Landscape: Pascale Richter; Artist: Lorraine Pellegrini.
— Structural system: Kesser; Plasterwork: Alvanti; Joinery: Vollmer; Roofing: Beyer; Waterproofing: Ried Étanche.

Saverne, sixth-form college, 2003
— Lead architect: Dominique Coulon; Project supervision: Arnaud Eloudyi; Architects: Caroline Cavé, Paul Le Quernec, Rémy Valantin.
— Structure: Batiserf Ingénierie; Mechanical plumbing: BET Gilbert Jost; Community kitchens: Écotral; Cost control and monitoring: C2Bi.
— Structural system: Alsacienne du bâtiment; Plasterwork: Alvanti; Joinery: Vollmer.

Marmoutier, infant school, 2006
— Lead architect: Dominique Coulon; Project and construction site supervision: Olivier Nicollas; Architects: Sarah Brebbia, Arnaud Eloudyi, Steve Letho Duclos.
— Structure: HN Ingénierie; Mechanical plumbing: BET Gilbert Jost; Cost control and monitoring: E3 Économie; Landscape: Bruno Kubler.

Montreuil, theatre, 2007
— Lead architect: Dominique Coulon; Project supervision: Steve Letho Duclos; Architects: Sarah Brebbia, Arnaud Eloudyi, Olivier Nicollas; Construction site supervision: Bertrand Meurice Architecte.
— Structure: Batiserf Ingénierie; Mechanical plumbing: BET Gilbert Jost; Cost control: E3 Économie; Scenographer: Jean-Paul Chabert; Acoustics: Euro Sound Project.

Maizières-lès-Metz, conservatoire, 2009
— Lead architect: Dominique Coulon; Project supervision: Steve Letho Duclos, Sarah Brebbia; Architects: Arnaud Eloudyi, Olivier Nicollas.
— Structure: Batiserf Ingénierie, Omnis Bâtiment, Del Ben Walter; Mechanical plumbing: BET Gilbert Jost; Cost control: E3 Économie; Acoustics: Euro Sound Project.
— Structural system: Zannier construction; Plasterwork: Küpeli.

La Courneuve, school complex, 2010
— Lead architects: Dominique Coulon, Olivier Nicollas; Architects: Sarah Brebbia, Benjamin Rocchi, Arnaud Eloudyi, Florence Haenel.
— Structure: Batiserf Ingénierie; Mechanical plumbing: BET Gilbert Jost; Cost control: E3 Économie; Landscape: Bruno Kubler.
— Structural system: SNRB; Exterior joinery: Vollmer; Plasterwork: Luso Plaque & Plâtre; Interior joinery: Bonnardel; Finish: Art Maniac; Heating, plumbing and ventilation: Foret; Electricity: Rezza.

Anzin, media library, 2010
— Lead architect: Dominique Coulon; Project supervision: Olivier Nicollas; Architects: Sarah Brebbia, Steve Letho Duclos; Construction site supervision: Olivier Werner Architecte.
— Structure: Batiserf Ingénierie; Mechanical plumbing: BET Gilbert Jost; Cost control: E3 Économie; Acoustics: Euro Sound Project.

Isbergues, cultural centre, 2013
— Lead architects: Dominique Coulon, Steve Letho Duclos; Architects: Gautier Duthoit, Olivier Nicollas; Construction site supervision: Olivier Werner Architecte.
— Structure: Batiserf Ingénierie; Mechanical plumbing and High Environmental Quality: BET Gilbert Jost; Cost control: E3 Économie; Acoustics: Euro Sound Project; Scenographer: Changement à Vue.

Bagneux, swimming pool, 2014
— Lead architects: Dominique Coulon, Benjamin Rocchi; Architects: Arnaud Eloudyi, Sarah Brebbia, Gautier Duthoit; Construction site supervision: Olivier Werner Architecte.
— Structure: Batiserf Ingénierie; Mechanical plumbing: Alto Ingénierie; Cost control: E3 Économie; Acoustics: Euro Sound Project.
— Structural system: Cari; Roofing and waterproofing: DBS; Exterior joinery: Reithler; Exterior insulation: SPR Bâtiment et Industrie; Stainless steel pools: Myrtha Pools; Interior joinery: Darbois; Metal works: ERI; Plasterwork and painting: Luso Plaque & Plâtre; Concrete slab and tiled floors: Koehler & Fils; Cast floors: Étandex; Elevators: Euro-Ascenseurs; Electricity: Huard; Heating, ventilation, air conditioning, plumbing, drainage and water treatment: Guiban; Sauna and hammam: Suede Sauna.

Buhl, nursery, 2015
— Lead architects: Dominique Coulon, David Romero-Uzeda, Olivier Nicollas; Architects: Javier Gigosos Ruipérez, Diego Bastos-Romero, Gautier Duthoit; Construction site supervision: David Romero-Uzeda.
— Structure: Batiserf Ingénierie; Mechanical plumbing: Solares Bauen; Electricity: BET Gilbert Jost; Cost control and monitoring: E3 Économie; Acoustics: Euro Sound Project; Kitchens: Écotral; Landscape: Philippe Obliger.
— Earthworks, roadworks and structural system: STP Mader; Waterproofing: SMAC; Exterior joinery: Vollmer; Metal works: Muller-Rost; Exterior insulation: Somren; Scaffolding: Loc'Echaf; Interior joinery and furniture: Hunsinger; Plasterwork: Somegyps; Concrete slabs: STP Mader; Tiled floors: Multisols; Glued floors: Hertzog; Painting and cleaning: Somren; Green areas: Parcs et Jardins Wittersheim; Electricity: Vincentz; Heating and ventilation: Maison Xavier Fruh; Plumbing and drainage: Labeaune; Kitchen: M.E.A.

Belfort, conservatoire, 2015
— Lead architects: Dominique Coulon, Steve Letho Duclos; Architects: Guillaume Wittmann, Lukas Unbekandt, Diego Bastos-Romero; Construction site supervision: Steve Letho Duclos, Lukas Unbekandt; Facade artists: Max Coulon, Gabriel Khokha.
— Structure: Batiserf Ingénierie; Mechanical plumbing: Solares Bauen; Electricity: BEE.FL; Cost control: E3 Économie; Acoustics: Euro Sound Project.
— Earthworks and roadworks: Eurovia; Structural system: Albizzati Père & Fils; Waterproofing: Soprema; Metal works: Antonietti; Exterior joinery: Hunsinger; Plasterwork: Curti; Interior joinery: Negro Père & Fils; Wood flooring: STTS; Glued floors: Mirolo Père & Fils; Cast floors: Floorcolor; Tiled floors: Petracca; Concrete slabs: De Stefano; Painting: Curti; Heating and ventilation: Eimi; Plumbing and drainage: Beyler; Electricity: Zanelec; Exterior insulation: Pôle Bâtiment; Elevators: Schindler.

Montpellier, school complex, 2015
— Lead architects: Dominique Coulon, Steve Letho Duclos; Architects: Fanny Liénart, Olivier Poulat; Construction site supervision: Steve Letho Duclos, Olivier Poulat.
— Structure: Batiserf Ingénierie; Mechanical plumbing: Solares Bauen; Electricity: BET Gilbert Jost; Cost control: E3 Économie; Acoustics: Euro Sound Project; Landscape: Bruno Kubler.
— Structural system, roadworks and networks: BEC Construction; Special foundations and poles: Franki Fondations; Metal frame: CIM Massol; Waterproofing: Soprema; Exterior joinery and sun protection: Mistral Fenêtres; Exterior insulation: Iso Therm Habitat; Metal works: Serrurerie Delmas; Exterior works: Colas; Green areas: Pousse Clanet; Interior joinery: Ducrot; Plasterwork and ceilings: Société frontignanaise de Plâtrerie; Glued floors: SPC; Tiled floors: Art et Technique du Bâtiment; Painting: Languedoc Chantier; Elevators: CFA; Electricity: SPIE Sud-Ouest; Heating, ventilation and drainage: Temperia.

Colombes, school complex, 2015
— Lead architects: Dominique Coulon, Olivier Nicollas; Architects: Guillaume Wittmann, Émilie Brichard, Jean Scherer, David Romero-Uzeda, Diego Bastos-Romero, Aurélie Martel, Gauthier Duthoit.
— Structure: Batiserf Ingénierie; Mechanical plumbing: Solares Bauen; Electricity: BET Gilbert Jost; Cost control: E3 Économie; Acoustics: Euro Sound Project; Ergonomist: Defacto; Kitchens: Écotral; Landscape: Bruno Kubler.
— Earthworks, structural system, waterproofing, elevators and metal works: SNRB; Facades: SEE Simeoni; Exterior joinery: Hunsinger; Interior joinery: Millet; Wood flooring: Prodesign; Heating, ventilation and drainage: Brunier; Electricity: Rezza; Photovoltaics: Solstyce.

Orbec, retirement home, 2015
— Lead architects: Dominique Coulon, Benjamin Rocchi; Architects: David Romero-Uzeda, Olivier Nicollas, Chang Zhang, Javier Gigosos Ruipérez, Pedro Rodríguez Ruipérez, Ania Klukowski, Gautier Duthoit; Construction site supervision: Émilie Brichard, Jean Scherer.
— Structure: Batiserf Ingénierie; Mechanical plumbing and electricity: BET Gilbert Jost; Cost control: E3 Économie; Acoustics: Euro Sound Project; Kitchens: Écotral; Landscape: Bruno Kubler.
— Earthworks: Langevin TP; Special foundations: Pieux Ouest; Structural system and drainage: Gagneraud; Roadworks: Colas; Green areas: Leblois Environnement; Waterproofing: SEO; Exterior joinery: ACD Ernoult; Facades: DSA Atlantique; Metal works: R2C; Plasterwork: Plâtres Modernes Claude Jobin; Interior joinery: Perrin; Tiled floors: Revnor; Glued floors: Patrizio; Painting: Durand; Elevators: Otis; Electricity: Eiffage Énergie; Heating, ventilation and plumbing: Sanichauffage; Kitchen and cold storage: MBI.

Clamart, sports hall, 2015
— Lead architect: Dominique Coulon; Architects: David Romero-Uzeda, Olivier Poulat, Chang Zhang, Steve Letho Duclos, Florence Haenel; Competition: Olivier Nicollas; Construction site supervision: Olivier Poulat.
— Structure: Batiserf Ingénierie; Mechanical plumbing and electricity: BET Gilbert Jost; Cost control: E3 Économie; Acoustics: Euro Sound Project; Landscape: Bruno Kubler.
— Asbestos disposal and demolition: Colas; Envelope and exterior facilities: SNRB; Elevators: SEC France Ascenseurs; Metal works, fence and gates: RS2i Bâtiment; Plasterwork, ceiling, interior joinery, signage and furniture: NBA; Tiled floors: De Cock; Painting and glued floors: Art Maniac; Plumbing, heating and ventilation: Sert; Sports equipment: Sport France.

Thionville, media library, 2016
— Lead architects: Dominique Coulon, Steve Letho Duclos; Architects: Gautier Duthoit, Thibaut Muller, Lukas Unbekandt; Construction site supervision: Steve Letho Duclos.
— Structure: Batiserf Ingénierie; Mechanical plumbing: Solares Bauen; Electricity: BET Gilbert Jost; Cost control: E3 Économie; Acoustics: Euro Sound Project; Landscape: Bruno Kubler.
— Earthworks and roadworks: Costantini; Special foundations: Soletanche Bachy; Structural system: Cari; Metal frame: ERTCM; Waterproofing: Soprema; Exterior metal joinery and glass: MGE + Socomet; Metal works: SMF; Exterior isolation and facade: Isola; Scaffolding: Kapp; Plasterwork: Kupeli; Interior joinery: Hunsinger; Concrete slab and tiled floors: Batipro Carrelage; Glued floors: Debra; Cast floors: Guinamic; Interior painting and cleaning: Appel; Elevators: Feller; Green areas: ISS; Drainage: Costantini; Plumbing drainage, heating and ventilation: Lorry; Electricity and VDI cabling: Ineo; Scenic works: Europodium; Audiovisual scenic equipements: Michelsonne.

Freyming-Merlebach, theatre, 2017
— Lead architects: Dominique Coulon, Olivier Nicollas; Architects: Jean Scherer, David Romero-Uzeda, Ali Ozku, Fanny Liénart, Grégoire Stouck, Diego Bastos-Romero, Margot Machin; Competition: Olivier Nicollas; Construction site supervision: Olivier Nicollas.
— Structure: Batiserf Ingénierie; Mechanical plumbing: Solares Bauen; Electricity: BET Gilbert Jost; Cost control: E3 Économie; High Environmental Quality: Solares Bauen; Acoustics: Euro Sound Project; Scenographer: Changement à Vue; Roads and networks: Lollier Ingénierie.
— Earthworks and roadworks: Colas; Structural system: Cari-Fayat; Metal frame: ERTCM; Waterproofing: Couvrest; Exterior steel joinery: Socomet; Ventilated facades: Deobat; Metal works: Muller; Interior joinery and furniture: Jung; Plasterwork: Nespola + Werey Stenger; Glued floors: SGR; Floor and wall tiles: Multi Services; Interior painting and cleaning: Debra; Elevators: Ascelec; Scaffolding: Kapp; Electricity: ETA; Heating and ventilation: Schaeffer; Plumbing and drainage: Lorry; Locksmithing, machinery and scenic carpentry: Caire; Scenic curtains and drapes: Azur Scenic; Theatre armchairs: Delagrave; Scenic lighting and audiovisual media: Système Son.

Pélissanne, media library and garden, 2018
— Lead architects: Dominique Coulon, Gautier Duthoit, Jean Scherer ; Architects: David Romero-Uzeda, Javier Gigosos Ruipérez, Diego Bastos-Romero, Olivier Poulat, Margot Machin, Thomas Buckenmeyer, Florent Revel, Théo Petit, Yannick Signani.
— Structure: Batiserf Ingénierie ; Mechanical plumbing and electricity: BET Gilbert Jost ; Cost control: E3 Économie ; Acoustics: Euro Sound Project ; Roads and networks: Lollier Ingénierie ; Landscape: Bruno Kubler.
— Demolition and structural system: COSEPI France ; Roofing and waterproofing: SMED ; Aluminium exterior joinery: SMAB ; Wood exterior joinery: Vollmer ; Facade renovation and scaffolding: Atrium Bâtiment ; Metal works: SFM du Luberon ; Interior joinery: Concept Parachini, Menuiserie Bareau ; Wood flooring: Singer ; Tiled floors: SPTB ; Plasterwork, interior painting and cleaning: Provence Peinture Revêtement ; Elevators: CFA ; Electricity: Ylioss ; Heating, ventilation, plumbing and drainage: STME ; Exterior works: Eurovia ; Furniture: IDM ; Signage: Polsud Communication.

Pictures

Every effort has been made to trace all copyrights holders and obtain permission to reproduce the present material. The publisher and authors sincerely apologize for any mistakes or omissions and would be grateful if notified of any corrections that should be incorporated in future reprints or editions of this publication.

For the illustrations, pages 64 and 129: A © Luca Merlini. A © Peter Märkli. D Photograph: Cemal Emden © ADAGP, Paris, 2020. E Aldo Rossi © Rights reserved, Eraldo Consolascio, Fabio Reinhart, Bruno Reichlin. Photograph: © Centre Pompidou, MNAM-CCI, Dist. RMN-Grand Palais/ Georges Meguerditchian. F © Sou Fujimoto. Photograph: © Dominique Coulon. G © F.L.C. /ADAGP, Paris, 2020. I © Fonds Parent. SIAF/Cité de l'architecture et du patrimoine/Archives d'architecture du XXe siècle. J © Álvaro Siza Vieira. Photograph: © Luís Ferreira Alves. K © Tezuka Architects. L © ADAGP, Paris, 2020. N © F.L.C./ ADAGP, Paris, 2020.

For the photographs, pages 50–51: Martin Argyroglo. Pages 175–177, 178 middle and bottom, 181–185, 186 bottom: Clément Guillaume. Pages 16–49, 57–63, 85 middle, 88: Jean-Marie Monthiers. Pages 12–13, 68–71, 85 top and bottom, 93, 94 left, 100, 111 bottom, 132–133, 145, 148–173, 189–196, 200–204, 205–209, 213–214, 218–220, 226–243, 248–261, 268, 292–301, 302–316, 317 bas, 318–319, 321–323, 328–336, 338, 344, 355–356, 360–369: Eugeni Pons. Page 197: Les 4 Vents. Pages 7–10, 86, 94 right, 101, 111 middle, 113, 131, 134, 139, 142–143, 178 top, 186 top, 187, 210, 216–217, 221, 271–286, 317 top, 325, 337: David Romero-Uzeda.

We would like to warmly thank all artists and architects who graciously granted us the reproduction rights of their works, as well as all who participated in the making of Dominique Coulon et Associés' projects and of this monograph.

Dominique Coulon was born in the Jura region of eastern France in 1961, and founded his practice in 1989 after studying in Strasbourg and Paris-Belleville. He travelled in America and Europe in 1991 on a Villa Medici 'Hors les Murs' grant. In 2007 he began teaching at the national school of architecture (ENSA) in Strasbourg, where he created a master's programme entitled 'Architecture and Complexity', working across disciplines to achieve a different way of thinking about architectural projects.

Dominique Coulon et Associés
1989–

Fatiha Almi
Ilia Anastassov
Marie Auberti
Ariane Azuelos
Sophia Babouri
Leatitia Ballarin
Diego Bastos-Romero
Michel Bayer
Mathilde Blum
Daria Boeva
Thomas Bonnet
Sarah Brebbia
— partner (2008–2013)
Émilie Brichard
Thomas Buckenmeyer
Caroline Cave
Houyam Cariou
Gwladys Celestin
Marion Costa
Dominique Coulon
— founder
Manon Cuccu
Mehmet Davaz
Léa Delpech
Valerija Denisova
Katia Dulck
Gautier Duthoit
Arnaud Eloudyi
Nicolas Etienne Hauck
Claudia Fong
Estelle Fort
Thibaut Foulon
Valérie Gangloff
Manon Genevois
Delphine George
Sophie Georgel
Javier Gigosos Ruipérez
Aurélien Gœpp
Olivier Greder
Annick Guillemette
Florence Haenel
Marine Joli
Laura Kaczmarek
Ania Klukowski
Blandine Kuntz
Armelle Legadec
Paul Le Quernec
Steve Letho Duclos
— partner (2011–)
Hannes Libis
Fanny Liénart
Margot Machin
Virginie Maglaive
Aurélie Martel
Hugo Maurice
Caroline Metzger
Thibaut Muller
Clara Neumann
Olivier Nicollas
— partner (2008–2020)
Alexandre Otto
Ali Ozku
Adrien Petit
Olivier Poulat
Alexandre Puech
Audrey Redelsperger
Florent Revel
Jan Richter
Pascale Richter
— partner (1995–2000)
Benjamin Rocchi
— partner (2013–2020)
Pedro Rodriguez Ruipérez
David Romero-Uzeda
Alex Rothenburger
Amina Sahaoui
Hélène Schaeffer
Jean Scherer
Yannick Signani
Grégoire Stouck
Lukas Unbekandt
Rémi Valantin
Guillaume Wittmann
Chang Zhang

Dominique Coulon
Crossings

Publisher
Actar Publishers, New York, Barcelona
www.actar.com

Concept
Dominique Coulon
Manon Cuccu
Sophie Georgel
David Romero-Uzeda

Texts of the projects
Dominique Coulon

Contributions
Claude Bonnet
Étienne Butzbach
Luca Merlini
Daniel Payot
Alexandra Pignol
Richard Scoffier

Translation from French to English
Andrew Ayers (projects)
Katherine Parsons (conversations)

Copy editing and proofreading
Manon Cuccu
Sophie Georgel
Clara Neumann

Plans and drawings
Diego Bastos-Romero
Isabella De Carvalho Ferreira
Cristian Garvia Mendivil
Sophie Georgel
Javier Gigosos Ruipérez
Osvaldo Gounon
Luc Kuster
Lion Rust

Photographs
Clément Guillaume
Jean-Marie Monthiers
Eugeni Pons
David Romero-Uzeda

Book design and layout
Clara Neumann

Typefaces
Akzidenz Grotesk, Garamond Premier

Paper
Munken Polar 120 g/m²

Printing
Offizin Scheufele, Stuttgart

Binding
Josef Spinner Großbuchbinderei, Ottersweier

Distribution
Actar D, Inc. New York, Barcelona

440 Park Avenue South, 17th Floor
New York, NY 10016
T +1 212 966 2207
salesnewyork@actar-d.com

Roca i Batlle 2–4
08023 Barcelona
T +34 933 282 183
eurosales@actar-d.com

English ISBN: 978-1-948765-31-2
LCCN: 2017956612
French edition available

Printed in Germany, Europe
Publication date: November 2020

BASICS
MAISONS PAYSANNES DE L'ANCIENNE FRANCE
France septentrionale